International Political Economy Series

Series Editor
Timothy M. Shaw
University of Massachusetts Boston
Boston, USA

Emeritus Professor
University of London
London, UK

The global political economy is in flux as a series of cumulative crises impacts its organization and governance. The IPE series has tracked its development in both analysis and structure over the last three decades. It has always had a concentration on the global South. Now the South increasingly challenges the North as the centre of development, also reflected in a growing number of submissions and publications on indebted Eurozone economies in Southern Europe. An indispensable resource for scholars and researchers, the series examines a variety of capitalisms and connections by focusing on emerging economies, companies and sectors, debates and policies. It informs diverse policy communities as the established trans-Atlantic North declines and 'the rest', especially the BRICS, rise.

NOW INDEXED ON SCOPUS!

More information about this series at
http://www.palgrave.com/gp/series/13996

Logan Cochrane · Nathan Andrews
Editors

The Transnational Land Rush in Africa

A Decade After the Spike

palgrave
macmillan

Editors
Logan Cochrane
Global and International Studies
Ottawa, ON, Canada

College of Public Policy
HBKU, Qatar

Nathan Andrews
Global and International Studies
University of Northern British Columbia
Prince George, BC, Canada

ISSN 2662-2483 ISSN 2662-2491 (electronic)
International Political Economy Series
ISBN 978-3-030-60788-3 ISBN 978-3-030-60789-0 (eBook)
https://doi.org/10.1007/978-3-030-60789-0

This Palgrave Macmillan imprint is published by the registered company Springer Nature Switzerland AG
The registered company address is: Gewerbestrasse 11, 6330 Cham, Switzerland

Acknowledgments

This book has come together as a result of collaborative efforts. We are therefore greatly indebted to everyone who has contributed to the project in any shape or form. Firstly, we acknowledge the financial support of the Social Sciences and Humanities Research Council of Canada as part of its Insight Development Grant program (2019–2021). Although the project funded (i.e. *The Global Land Rush, Inequalities and Livelihoods: Enabling Environments for Strengthening Food Security in Ethiopia and Ghana*) specifically focuses on two countries in Africa for which research is ongoing, the funding helped us to hire research assistants who worked in different capacities to support this final output. Secondly, we appreciate the efforts of our contributors many of whom received "cold emails" from us, which served as our first introduction—and yet committed to doing their part to make the publication of this volume a success. Thirdly, we wish to thank both Danielle Legault and Charlotte Connolly for their editorial assistance, which facilitated the rapid finalization of the book. Finally, we are grateful for the supportive network of scholars we are part of. In particular, we thank Professor Tim Shaw (*Palgrave IPE series editor*) for convincing us about the usefulness of such a collection on the land issue in Africa since the 2007/2008 commodity price hikes. In taking on the challenge, we have learned so much and also connected with more people interested in this topic than we would have otherwise. Furthermore, we greatly appreciate the thoughtful feedback received from the anonymous peer reviewers of our book as well as colleagues like Lorenzo

Cotula, Tor Benjaminsen, David Deng and Tsegaye Moreda who were all very eager to endorse this book. It feels really great to receive such enormous peer support for our scholarship.

Praise for *The Transnational Land Rush in Africa*

"Drawing on in-depth country studies from across the African continent, this important new book offers invaluable insights not only on the longer-term impacts of extractivism, but also on connecting international processes to local dynamics and – ultimately – challenging Eurocentric accounts of IPE as a discipline and a field of inquiry."

—Lorenzo Cotula, *International Institute for Environment and Development (IIED)*

"Through an open and empirical approach, this book investigates what happened to the African land rush a decade later. While the overall story told sounds familiar with its cast of winners and losers, the book provides new insights, updated knowledge and important nuance to the intricate political economy of land governance in Africa."

—Tor A. Benjaminsen, *Norwegian University of Life Sciences*

"This edited book, which puts together a collection of relevant works based on a range of studies in many African countries, is an exemplary political economy analysis of what has happened across Africa since the contemporary global land grabbing occurred more than a decade ago. While the topic and questions addressed may sound familiar to many readers who have been tracking the issue over the last decade, this volume provides a much needed up to date information, critical insights and nuanced analysis, which place it among the best in Africa's land rush scholarship and beyond."

—Tsegaye Moreda, *International Institute of Social Studies (ISS), Erasmus University Rotterdam*

"While the stories have faded from the headlines in the decade or so since the trend first emerged, discussions about the implications of large-scale land investments have persisted among academics and development practitioners. The Transnational Land Rush in Africa manages to both highlight emerging trends and provide an analysis that is rich in contextual detail. The book is an important and timely contribution to discourses on the nexus between law, power and economic development in Africa."

—David Deng, *Human Rights Lawyer and Researcher, Detcro LLC*

Contents

Notes on Contributors

Nathan Andrews is an Assistant Professor of Global and International Studies at the University of Northern British Columbia, where he received a University Excellence Award in Research in May 2019. His ongoing research examines the international political economy/ecology of resource extraction and development. Dr. Andrews is currently undertaking a project that explores the connections between the global land rush, food security and livelihoods in Ghana and Ethiopia. In addition to his core research focus, he is also broadly interested in global governance, international relations and qualitative research methodology. His research has been published in high-impact journals such as *International Affairs*, *World Development*, *Resources Policy*, *Energy Research & Social Science*, *Extractive Industries & Society*, *Commonwealth & Comparative Politics*, and *Third World Quarterly*, among others. Dr. Andrews' recent monograph is *Gold Mining and the Discourses of Corporate Social Responsibility in Ghana* (Palgrave Macmillan, 2019). He has also co-authored *Oil and Development in Ghana: Beyond the Resource Curse* (Routledge, 2021) and co-edited *Corporate Social Responsibility and Canada's Role in Africa's Extractive Sectors* (University of Toronto Press, 2020). He has consulted for international organizations such as the African Development Bank, the International Committee for the Red Cross, and the Geneva Centre for Security Sector Governance.

John Hopeson Anku is a M.A. Student in International Studies-International Development and a Research Assistant at the University of Northern British Columbia. He holds degrees in Political Science and International Affairs from University of Ghana. His current research examines how farmers are experiencing and responding to processes of land grabbing in selected agrarian communities in Ghana.

Noah Echa Attah is a Professor of African Economic History and Development in the Department of History and Diplomatic Studies at the Federal University of Kashere in Nigeria. He holds a Ph.D. and an M.A. in History from the University of Ibadan, Nigeria, as well as a B.A. in History from Lagos State University, Ojo, Nigeria. He received the African Peacebuilding Network (APN) Individual Research Grant from the Social Science Research Council (SSRC) in 2017 for his project, "Large-Scale Land Acquisition in Nigeria: Interrogating the Conflict Trajectories and Critical Issues for Pro-Poor Peacebuilding."

Logan Cochrane is an Associate Professor in the College of Public Policy at HBKU in Qatar and an Assistant Professor of Global and International Studies at Carleton University, Canada, as well as an Adjunct Professor at the Institute of Policy and Development Research at Hawassa University, Ethiopia. Logan edited *Ethiopia: Social and Political Issues* (2019) and has published over fifty academic articles. For the last fifteen years, he has worked in non-governmental organizations internationally, including in Afghanistan, Benin, Burundi, the Democratic Republic of the Congo, Egypt, Ethiopia, Qatar, South Africa, South Sudan, Tanzania and Uganda. Logan has served as a Director for two non-governmental organizations, and worked as a consultant with clients that have included Save the Children, Management Sciences for Health, The Liaison Office, UNICEF and UNAIDS.

Melisew Dejene is an Assistant Professor of Development Studies as well as Journalism and Communication at the Institute of Policy and Development Research, Hawassa University, Ethiopia.

Ashley Fent is a postdoctoral fellow in geography at Vassar College. She has conducted research in Senegal since 2011, and specializes in resource controversies, land issues and environmental change.

Marie Gagné is a postdoctoral fellow at Concordia University. She holds a Ph.D. in Political Science from the University of Toronto, with a specialization in development studies. Her research enquires into various themes of critical importance for agrarian livelihoods: land access, agricultural development, natural resources management and food security. Her work was funded by the Social Sciences and Humanities Research Council of Canada (SSHRC), the Ontario Graduate Scholarship (OGS) Program and the International Development Research Centre (IDRC), among others. She also has extensive professional experience in conducting research for rural development policy.

Solomon Peter Gbanie is a geographer at Fourah Bay College, University of Sierra Leone with over ten years of research and teaching experience. Gbanie's approach blends geospatial science technologies with social science research frameworks to understand environmental change. Using mix methods, his research explores landscape dynamics in post-conflict contexts using fragmentation and aggregation as indices of land cover and ecosystem change. Dr. Gbanie holds a Ph.D. in Geography (2015) from the University of New South Wales, Australia, and has collaborated with geographers and engineers from the University of New South Wales, Australia, the University of Wisconsin, United States (US) and University of Bath, United Kingdom (UK). He recently served as a local collaborator and Co-Principal Investigator on two projects: *Land Use, Microclimate and Water Quality Nexus: Implications for Human Health in the Rokel–River Basin, Sierra Leone* and *GCRF - Mapping Opportunities for Improving the Environmental Sustainability of Artisanal Gold Mining in Sierra Leone.* He is currently a co-investigator and local collaborator on a research entitled: Green rooted agriculture association (GRASS): Community led pairing of urban agriculture and phytoremediation in Sierra Leone (British Academy Funding, 18/11/19–17/11/2).

Steffi Hamann is Assistant Professor of Political Science and International Development Studies at the University of Guelph. Prior to pursuing an academic career in Canada, she worked for the German Development Agency (GIZ). Her research explores the impacts of private-sector investments in the African agro-industrial sector. She has conducted extensive field research in Cameroon and is a recipient of the Kari Polanyi-Levitt prize, awarded by the Canadian Association for the Study of International Development. Steffi's most recent research project is a comparative examination of investment promotion policies in sub-Saharan Africa.

Dr. Chris Huggins is an Assistant Professor at the School of International Development and Global Studies, University of Ottawa. He holds a Ph.D. in Geography (specialization in political economy) from

Carleton University, Canada. His research interests include critical political economy, natural resource management, land rights, and livelihoods approaches, with a geographical focus on several African countries, particularly Rwanda, the Democratic Republic of Congo (DRC), and Tanzania. He published a monograph, *Agricultural Reform in Rwanda: Authoritarianism, Markets and Zones of Governance* in 2017 with Zed Books. He is a member of the editorial board of the *Nokoko Journal of African Studies* and is a non-Resident Fellow of the African Centre for Technology Studies in Nairobi.

Prosper B. Matondi is the Executive Director of Ruzivo Trust, an independent think tank based in Harare, Zimbabwe. He has undertaken research on land and agrarian reform and natural resources governance more broadly for the last 25 years. He co-edited a book, *Biofuels, Land Grabbing and Food Security in Africa* (Zed Books, 2011) and is the author of *Zimbabwe's Fast Track Land Reform Programme* (ZED Books, 2012).

Ricarda Roesch is a research associate and Ph.D. student at the Friedrich-Alexander-University of Erlangen-Nuremberg. Her research focuses on the negotiation of the right to Free, Prior, and Informed Consent (FPIC) in Liberia from a legal anthropological and feminist perspective. It is funded by the Heinrich-Boell-Foundation. She holds an LL.B. from the Hanse Law School, University of Bremen and an LL.M. from the School of Oriental and African Studies, University of London.

Blair Rutherford is a Professor of Anthropology in the Department of Sociology and Anthropology at Carleton University in Ottawa, Canada. He has conducted ethnographic research in four sub-Saharan African countries for over the course of 25 years. Among other publications, he is the author of *Working on the Margins: Black Workers, White Farmers in Postcolonial Zimbabwe* (Zed Books and Weaver Press, 2001) and *Farm Labor Struggles in Zimbabwe: The Ground of Politics* (Indiana University Press, 2017).

Adam Sneyd is Associate Professor of Political Science and International Development Studies at the University of Guelph. His research focuses on the political economy of commodities and development, particularly in sub-Saharan Africa. His latest major project, funded by an Insight Grant from the Social Sciences and Humanities Research Council (SSHRC), examines the politics of "responsible" business practices in Cameroon.

Adam is widely published and has authored two books on the global politics of the cotton industry. His third book, *Politics Rules: Power, Globalization and Development*, explores the political contestations that shape contemporary development challenges.

Dr. Alec Thornton is a Senior Lecturer in Geography in the School of Science at University of New South Wales (UNSW) Canberra, Australia. He is also Academic Co-Lead for Africa at the Institute for Global Development, UNSW Sydney. Alec combines critical theory and participatory research methods to explore the role of social movements in struggles for food and environmental justice. He is Senior Research Associate in the School of Humanities and the School of Tourism & Hospitality at the University of Johannesburg. Alec was Vice-President of the African Studies Association of Australasia and the Pacific (AFSAAP) from 2010 to 2017. He served as co-editor of the *Australasian Review of African Studies* (ARAS) from 2015 to 2018 and as an editorial board member of *Urban Forum* from 2010 to 2016 and Applied Geography from 2009 to 2015. He also the "Sustainable Urban and Rural Development" Section Editor for the journal, *Sustainability* (MDPI, Switzerland). Alec is currently project lead for a collaborative study of urban green infrastructure and economic development in sub-Saharan African cities.

Patrick Wight is a Ph.D. candidate in the Departments of Political Science and International Development at the University of Guelph. His dissertation is titled, "The Limitations of Liberal Institutionalism in South Sudan: Explaining the International Community's Inability to Bring About Lasting Peace and Build an Empirical State." Field research for this project took during the South Sudan peace process and involved three separate trips to Ethiopia and Kenya from 2014 to 2019.

Acronyms

ACD	African Commercial Development
ACDI-VOCA	Agricultural Cooperative Development International–Volunteers in Overseas Cooperative Assistance
ADP	Agricultural Development Projects
ARCSS	Agreement on the Resolution of the Conflict in South Sudan
ARDA	Agriculture and Rural Development Authority
BIET-Ghana	Base for Industrial and Environmental Technology Ghana
CA	Community Assembly
CARG	Conseil Agricole Rural de Gestion
CATs	Community Awareness Teams
CDC	Cameroon Development Corporation
CEDASS	Canadian Economic Development Assistance for South Sudan
CES	Central Equatoria State
CFLEDD	Coalition of Women Leaders for the Environment and Sustainable Development
CFMA	Community Forest Management Agreement
CFMB	Community Forest Management Body
CFMP	Community Forest Management Plan
CFOCs	Community Forest Organizing Committees
CLA	County Land Authority
CONAREF	National Land Reform Commission
CPA	Comprehensive Peace Agreement
CRL	Community Rights Law
CSOs	Civil Society Organizations
CUC	Commercial Use Contract
DRC	Democratic Republic of the Congo

EC	Executive Committee
EES	Eastern Equatoria State
EHSIA	Environmental Health and Social Impact Assessment
EIA	Ethiopian Investment Agency
ENDC	Eastern Nigerian Development Corporation
EPA	Environmental Protection Agency
EPRDF	Ethiopian Peoples' Revolutionary Democratic Front
ETC	Equatoria Teak Company
FAO	Food and Agriculture Organization
FDA	Liberian Forestry Development Authority
FDI	Foreign Direct Investment
FIFES	Forest Incomes for Environmental Sustainability
FTLRP	Fast Track Land Reform Programme
GCC	Gulf Cooperation Council
GDP	Gross Domestic Product
GHI	Global Hunger Index
GoSS	Government of Southern Sudan
ha	Hectare
ICSS	Interim Constitution of Southern Sudan
IDPs	Internally Displaced Persons
IFC	International Finance Corporation
IFPRI	International Food Policy Research Institute
IIED	International Institute for Environment and Development
ILC	International Law Commission
IPA	Investment Promotion Agency
IPE	International Political Economy
ISPO	Irrevocable Standing Payment Order
IUCN	International Union for Conservation of Nature
JAM	Joint Aid Management
JTF	Jatropha Technology Farm
km	Kilometer
LCCs	Land Consultative Committees
LSLA	Large-Scale Land Acquisition
MALAO	Malen Affected Land Owners and Land Users Association
MDC	Movement for Democratic Change
MLRR	Ministry of Lands and Rural Resettlement
MoAMID	Ministry of Agriculture Mechanisation and Irrigation Development
MoU	Memorandum of Understanding
NACRDB	Nigeria Agricultural, Cooperative and Rural Development Bank
NFRL	National Forestry Reform Law
NGOs	Non-Governmental Organizations
NNPC	Nigeria National Petroleum Corporation

NPIA	National Agricultural Investment Plan
NTD	Nile Trading and Development
NTFP	Non-Timber Forest Product
OWR	Okapi Wildlife Reserve
PHP	Plantations du Haut Penja
PLAAS	Programme for Land and Agrarian Studies
PLCs	Payam Land Councils
PROSPER	Peoples, Rules, and Organizations Supporting the Protection of Ecosystem Resources
PUPs	Private Use Permits
R-ARCSS	Revitalized Agreement on the Resolution of the Conflict in South Sudan
REDD+	Reducing Emissions from Deforestation and Forest Degradation
RRDC	Rainforest Resources Development Centre
RSPO	Roundtable on Sustainable Palm Oil
SAC	Socfin Agricultural company
SER	Socio-Economic Resource Reconnaissance
SGSOC	Sithe Global Sustainable Oils Cameroon
SHOG	Smallholder and Out Grower
SLIEPA	Sierra Leone Investment and Export Promotion Agency
SNNP	Southern Nations Nationalities and Peoples
SPLM/A	Sudan People's Liberation Movement/Army
SRLG	Sudan Rural Land and Governance
SSLA	South Sudan Legislative Assembly
SSLC	Southern Sudan Land Commission
TCSS	Transitional Constitution of South Sudan
TSCs	Forest Management Contracts (FMCs) and ten Timber Sale Contracts
UBRBDA	Upper Benue River Basin Development Authority
UK	United Kingdom
UN	United Nations
US	United States
USAID	United States Agency for International Development
USSR	Union of Soviet Socialist Republic
VPA	Voluntary Partnership Agreement
VPA-FLEGT	European Union's Forest Law Enforcement, Governance and Trade Facility
WFP	World Food Program
ZANU-PF	Zimbabwe African National Union Party—Patriotic Front
ZERA	Zimbabwe Energy Regulatory Authority

List of Figures

List of Tables

CHAPTER 1

International Political Economy and the Land Rush in Africa: Trends, Scale, Narratives, and Contestations

Nathan Andrews and Logan Cochrane

Introduction

The International Political Economy (IPE) of land is a contested arena, both in terms of scholarly discourse and practical engagement (see Zoomers 2011; Borras et al. 2012; Lavers 2012; Moreda and Spoor 2015; Andrews 2018; Hall 2019; Woods 2020). The rapid rise in global commodity prices in 2007 and 2008 resulted in agricultural and supply chain crises and led to increased levels of hunger and rioting worldwide.

N. Andrews
Global and International Studies, University of Northern British Columbia, Prince George, BC, Canada
e-mail: nathan.andrews@unbc.ca

L. Cochrane (✉)
Global and International Studies, Carleton University, Ottawa, ON, Canada

College of Public Policy, HBKU, Qatar

L. Cochrane and N. Andrews (eds.), *The Transnational Land Rush in Africa*, International Political Economy Series,
https://doi.org/10.1007/978-3-030-60789-0_1

The commodity price spike catalyzed global capital to search for new avenues in the pursuit of high financial returns, a phenomenon which is highlighted as one of the key factors that drove Africa's contemporary land rush. At least 56 million hectares of the African continent were acquired between October 2008 and August 2009 (Cotula 2012; Hall et al. 2015). This collection of works explores the ramifications and ongoing effects of Africa's 'land grabbing' processes a decade after this tumultuous period. Despite the emergence of 'best practices' and legal directives (e.g. Cook and Chambers 2019), as well as efforts to push for greater transparency in land acquisition (Scoppola and Prontera 2018), the exploitative nature of Africa's contemporary land rush did not stop with the commodity price spike.

Africa is a focal point in the global land rush and thus the continent is frequently centred in scholarly debates on the topic (ElHadary and Obeng-Odoom 2012; Boone 2017; Berry 2017; Chimhowu 2019; Walker et al. 2019; Santiago 2019; Ochieng 2020). Determining the extent of land investments in Africa is difficult due to a lack of transparent data and the range of metrics utilized such as land available, land committed, and land leased. The amount of land estimated to have been leased or acquired and finalized through signed contracts in Africa during the 2007/2008 period, approximately 15.2 million hectares, represents an area larger than the size of Portugal and Switzerland combined. Globally, 49.7 million hectares were reported as leased through concluded contracts, an area equivalent to the size of Spain (Land Matrix 2018). These figures most likely underestimate the total level of land sold or leased in Africa since many deals are not reported in national and international databases such as the Land Matrix, as discussed in several chapters in this volume.

To further complicate the issue, dominant narratives about the 2007/2008 land rush found in the media, reports from intergovernmental and non-governmental agencies, and some research contain inaccuracies or are not supported with adequate evidence, such as the origin of the investors driving the land rush (e.g. Cochrane and Amery 2017). Land deals have undermined the viability of pastoralist lives and livelihoods by exchanging small-scale family operations for large commercial ones. Foreign investments in land have thus created new vulnerabilities as people who have lost their land are coerced to take up temporary or seasonal labour opportunities. Meanwhile, large land deals create enormous wealth for a few elites through the export of agricultural commodities. Food insecurity may increase as a result of growing agricultural production, alongside other social injustices (Maxwell and Wiebe 1999; Daley 2005; Muraoka et al. 2018).

This book re-visits dominant narratives by offering a broad set of country studies from across the African continent. In selecting the cases, we identified countries with the largest amount of leased or acquired land using 2019 data from the Land Matrix. In addition, we purposively added other countries that experienced unique circumstances in relation to large-scale land acquisitions, such as Senegal. We then invited experts knowledgeable about the identified countries to contribute to this collection, as opposed to an open call which may have resulted in multiple contributions for a single country. Our objective was to compile a volume that represents a diversity of experiences from across the continent. This book includes chapters on the Democratic Republic of the Congo, South Sudan, Cameroon, Ethiopia, Senegal, Liberia, Sierra Leone, Nigeria, and Zimbabwe. Other authors were solicited to write on Gabon, Ghana, Madagascar, Mozambique, Sudan, and Tanzania, but these works are not included in the final volume for a range of reasons.[1]

We provided contributors with a set of research questions to produce a coherent volume that covered similar issues across the country studies. Specifically, we encouraged engagement with macro-level, political economy analyses so as to provide a valuable collection for researchers and students alike. In addition to providing an update a decade after the 2007/2008 commodity price spike, this volume challenges some of the widely held assumptions about the African 'land rush,' including its extent, the evolving resistance to it, and the legal landscapes which define and shape its component parts (e.g. Cochrane 2012, 2016; Cochrane and Skjerdal 2015). The collection also challenges assumptions about the actors involved in processes of land grabbing; mainstream narratives tend to focus on investors from particular locations while others are rendered invisible (Cochrane and Amery 2017; Hall 2019). This chapter situates the book within the broader IPE debates around the land issue and

[1] These countries are characterized by a similar environmental setting, that is, the tropical savannah range. We thank Danielle Legault for pointing this aspect out, as we realized the need to appreciate the specific agro-ecologies of the countries where investors acquired the most land. Indeed, only one country (Sudan) resides primarily outside of the tropical climate setting (as per the Koppen-Geiger classification).

provides a discussion of the book's scope, including a chapter-by-chapter analysis. We conclude with a reflection on areas for future research.

Land and the International Political Economy: Contributions and Silences

There is an abundance of books (e.g. Cotula 2009; Pearce 2012; Liberti 2013; Hall et al. 2015; Kapoor 2017; Edelman et al. 2017; Levien 2018; Cook and Chambers 2019) and journals, such as *Geoforum*, *Journal of Peasant Studies*, *Journal of Agrarian Change*, *Land Use Policy*, *Review of African Political Economy*, *World Development*, *Journal of Development Studies*, and *Third World Quarterly*, among other publications, which engage with the politics and processes of 'land grabbing.' The land question, however, is not featured in mainstream IPE discussions, even though these 'grabbing' processes involve political and economic actors and networks operating at both the global and local scales. A recent review of the future of IPE helps to explain the absence of the land and agrarian question in mainstream discussions as a consequence of the Eurocentrism embedded in both classical and contemporary accounts of political economy (Johnson et al. 2013; see also Blyth 2009).

The Eurocentrism of IPE is problematic for two reasons. Firstly, it focuses on processes of order and stability, or, in other words, the reproduction of the status quo. This parochial preoccupation explains the discipline's disinterest in agrarian politics and those contestations which tend to create chaos by questioning, destabilizing, or otherwise decentering the agency of powerful actors. The absence of discussion on transnational 'land grabs' in IPE is underscored by the tendency of leading researchers to avoid 'studying down,' that is, researching populations that are vulnerable and often marginalized from mainstream discourses. Secondly, the Eurocentric foundations of IPE leads mainstream accounts to defend, promote, or even celebrate 'Western civilization as the highest or ideal referent in the world' (Hobson 2013, 1024). This becomes obvious when one examines the scope and the foci of contributions in leading journals such as *Review of International Political Economy* (RIPE) or even *New Political Economy*, although recognizing that the latter publication has a more progressive and inclusive orientation to research and knowledge production than the former.

IPE appears to be dominated by white people and Western perspectives when one investigates who is producing knowledge, where such knowledge comes from, and who has access to it. The editorial board membership of leading IPE journals, including the two mentioned above, reflect this reality. As Cohen (2008) argued over a decade ago, in IPE, the 'rest of the world' does not exist. We posit that the discursive practices and material mechanisms of knowledge mobilization and production that contribute to writing the rest of the world out of the intellectual history of IPE in particular and international relations in general are also responsible for the erasure of the land question (see Jones 2005; Lavelle 2005; Andrews and Okpanachi 2012; Odoom and Andrews 2017; Andrews 2020). The primacy given to positivism, objectivity, and reductionism in core IPE contributions (Weber 2015) has relegated the land question as a particularly 'local' dynamic and thus the domain of anthropologists or sociologists, for example.

The points raised above are not meant to unnecessarily essentialize the domain of IPE or argue that our book is central to IPE (though the nexus between the transnational land rush and IPE is explicit). Rather, we seek to challenge the Eurocentric status quo of IPE by demonstrating how and why *land*, though sometimes considered a 'local' resource and an issue relevant to that scale of analysis, is of interest to a globalized assemblage of actors and networks, including international organizations, Non-Governmental Organizations (NGOs), think tanks, transnational corporations, governments, and private individuals. To be sure, existing scholarship highlights the intricate relationships among these diverse actors and explores a range of processes underlying large-scale land acquisitions within the broader context of political economy (see Hall 2011; Cotula 2012; Zoomers and Kaag 2014; Cochrane and Amery 2017; Baaz et al. 2017; Ayelazuno 2019; Santika et al. 2019; Borras et al. 2020a). Specifically, scholars have drawn attention to the polycentric or 'hybrid' forms of governance that surround land transactions, including the ownership, access, and use of such natural resources (Zoomers 2010; Pedersen 2016; Margulis et al. 2016; Collins et al. 2019; Miller et al. 2020). These contributions reveal 'land grabs' to be a truly global phenomenon requiring a multi-scalar assessment. We believe this book draws from, and adds to, wider IPE discussions by dissecting the local, national, and transnational dynamics of land acquisitions.

Scope and Structure of the Book

Investors from around the world have been rapidly acquiring land in Africa on an unprecedented scale since the commodity price spike of 2007/2008. Land is often leased or sold without due process or compensation for affected citizens, resulting in what many advocates call 'land grabbing.' International actors and some governments have been advocating for transparency with regard to these large-scale land acquisitions. Following the commodity price spike of 2007/2008, the acquisition of land by investors rapidly increased, with tens of millions of hectares of land being leased or purchased. Data, however, was sparse in the immediate years and many claims turned out to be inaccurate. Governments in Africa have also defined and refined their laws, policies, and regulatory processes in the past decade. This volume provides up-to-date information on what has happened since the 2007/2008 African 'land rush' by providing case studies for those countries which were most heavily impacted by the phenomenon. In so doing, it provides detailed, long-term assessments of a broad range of national contexts, making it a critical resource for students, researchers, advocates, and policymakers. Beyond the specific question of land and investment, this book also sheds light on the broader political economy of development in Africa.

We recognize the challenges imposed by terminology such as 'land grab' and 'large-scale land acquisition,' where the former implies illegality and the latter legality. The book's title uses 'land rush' to skirt these ambiguities. The relevance or accuracy of terminology depends on each country's unique context, as highlighted by this collection of country studies. We are also cognizant that, in some countries, it is not a few wealthy foreign investors but a large number of smaller domestic investors who have driven the 'land rush.' Contributors to this volume elaborate on such country-specific trends. Lastly, we do not frame the 'land rush' phenomenon exclusively within the agricultural context, as much land has been obtained for other purposes, including mining, forestry, and tourism (see Ayelazuno 2011, 2019; Hall 2011; German et al. 2013; Osabuohien 2014; Jayne et al. 2014; Andrews 2018; Van Bockstael 2019). We do, however, focus on recent experiences between 2008 and 2019, recognizing that this poses some limitations. Some chapters have addressed this gap. The chapter on Zimbabwe, for instance, traces the 'land rush' phenomenon back to the early 2000s to the country's Fast Track Land Reform Program, which has deep roots in historical struggles and processes of legally enforced displacement between 1900 and 1950, long before the period emphasized by this book (see Matondi 2012; Chamunogwa 2019). Each chapter explores the history, development, and current context of the 'land rush,' which provides much needed nuance to a discourse and discipline driven by country- and investment-specific studies, to the exclusion of long-term, macro-scale analyses of trends.

This volume addresses a critical gap in the IPE of development in different African countries. The chapters are organized into three sub-themes to create coherence across the various case studies and to offer a comprehensive resource for researchers, students, and policy practitioners interested in the 'land rush' in Africa and beyond: (1) the land-development nexus; (2) informality and 'new' customary land tenure landscapes; and (3) formalization, domestic agency, and legacies of legal pluralism. The chapters provided herein answer a similar set of questions while allowing contributors to draw upon their theoretical, methodological, and context-specific interests. Each chapter includes an overview of country trends, the relevant governance structures (regulation, land tenure, and policy and law), and a discussion of the impacts of land acquisitions on livelihoods and resulting inequalities. Together, the surveyed themes allow for comparative analysis in the Introductory and Concluding chapters and ensure a consistent structure for the various case studies.

The Land-Development Nexus: Grand Discourses, Social Injustice and Contestations

Chapter 2 by Hamann and Sneyd employs a critical development studies framework to dissect the land-development nexus. The Cameroonian case demonstrates how large-scale land acquisitions serve extractive functions and thereby exacerbate economic and social inequalities. This perspective challenges prevailing neoliberal discourses in Cameroon and elsewhere that privilege the privatization and commoditization of land as a solution to economic stagnation and social marginalization. The World Bank and other international organizations have promoted such ideas while drawing global attention to Africa's vast 'idle' lands and resources. The practice of land grabbing as a 'development' strategy forms part of a broader capitalist logic underlying the land rush across the continent (see Cotula 2009; Lavers 2012; ElHadary and Obeng-Odoom 2012).

Hamann and Sneyd document the various forms of resistance provoked by contentious 'land grabs' in Cameroon for the purpose of agricultural projects, 20 of which were concluded as of late 2019. Although international peasant movements, such as *La Vía Campesina*, have not played a prominent role across the African continent, this chapter reveals the significant rise in opposition to corporate-driven agriculture in the Cameroonian case. Numerous communities have experienced displacement and other forms of social injustice as a result of land acquisitions. However, there is also persistent 'push-back' from social movements. Contestation at the 'grassroots' level is juxtaposed with the influence of elite politicians and community leaders, such as powerful chiefs and dignitaries who sit on Land Consultative Committees, who tend to benefit personally from land deals at the expense of the broader population. These actors can either delay or accelerate land transaction processes. Hamann and Sneyd argue that elites possess a considerable amount of power and influence in their communities and networks via strategic acts of patronage. The chapter highlights the need for land reform in Cameroon, where there are tenure regulations that date back to the 1970s, to address the systemic and structural injustices that result in the marginalization of disadvantaged groups.

Like other African countries, the Government of Senegal identified agriculture and mining as a pathway to development, with foreign investment needed to fast track economic objectives. Gagné and Fent (Chapter 3) explore how global capitalism is presented as a 'win-win' for investors and governments without attention to the inherently extractive nature of wealth acquisition. Abate (2020) and Manda et al. (2020) drawing on experiences in Ethiopia and Zambia, respectively, highlight how partnerships between public and private actors influence policy and investment conditions in favour of elites at the expense of people and the environment. In Senegal, the promises of development promoted by government and investors alike have failed to materialize. The authors posit three key reasons for this failure: effective citizen mobilization against large-scale land acquisitions, changing government priorities, and investor-related challenges. Above all, the experience in Senegal demonstrates the power of mass mobilization, as this factor largely produced or contributed to the latter two. For example, the fluctuation in government stances was in direct response to public protest and contestation. Investor-related issues included a lack of social licence but also weak capacity and an inability to acquire sufficient funding for proposed projects. These failings of the land rush in Senegal, however, did not mean a victory for the people against corporate-driven agriculture. Gagné and Fent point out, in many instances, lands unjustly taken from Senegalese citizens remain out of their hands.

Extractivism, of which there are many analyses (see, for example, Bebbington et al. 2013 and the virtual issue this article was a part), is applied to the case of Senegal using three case studies, namely Jatropha Technology Farm, an agricultural project, and the Senhuile and Niafarang projects, both mining ventures. All three initiatives were sites of resistance and contestation. Gagné and Fent provide original data collected during extensive stays in the study areas. According to the authors, the democratic history of Senegal contextualizes the mass mobilization against foreign investment in land and resources and reflects the importance of political institutions, particularly the country's long tradition of decentralized structures as documented in the work of Acemoglu and Robinson (2013). The prominence and strength of civil society is seen as instrumental to the widespread and successful resistance against land grabbing processes, a unique factor not common to other experiences on the continent. Senegalese civil society is supported by international allies and solidarity movements, such as GRAIN, who conduct research and engage in advocacy globally. While there are some parallels between Senegal and Cameroon (see Chapter 2) with regard to resistance, the local population of Senegal stands out; not only were activists and communities successful in contesting and resisting foreign investors, but they were also able to influence domestic politics and national elites to shift their policy position, effectively putting an end to several large-scale land acquisitions and investments, including state-sponsored ones.

Wight, in his analysis of South Sudan's land rush in Chapter 4, presents three forms of land tenure, namely investor leasehold, rural customary, and urban freehold, and then discusses how these systems impact the ways in which land acquisitions occur. Similar to other cases in this collection (e.g. in Cameroon and Senegal), the amount of land acquisitions reported in South Sudan is not accurate since some acquisitions never occurred while industrial operations did not materialize in other cases. Although many other countries were similarly impacted by the peak in foreign investment in land in the late 2000s, South Sudan offers unique insights into the 'push' and 'pull' factors for investors. Wight opines that foreign investment possesses a greater likelihood for negative consequences when state actors hold questionable or weak authority. Some of the negative impacts surveyed by Wight include the unjust usurpation of land, elite capture, the emergence of conflict, the marginalization and exclusion of minorities, the continuation and exacerbation of gendered disparities, and adverse impacts on livelihoods. The experience of South Sudan demonstrates that investors are more hesitant to invest, and investments more likely to fail, when there is significant uncertainty emanating from fragility and conflict. Although many investors acquired land in South Sudan between 2007 and 2013—in one of Africa's largest land acquisitions—most investment ended (formally or practically) following the civil war of 2013. A key contribution of this chapter is its discussion on how the areas of tenure, law, and regulation impact on foreign investment in land in South Sudan.

Drawing upon detailed analyses of three case studies in Nigeria, Attah (Chapter 5) explores the extent to which development narratives have materialized and whether the counternarrative of dispossession and marginalization more accurately reflects the country's reality. Attah examines the ways 'land grabs' are defined and the rationales underlying the decision to sell or lease land to foreign investors, as provided by intergovernmental agencies, international financial institutions, and governments. As with most chapters in this volume, the national legal context is key to understanding country-specific political economy dynamics. This volume's historical review of law and tenure as it pertains to the land question reveals that the dichotomies between the informal and formal, the customary and statutory, have been blurred, fluid, and subject to change, as the cases of Ethiopia, Nigeria, and Liberia demonstrate. In the case of Ethiopia (Chapter 8), federal governance regimes are integrated into decentralized power structures on account of the country's specific legal history, which in turn has impacted the ability to sell or lease land over time. The role of Zimbabwean investors in Kwara State of Nigeria elucidates how interconnected national governments are in processes of land acquisition, not only in terms of approving land sales but also in providing infrastructure, financing, and a range of other incentives. The three detailed case studies surveyed by Attah include the Zimbabwean-owned Shonga Farms, the Singaporean-owned Wilmar International, and the American-owned Dominion Farms. These projects provide a spectrum of outcomes, from investment failure to extractive bonanza, in Attah's study of the commercial farming complex.

All three Nigerian cases showcase how supposed development 'dreams' become nightmares for individuals and communities living in affected areas. Attah believes that the disenfranchisement and impoverishment of local people belies the promises of hegemonic development narratives used to justify large-scale land acquisitions. Some foreign investors may earn profits, but Nigeria and Nigerians are left with greater food insecurity, lost livelihoods, environmental crises, and conflict. In another comparative case study of Indonesia, Santika et al. (2019, 105) found that the impacts of land grabbing on poverty are 'not uniformly positive, not negative.' Instead, the socio-economic factors affecting development outcomes are dependent upon local factors, such as whether wage labour was already the predominant source of livelihood prior to the imposition of foreign investment projects. The perspective of Santika et al. is juxtaposed with that of Gagné and Fent who focus on the capacity of local populations to resist the incursion of foreign investors in Senegal in Chapter 3. Despite these variations, Santika et al. (2019), Attah, and Gagné and Fent all acknowledge the potential of negative socioeconomic outcomes and environmental degradation. The chapter by Attah opens up the possibility for re-negotiation and reform in laying bare the rationales used to promote, justify, and perpetuate exploitative forms of the land rush (see also Walker et al. 2019).

Informality and 'New' Customary Land Tenure Landscapes

Roesch analyses the land rush in Liberia (Chapter 6) through the lens of 'community forestry,' as the most recent manifestation or pathway through which land acquisition occurs. As in other cases (e.g. South Sudan and Nigeria), this chapter highlights the challenges posed by new governance structures without foundations in customary land regimes and the complex entanglements of NGOs, donors, and companies within land management processes. Roesch critically assesses the deployment of supposed community-based approaches, arguing that they are not as participatory as assumed. The international advocacy surrounding new modalities of land acquisition is further complicated by a complex post-war setting with a myriad of different actors and interests at play. Unique to this chapter is the role of official development assistance, specifically USAID and intergovernmental actors. The examples provided in this chapter blur the traditional lines between the private sector and 'development' actors. Roesch draws upon primary data and in-depth fieldwork to offer a detailed analysis of two case studies, presenting ethnographic experiences at the micro-level to provide more nuance at the macro-level. Roesch brings the macro-data to life by opening windows into how the land rush looks, sounds, and feels at its sites of interaction. The case studies trouble and complicate the assumptions of dominant narratives and challenge readers to critically reflect on the lives and livelihoods affected by the land rush, which are too often subsumed by abstract and dehumanizing statistics.

Similar to other African contexts examined in this book, large-scale land acquisitions for agribusiness (e.g. sugar cane and oil palm plantations) has been a constant feature in Sierra Leone. Gbanie and Thornton (in Chapter 7) explore the Sierra Leone case study by critically interrogating narratives of beneficiation, job creation, and economic development which often surround agribusiness investments. Contrary to 'win-win' expectations, land deals have resulted in devastating impacts on rural livelihoods as local populations lose their right to access land which hitherto supported their subsistence and thus food sovereignty. Sierra Leone is divided into 16 districts and 199 chiefdoms, with land lease transactions involving three main actors: (1) the landholding family, (2) the Chiefdom Council headed by the Paramount Chief, and (3) the land user. Up until 2009, the Government of Sierra Leone did not possess direct stakes in land lease arrangements, although it typically served as a facilitator of large-scale lease negotiations. Since 2009, there has been a payment sharing arrangement for leases between landowners (50%), the Chiefdom Council (20%), the District Council (20%), and the central government (10%).

In Chapter 8, Matondi and Rutherford examine large-scale land acquisitions for sugar cane plantations in Zimbabwe. Sugar cane is considered a 'green' fuel and is being leveraged by the Zimbabwean government to reduce fuel import levels and to generate employment at the local and national levels. The authors discuss the Chisumbanje bio-ethanol project, which resulted from government efforts to address the impacts of economic decline on Zimbabwe's agriculture sector since the 2000s. Zimbabwe is another exemplary case which contests the prevailing notion in the 'land grab' literature that large-scale land acquisitions are exclusively 'transnational' or 'international.' In Zimbabwe, large-scale land transactions are underpinned by partnerships between public and private actors, with land being primarily owned, used, and leased by state-owned entities. The Chisumbanje bio-ethanol project involves 9000 hectares of land acquired as a lease from the Agricultural and Rural Development Authority (ARDA). However, agrarian users 'owned' the land on customary basis and subsequently challenged this development. The highly secretive nature of the land deal raised concerns around the rights, wellbeing, and livelihoods of the local population who were not considered in the government's national strategy to address the dual economic and energy crisis through investments in arable land.

The Zimbabwe case study speaks to the development contradictions inherent to 'land grabs,' which reflect many of the experiences documented in this book and elsewhere (see Cotula 2012; de LT Oliveira 2013; Ballvé 2013; Broegaard et al. 2017; Schoenberger et al. 2017; Levien 2018). These contradictions are amplified in Zimbabwean politics where the commercial usurpation of communal lands is justified in the name of 'national interest' (Rutherford 2017; Matondi 2012). All land in Zimbabwe is owned by the state and administered by the Ministry of Lands and Rural Resettlement (MLRR), in conjunction with other ministries depending on the enterprise. The complexity of customary-statutory regimes is heightened by the multiplicity of players and their overlapping roles, such as the Ministry of Agriculture Mechanisation and Irrigation Development (which was central in the lease agreement that established the Chisumbanje bio-ethanol project) and the Zimbabwe Energy Regulatory Authority (which possesses an interest in promoting green energy solutions), among other public and private interests. The intense politicization of land governance at the local and national scales and its intersection with other domestic issues amplify the socio-economic marginalization of affected communities in Zimbabwe (see also Scoones et al. 2011; Rutherford 2012; Makate et al. 2019; Chamunogwa 2019; Chipato et al. 2020).

The findings from the chapters on Sierra Leone and Zimbabwe are symptomatic of what Chimhowu (2019) characterizes as the 'new' African customary tenure regime which distinguishes registered land from unregistered land. New class dynamics are created and institutional power relations altered as governments cease control of traditional or local land lease negotiations. Changes to the local 'ranking order' involves schisms between traditional 'big shots' and 'new elites.' Tzouvala (2019) describes how emerging instruments designed to regulate the transnational land rush are falling short of expectations. In the case of Sierra Leone, for instance, all chiefs are delegated some control or decision-making power over land transactions. However, certain chiefs are considered 'Kingpins' who profit disproportionately from land deals at the expense of other members of their lineage (see Ryan 2018). The job creation and other transformational benefits purportedly associated with land deals fail to materialize. Land holding communities find themselves locked in agreements that can last for more than 50 years, further compounding the negative ramifications of large-scale land acquisitions on local populations.

Formalization, Domestic Agency, and Legacies of Legal Pluralism

For the case of Ethiopia, Dejene and Cochrane (in Chapter 9) illustrate how social differentiation can be used to assess the micro-level outcomes of foreign land deals. The authors deploy the Land Matrix database to examine foreign land transactions involving deals of more than 200 hectares of land. The rapid growth in land deals in Ethiopia during and after the 2007/2008 commodity price spike created expectations that these investments would contribute to economic development through increased foreign currency reserves, technology transfer, increased production, and widespread employment. Promised developmental outcomes, however, did not materialize. Existing scholarship documents the devastating impacts of such large-scale land acquisitions (see Cochrane and Skjerdal 2015; Maru and Rutten 2015; Teklemariam et al. 2016). Dejene and Cochrane reveal the harmful impacts on regions such as Gambella and Benishangul-Gumuz in Ethiopia where minority rights were disregarded for the sake of 'national interest.' The authors contend that, with the right approach and in the right context, the impacts of land investment on livelihoods and incomes can be positive (see also Baumgartner et al. 2015). As noted in the chapter, contract farming may provide avenues by which investments can be profitable for foreign investors while maintaining the integrity of livelihoods and land tenure. Some criticize this outcome as 'stabilizing' poverty (e.g. Wendimu et al. 2015), while others highlight the potential for positive outcomes beyond contract modalities (e.g. Santiago 2019).

The theme of formalization is important to Dejene and Cochrane's chapter on Ethiopia. The introduction of a new land lease policy in 2013 institutionalized limits for leases and created provisions for stronger enforcement regulation, which has resulted in a drop in foreign investment or, in some cases, the annulment of existing leases. This chapter builds upon the work of other scholars such as that of Lavers (2016) which re-position the agency of the state in the land rush debate.

The history of land formalization in Ethiopia is highly politicized and involves multiple trajectories and developments, like other African countries affected by age-old land use conflicts (see Chimhowu and Woodhouse 2006; Berry 2017; Boone 2017; Mwendwa et al. 2018). Despite recent legislative changes, tensions surrounding land leases in Ethiopia continue due to a constitutional provision which institutionalizes land as a state property. Since 2008, all leases over 1000 hectares are to be handled by the federal government. Dejene and Cochrane examine how regulatory incentives underlie increases in foreign land deals; though meant to facilitate greater economic benefits for Ethiopia, these investor-oriented incentives have led to 'a race to the bottom.' Cheap land, weak regulation, low labour costs, and high tax breaks contribute to the impoverishment of Ethiopia's 'emerging' regions that bear the brunt of large-scale land deals. This chapter reveals the complexities of formalization as well as the intricate role of government in foreign land acquisitions.

In Chapter 10, Huggins deploys a political economy approach to highlight the hybrid legalities and institutional structures surrounding the land rush and its gendered ramifications. Drawing on four case studies in the Democratic Republic of the Congo (DRC), Huggins illustrates how large-scale land transactions can result in problematic outcomes for different stakeholders, especially groups traditionally excluded from the material gains of foreign transactions. The chapter underpins the multiscalar and intersectional lens needed to effectively understand land rush dynamics and their manifestation in specific sites. The hybridity of the land tenure system in the DRC is rooted in the late 1800s, specifically the State Land Decree of 1885, and a complex mixture of colonial and post-colonial legislation, such as the 1973 Land Law, the 2002 Forestry Law, the 2006 Constitution, and the 2011 Agricultural Law, among others. These different legislative instruments compete in an environment where the distinction between what is customary and what is 'formal' is not clear-cut. Legal pluralism serves as a double-edged sword in the land tenure systems examined in this book and beyond (see Hamann and Sneyd in this volume; Unruh 2003; Tegnan 2015; Andrews 2016; Baaz et al. 2017; Bisoka et al. 2020; Suhardiman et al. 2019). The 'land grabs' for oil palm plantations, mining, logging and agri-business parks, Huggins argues, demonstrates how legal ambiguities can result in conflicts between investors and host communities on the one hand, and dispossessed communities and political leaders, on the other. Like the case of Ethiopia, the DRC government is working in tandem with foreign actors and networks, leveraging legal uncertainties for the benefit of a small but growing class of domestic elites, at the detriment and further marginalization of rural smallholder farmers who depend on the land as a source of livelihood.

Concluding Remarks

The chapters provide an important contribution to understandings of the transnational land rush in Africa. The political economy framework guiding this collection enables critical insights into the policies, laws, regulations, and formal and informal decision-making processes (i.e. politics) that impact land acquisition processes and the ensuing socio-economic benefits and harms of land transactions (i.e. economics). The three intersecting areas of climate change, human rights, and social differentiation do not receive significant attention in this volume, which we see as an opportunity for future research. The land rush impacts livelihoods and the future of food security (see Gyapong 2020), with climate change expected to exacerbate local vulnerabilities. Mason-D'Croz et al. (2019) estimate that an additional 16 million people in Africa will be at risk of hunger by 2030 due to the impacts of climate change. Much of the current academic discourse focuses on the immediate or short-term impacts of the land rush. However, recent scholarship in Myanmar suggests that we should broaden our horizons due to the ever-present threat of the climate crisis (Borras et al. 2020b).

While many works in this collection focus on law, policy, and regulation, few focus on the concept of human rights in relation to the land rush. Authors such as Ashukem (2019) put forward approaches grounded in human rights as a way to assess the meaning and impacts of the land rush, as opposed to those based in national law and policy. These prefigurative types of critiques enable the envisioning of futures beyond existing frameworks and deepen our engagement with the resistance to the land rush. Human rights discourses, however, are not without issue and are most often driven by intergovernmental organizations and institutions based in the Global North, as Ibhawoh (2018) reminds us in his review of the problematic role played by "human rights" in Africa's history.

Finally, macro-level analyses tend to obfuscate the individual and group manifestations of inequality. Social differentiation, including age, ability, gender, ethnicity, religion, geographic location, marital status, economic status, educational attainment, legal status, and political affiliation, among others, is made invisible by macro-level data. Qualitative data and case studies highlight how the land rush has affected particular people, such as the gendered impacts of 'land grabs' (Hajjar et al. 2019; Lanz et al. 2019; Ndi 2019). The range of experiences related to power, class, ethnicity, and livelihoods are sometimes lost in this volume due to its broad scope and macro-level approach. Other works (see, for example, Barbesgaard 2019; Moreda and Spoor 2015; Regassa et al. 2019) document the differentiated impacts of the land rush and how practices of 'grabbing' replicate or multiply existing forms of marginalization, vulnerability, and discrimination. Increased attention to these differentiated impacts in detailed case studies can influence our engagement with, and understanding of, quantitative and macro-level data. We expect future work on the land rush topic and the intersecting issues of climate change, food security, human rights, and social differentiation to complement this volume.

References

Abate, Abebe Gizachew. 2020. The effects of land grabs on peasant households: The case of the floriculture sector in Oromia, Ethiopia. *African Affairs* 119: 90–114.

Acemoglu, Daron, and J.A. Robinson. 2013. *Why nations fail: The origins of power, prosperity, and poverty*. New York: Crown Business.

Andrews, Nathan. 2016. Challenges of corporate social responsibility (CSR) in domestic settings: An exploration of mining regulation vis-à-vis CSR in Ghana. *Resources Policy* 47: 9–17.

Andrews, Nathan. 2018. Land versus livelihoods: Community perspectives on dispossession and marginalization in Ghana's mining sector. *Resources Policy* 58: 240–249.

Andrews, Nathan. 2020. International Relations (IR) pedagogy, dialogue and diversity: Taking the IR course syllabus seriously. *All Azimuth: A Journal of Foreign Policy and Peace*. https://doi.org/10.20991/allazimuth.716687.

Andrews, Nathan, and Eyene Okpanachi. 2012. Trends of epistemic oppression and academic dependency in Africa's development: The need for a new intellectual path. *Journal of Pan African Studies* 5 (8): 85–104.

Ashukem, Jean-Claude. 2019. A human rights-based approach to foreign agricultural investments in Uganda. *African Journal of International and Comparative Law* 27 (2): 268–291.

Ayelazuno, J. 2011. Continuous primitive accumulation in Ghana: The real-life stories of dispossessed peasants in three mining communities. *Review of African Political Economy* 38 (130): 537–550.

Ayelazuno, Jasper Abembia. 2019. Land governance for extractivism and capitalist farming in Africa: An overview. *Land Use Policy* 81: 843–851.

Baaz, Mikael, Mona Lilja, and Allison Östlund. 2017. Legal pluralism, gendered discourses, and hybridity in land-titling practices in Cambodia. *Journal of Law and Society* 44 (2): 200–227.

Ballvé, Teo. 2013. Grassroots masquerades: Development, paramilitaries, and land laundering in Colombia. *Geoforum* 50: 62–75.

Barbesgaard, Mads. 2019. Ocean and land control-grabbing: The political economy of landscape transformation in Northern Tanintharyi, Myanmar. *Journal of Rural Studies* 69: 195–203.

Baumgartner, Phillip, Joachim von Braun, Degnet Abebaw, and Marc Muller. 2015. Impacts of large-scale land investments on income, prices and employment: Empirical analyses in Ethiopia. *World Development* 72: 175–190.

Bebbington, Anthony, Teresa Bornschlegl, and Adrienne Johnson. 2013. Introduction to development and change virtual issue 2. *Development and Change*. https://doi.org/10.1111/dech.12057.

Berry, Sara. 2017. Struggles over land and authority in Africa. *African Studies Review* 60 (3): 105–125.

Bisoka, A.N., C. Giraud, and A. Ansoms. 2020. Competing claims over access to land in Rwanda: Legal pluralism, power and subjectivities. *Geoforum* 109: 115–124.

Blyth, Mark. 2009. Torn between two lovers? Caught in the middles of British and American IPE. *New Political Economy* 14 (3): 329–336.

Boone, Catherine. 2017. Sons of the soil conflict in Africa: Institutional determinants of ethnic conflict over land. *World Development* 96: 276–293.

Borras Jr., Saturnino M., Jennifer C. Franco, Sergio Gómez, Cristóbal Kay, and Max Spoor. 2012. Land grabbing in Latin America and the Caribbean. *The Journal of Peasant Studies* 39 (3–4): 845–872.

Borras Jr., Saturnino M., Elyse N. Mills, Philip Seufert, Stephan Backes, Daniel Fyfe, Roman Herre, and Laura Michéle. 2020a. Transnational land investment web: Land grabs, TNCs, and the challenge of global governance. *Globalizations* 17 (4): 608–628.

Borras Jr., Saturnino M., Jennifer C. Franco, and Zau Nam. 2020b. Climate change and land: Insights from Myanmar. *World Development* 129: 104864.

Broegaard, Rikke Brandt, Thoumthone Vongvisouk, and Ole Mertz. 2017. Contradictory land use plans and policies in Laos: Tenure security and the threat of exclusion. *World Development* 89: 170–183.

Chamunogwa, Arnold. 2019. The negotiability of state legal and bureaucratic authority during land occupations in Zimbabwe. *Review of African Political Economy* 46 (159): 71–85.

Chimhowu, Admos. 2019. The 'new' African customary land tenure. Characteristic, features and policy implications of a new paradigm. *Land Use Policy* 81: 897–903.

Chimhowu, Admos, and Phil Woodhouse. 2006. Customary vs private property rights? Dynamics and trajectories of vernacular land markets in Sub-Saharan Africa. *Journal of Agrarian Change* 6 (3): 346–371.

Chipato, Fadzai, Libin Wang, Ting Zuo, and George T. Mudimu. 2020. The politics of youth struggles for land in post-land reform Zimbabwe. *Review of African Political Economy* 47: 59–77.

Cochrane, Logan 2012. Regulating corporate land purchases will reduce food insecurity. In *Food insecurity*, ed. Louise Gerdes, 99–112. Detroit: Greenhaven Press.

Cochrane, Logan. 2016. Land grabbing. In *Encyclopedia of food and agricultural ethics*, ed. P. Thompson and D. Kaplan. Dordrecht: Springer.

Cochrane, Logan, and Hussein Amery. 2017. Gulf cooperation council countries and the global land grab. *Arab World Geographer* 20 (1): 17–41.

Cochrane, Logan, and Terje Skjerdal. 2015. Reading the narratives: Resettlement, investment and development in Ethiopia. *Forum for Development Studies.* 42 (3): 467–487.

Cohen, Benjamin J. 2008. *International political economy: An intellectual history.* Princeton: Princeton University Press.

Collins, Andrea M., J. Andrew Grant, and Patricia Ackah-Baidoo. 2019. The glocal dynamics of land reform in natural resource sectors: Insights from Tanzania. *Land Use Policy* 81: 889–896.

Cook, Kate, and Matrix Chambers. 2019. *Due diligence, tenure and agricultural investment.* Rome: Food and Agriculture Organization.

Cotula, Lorenzo. 2009. *Land grab or development opportunity?: Agricultural investment and international land deals in Africa.* IIED.

Cotula, Lorenzo. 2012. The international political economy of the global land rush: A critical appraisal of trends, scale, geography and drivers. *Journal of Peasant Studies* 39 (3–4): 649–680.

Daley, Elizabeth. 2005. Land and social change in a Tanzanian village 2: Kinyanambo in the 1990s. *Journal of Agrarian Change* 5 (4): 526–572.

de LT Oliveira, Gustavo. 2013. Land regularization in Brazil and the global land grab. *Development and Change* 44 (2): 261–283.

Edelman, Marc, Ruth Hall, Saturnino M. Borras Jr., Ian Scoones, Ben White, and Wendy Wolford (eds.). 2017. *Global land grabbing and political reactions 'from below'.* New York: Routledge.

ElHadary, Yasin Abdalla Eltayeb, and Franklin Obeng-Odoom. 2012. Conventions, changes, and contradictions in land governance in Africa: The story of land grabbing in North Sudan and Ghana. *Africa Today* 59 (2): 59–78.

German, L., G. Schoneveld, and E. Mwangi. 2013. Contemporary processes of large-scale land acquisition in Sub-Saharan Africa: Legal deficiency or elite capture of the rule of law? *World Development* 48: 1–18.

Gyapong, Adwoa Yeboah. 2020. Land grabs, farmworkers, and rural livelihoods in West Africa: Some silences in the food sovereignty discourse. *Globalizations*: 1–16. https://doi.org/10.1080/14747731.2020.1716922.

Hajjar, Reem, Alemayehu N. Ayana, Rebecca Rutt, Omer Hinde, Chuan Liao, Stephanie Keene, Solange Bandiaky-Badji, and Arun Agrawal. 2019. Capital, labor, and gender: The consequences of large-scale land transactions on household labor allocation. *The Journal of Peasant Studies*. https://doi.org/10.1080/03066150.2019.1602520.

Hall, Ruth. 2011. Land grabbing in Southern Africa: The many faces of the investor rush. *Review of African Political Economy* 38 (128): 193–214.

Hall, Derek. 2019. Where is Japan in the land rush debate? *Canadian Journal of Development Studies*. https://doi.org/10.1080/02255189.2020.1678461.

Hall, Ruth, I. Scoones, and D. Tsikata. 2015. *Africa's land rush: Rural livelihoods and agrarian change*. Rochester: James Currey.

Hobson, John M. 2013. Part 1—Revealing the Eurocentric foundations of IPE: A critical historiography of the discipline from the classical to the modern era. *Review of International Political Economy* 20 (5): 1024–1054.

Ibhawoh, Bonny. 2018. *Human rights in Africa*. Cambridge: Cambridge University Press.

Jayne, T.S., A. Chapoto, N. Sitko, C. Nkonde, M. Muyanga, and J. Chamberlin. 2014. Is the scramble for land in Africa foreclosing a smallholder agricultural expansion strategy? *Journal of International Affairs*: 35–53.

Johnson, Juliet, Daniel Mügge, Leonard Seabrooke, Cornelia Woll, Ilene Grabel, and Kevin P. Gallagher. 2013. The future of international political economy: Introduction to the 20th anniversary issue of RIPE. *Review of International Political Economy* 20 (5): 1009–1023.

Jones, Branwen Gruffydd. 2005. Africa and the poverty of international relations. *Third World Quarterly* 26 (6): 987–1003.

Kapoor, Dip (ed.). 2017. *Against colonization and rural dispossession: Local resistance in South and East Asia, the Pacific and Africa*. London: Zed Books.

Land Matrix. 2018. *Data*. https://landmatrix.org/country/.

Lanz, Kristina, Elisabeth Prügl, and Jean-David Gerber. 2019. The poverty of neoliberalized feminism: Gender equality in a 'best practice' large-scale land investment in Ghana. *Journal of Peasant Studies*: 1–19. https://doi.org/10.1080/03066150.2019.1602525.

Lavelle, Kathryn C. 2005. Moving in from the periphery: Africa and the study of international political economy. *Review of International Political Economy* 12 (2): 364–379.

Lavers, Tom. 2012. 'Land grab' as development strategy? The political economy of agricultural investment in Ethiopia. *Journal of Peasant Studies* 39 (1): 105–132.

Lavers, Tom. 2016. Agricultural investment in Ethiopia: Undermining national sovereignty or a tool for state building? *Development and Change* 47 (5): 1078–1101.

Levien, Michael. 2018. *Dispossession without development: Land grabs in neoliberal India*. Oxford: Oxford University Press.

Liberti, Stefano. 2013. *Land grabbing: Journeys in the new colonialism*. London: Verso.

Makate, Clifton, Nelson Mango, and Marshall Makate. 2019. Socioeconomic status connected imbalances in arable land size holding and utilization in smallholder farming in Zimbabwe: Implications for a sustainable rural development. *Land Use Policy* 87: 104027.

Manda, S., A. Tallontire, and A.J. Dougill. 2020. Business 'power of presence': Foreign capital, industry practices, and politics of sustainable development in Zambian agriculture. *Journal of Development Studies* 56 (1): 186–204.

Margulis, Matias E., Nora McKeon, and Saturnino M. Borras Jr. (eds.). 2016. *Land grabbing and global governance*. New York: Routledge.

Maru, Shete, and Marcel Rutten. 2015. Impacts of large-scale farming on local communities' food security and income levels—Empirical evidence from Oromia Region, Ethiopia. *Land Use Policy* 47: 282–292.

Mason-D'Croz, Daniel, Timothy B. Sulser, Keith Wiebe, Mark W. Rosegrant, Sarah K. Lowder, Alejandro Nin-Pratt, Dirk Willenbockel, Sherman Robinson, Tingju Zhu, Nicola Cenacchi, Shahnila Dunston, and Richard D. Robertson. 2019. Agricultural investments and hunger in Africa modeling potential contributions to SDG2—Zero Hunger. *World Development* 116: 38–53.

Matondi, Prosper B. 2012. *Zimbabwe's fast track land reform programme*. London: Zed Books.

Maxwell, Daniel, and Keith Wiebe. 1999. Land tenure and food security: Exploring dynamic linkages. *Development and Change* 30 (4): 825–849.

Miller, Michelle Ann, Carl Middleton, Jonathan Rigg, and David Taylor. 2020. Hybrid governance of transboundary commons: Insights from Southeast Asia. *Annals of the American Association of Geographers* 1101: 297–313.

Moreda, Tsegaye, and Max Spoor. 2015. The politics of large-scale land acquisitions in Ethiopia: State and corporate elites and subaltern villagers. *Canadian Journal of Development Studies* 36 (2): 224–240.

Muraoka, Rie, Songqing Jin, and Thomas S. Jayne. 2018. Land access, land rental and food security: Evidence from Kenya. *Land Use Policy* 70: 611–622.

Mwendwa, G., A.K. Kiplagat, and J. Ngetich. 2018. The relationship between land use conflicts and land cover changes around Nairobi National Park. *Africa Environmental Review Journal* 3 (1): 188–199.

Ndi, Frankline. 2019. Land grabbing: A gendered understanding of perceptions and reactions from affected communities in Nguti Subdivision of South West Cameroon. *Development Policy Review* 37: 348–366.

Ochieng, Cosmas Milton Obote. 2020. Introduction. Rethinking land reform in Africa: New ideas opportunities and challenges. In *Rethinking land reform in Africa: New ideas, opportunities and challenges*, ed. by Cosmas Milton Obote Ochieng, 13–18. Abidjan: African Development Bank.

Odoom, Isaac, and Nathan Andrews. 2017. What/who is still missing in International Relations scholarship? Situating Africa as an agent in IR theorising. *Third World Quarterly* 38 (1): 42–60.

Osabuohien, E.S. 2014. Large-scale agricultural land investments and local institutions in Africa: The Nigerian case. *Land Use Policy* 39: 155–165.

Pearce, Fred. 2012. *The land grabbers: The new fight over who owns the earth*. Boston: Beacon Press.

Pedersen, Rasmus Hundsbaek. 2016. Access to land reconsidered: The land grab, polycentric governance and Tanzania's new wave land reform. *Geoforum* 72: 104–113.

Regassa, Asebe, Yetebarek Hizekiel, and Benedikt Korf. 2019. 'Civilizing' the pastoral frontier: Land grabbing, dispossession and coercive agrarian development in Ethiopia. *Journal of Peasant Studies* 46 (5): 935–955.

Rutherford, Blair. 2012. Shifting the debate on land reform, poverty and inequality in Zimbabwe, an engagement with Zimbabwe's land reform: Myths and realities. *Journal of Contemporary African Studies* 30 (1): 147–157.

Rutherford, Blair. 2017. *Farm labor struggles in Zimbabwe: The ground of politics*. Bloomington, IN: Indiana University Press.

Ryan, Caitlin. 2018. Large-scale land deals in Sierra Leone at the intersection of gender and lineage. *Third World Quarterly* 39 (1): 189–206.

Santiago, Anne Pitsch. 2019. Land grabbing or economic development? A modernisation debate enacted on Bugala Island, Uganda. *Journal of Contemporary African Studies*. https://doi.org/10.1080/02589001.2019.1607265.

Santika, Truly, Kerrie A. Wilson, Sugeng Budiharta, Elizabeth A. Law, Tun Min Poh, Marc Ancrenaz, Matthew J. Struebig, and Erik Meijaard. 2019. Does oil palm agriculture help alleviate poverty? A multidimensional counterfactual assessment of oil palm development in Indonesia. *World Development* 120: 105–117.

Scoones, Ian, Nelson Marongwe, Blasio Mavedzenge, Felix Murimbarimba, Jacob Mahenehene, and Chrispen Sukume. 2011. Zimbabwe's land reform: Challenging the myths. *Journal of Peasant Studies* 38 (5): 967–993.

Scoppola, Margherita, and Andrea Prontera. 2018. Transparency in Foreign Land Acquisitions: The role of institutions and information. *Development Policy Review*. https://doi.org/10.1111/dpr.12422.

Schoenberger, Laura, Derek Hall, and Peter Vandergeest. 2017. What happened when the land grab came to Southeast Asia? *The Journal of Peasant Studies* 44 (4): 697–725.

Suhardiman, Diana, John Bright, and Casper Palmano. 2019. The politics of legal pluralism in the shaping of spatial power in Myanmar's land governance. *The Journal of Peasant Studies*: 1–25. https://www.tandfonline.com/doi/abs/10.1080/03066150.2019.1656200.

Tegnan, Hilaire. 2015. Legal pluralism and land administration in west sumatra: The implementation of local and nagari governments' regulations on communal land tenure. *The Journal of Legal Pluralism and Unofficial Law* 47 (2): 312–323.

Teklemariam, Dereje, Hossein Azadi, Jan Nyssen, Mitiku Haile, and Frank Witlox. 2016. How sustainable is transnational farmland acquisition in Ethiopia? Lessons learned from the Benishangul-Gumuz Region. *Sustainability* 8 (3): 213.

Tzouvala, Ntina. 2019. A false promise? Regulating land-grabbing and the postcolonial state. *Leiden Journal of International Law* 32 (2): 235–253.

Unruh, Jon D. 2003. Land tenure and legal pluralism in the peace process. *Peace & Change* 28 (3): 352–377.

Van Bockstael, S. 2019. Land grabbing "from below"? Illicit artisanal gold mining and access to land in post-conflict Côte d'Ivoire. *Land Use Policy* 81: 904–914.

Walker, Julian Hugo, Barbara Lipietz, Victoria Ohaeri, Victor Onyebueke, and Oliver Ujah. 2019. Displacement and the public interest in Nigeria: Contesting developmental rationales for displacement. *Development in Practice*. https://doi.org/10.1080/09614524.2019.1694642.

Weber, Heloise. 2015. Is IPE just 'boring', 1 or committed to problematic meta-theoretical assumptions? A critical engagement with the politics of method. *Contexto Internacional* 37 (3): 913–944.

Wendimu, Mengistu, Arne Henningsen, and Peter Gibbon. 2015. Sugarcane outgrowers in Ethiopia: 'Forced' to remain poor? IFRO Working Paper 06, Department of Food and Resource Economics, University of Copenhagen.

Woods, Kevin M. 2020. Smaller-scale land grabs and accumulation from below: Violence, coercion and consent in spatially uneven agrarian change in Shan State, Myanmar. *World Development* 127: 104780.

Zoomers, Annelies. 2010. Globalisation and the foreignisation of space: Seven processes driving the current global land grab. *The Journal of Peasant Studies* 37 (2): 429–447.

Zoomers, Annelies. 2011. Introduction: Rushing for land: Equitable and sustainable development in Africa, Asia and Latin America. *Development* 54 (1): 12–20.

Zoomers, Annelies, and Mayke Kaag. 2014. *The global land grab: Beyond the hype*. London: Zed Books.

PART I

The Land-Development Nexus: Grand Discourses, Social Injustice and Contestations

CHAPTER 2

Agri-Business Development in Cameroon: Colonial Legacies and Recent Tensions

Steffi Hamann and Adam Sneyd

Introduction and Country Context

Cameroon's turbulent colonial period gave rise to large-scale plantations that remained the dominant feature of the country's agricultural sector throughout the twentieth century. While the influence of the German, British, and French empires plays a crucial role in shaping Cameroonian land relations until today, new actors from the domestic and international corporate sector have entered the market for the country's precious natural resources. Neoliberal policymaking drove the privatization of state-owned plantations and encouraged corporate investors to acquire land resources. As part of the fertile Congo Basin, the Central African country (Fig. 2.1) has been a site of intense land-related tensions for more than two centuries.

Large-scale land acquisitions in Cameroon proceeded in three major waves (Kenfack et al. 2016). The first wave entailed the appropriation of

S. Hamann (✉) · A. Sneyd
University of Guelph, Guelph, ON, Canada
e-mail: shamann@uoguelph.ca

L. Cochrane and N. Andrews (eds.), *The Transnational Land Rush in Africa*, International Political Economy Series,
https://doi.org/10.1007/978-3-030-60789-0_2

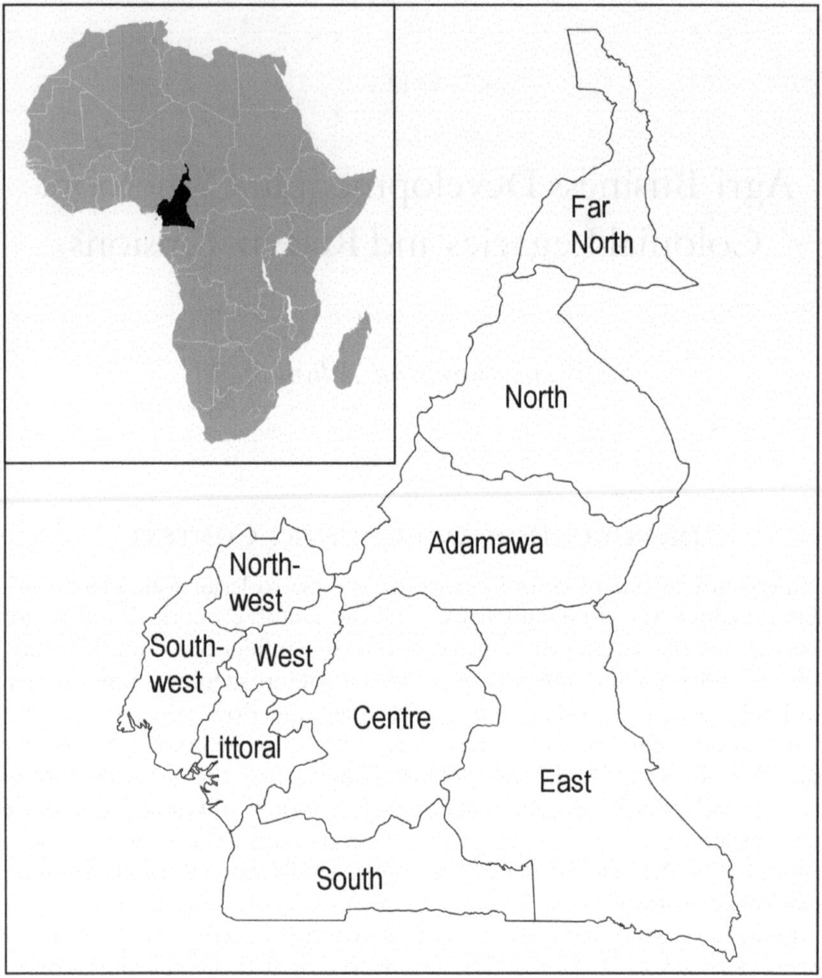

Fig. 2.1 Map of Cameroon (*Source* Created by the author using the online maps "Provinces of Cameroon EN" [Public Domain; see https://commons.wikimedia.org/wiki/File:Provinces_of_Cameroon_EN.svg#/media/File:Provinces_of_Cameroon_EN.svg] and "Locator map of Cameroon in Africa.svg" [CC BY-SA 3.0; see https://commons.wikimedia.org/wiki/File:Locator_map_of_Cameroon_in_Africa.svg#/media/File:Locator_map_of_Cameroon_in_Africa.svg])

fertile land tracts by European colonial entrepreneurs in the late 1800s (Hausen 1970; Epale 1985; Ewangue 2007). Under German rule, well over a dozen companies established cash crop plantations for the cultivation of coffee, cocoa, tobacco, rubber trees, bananas, and oil palms (Haupt 1984; Hamann 2017). Following Germany's defeat in World War I, the Cameroonian territory was divided into two separate League of Nations mandates. Incorporated into the colonial empires of France and Great Britain, the lucrative plantation economy continued to serve the extraction of economic surplus. The second major wave of land acquisitions was initiated in the two decades following decolonization and the 1961 unification of French and British Cameroon. Newly independent, the government invested heavily in agro-industrial expansion (Gerber 2008; Konings 2011). Numerous colonial possessions were nationalized and extended, leading to a boost in agricultural production on the one hand and increasing local resistance to growing land pressures on the other. The latest wave of large-scale land acquisitions in Cameroon took off in the beginning of the twenty-first century. It was chiefly a result of neoliberal reform policies symptomized by a government-led push for economic liberalization, agricultural commodification, and the privatization of production sites.

Both macroeconomic dynamics and deliberate policy change contributed to the most recent phase of land acquisitions. In the 1980s, soon after long-term dictator Paul Biya's ascent to power, Cameroon faced an economic downturn, experiencing negative growth rates and increased financial difficulties. The country was forced to accept drastic austerity measures imposed by the Bretton Woods institutions and, over the course of one and a half decades, implemented a series of structural adjustment programs in return for much-needed loans (World Bank 1989; African Development Bank 2002; African Development Fund 2005). Government spending was cut, and numerous state-owned enterprises were either closed or privatized. It was this period that saw a significant expansion in the influence of private actors in the country's economy.

The 2007/08 global food price crisis, combined with a rise in the demand for biofuel resources and growing financial sector interest, further boosted demand for agricultural land in sub-Saharan Africa (Kugelman 2013; Cotula 2013). Like other countries, Cameroon consequently increased its efforts to reap economic benefits from land-based transactions. Soon, reports emerged about land deals with foreign investors, particularly in the booming palm oil sector (Hoyle and Levang 2012).

The most spectacular case, which would later be termed the 'Herakles Debacle' (Bieleu 2012), involved an American investor professing the intention to set up a vast oil palm plantation in the Southwest region. It made for an astonishing tale involving unsustainable resource exploitation, corrupt back-door dealings, a blatant disregard for legal norms, and vigorous communal resistance. According to data from the Land Matrix, a total of 2,771,406 hectares (ha) have been subjected to land deals since the year 2000. As in several other cases highlighted in this volume (see, for example, Senegal in Chapter 3 and South Sudan in Chapter 4), the scale of actually realized deals is appreciably smaller. Concluded deals in Cameroon account for 2,065,998 ha, covering an area approximately the size of Slovenia. Timber, biofuel crops, and food products are the main drivers for large-scale land acquisitions in Cameroon.

We begin below with a brief outline of the theoretical framework and the methods used to study the Cameroonian case. We then proceed to detail the legal, policy, and regulatory context that shapes land transactions in the country. The core analysis focuses on agro-industrial deals in Cameroon's tropical region. We detail the land deals that have been registered in the Land Matrix and highlight the most prominent cases by drawing on published literature and field research findings. Three key insights can be distilled. Firstly, the land rush in Cameroon did not occur suddenly and neither was it driven primarily by the commodity price hike. Secondly, the perpetuation of conflictual land relations is a result of ineffective regulation. Thirdly, domestic actors, rather than foreign corporations, are of central importance for determining the outcomes of land-related investments in the country's agricultural sector.

Theoretical Framework

This case study employs on a critical development studies framework. It challenges core assumptions of the conventional view on socio-economic development, which postulates a process of national economic growth for impoverished countries that mimics the experience of highly industrialized nation-states. According to classical modernization thinkers, growth occurs through a set of identifiable stages that catapult national economies from traditional agricultural societies into an age of high mass-consumption (Rostow 1960). Inspired by the dominant economic philosophy of the post-war Truman era, this approach dates back to the mid-twentieth century and calls for technological innovation, specialization, and economies of scale. Modern-day market-liberal approaches echo the call for economic growth to promote development. In the agricultural sector, this calls for the industrialization of production processes, the commodification of agricultural resources, and a focus on export crops in order to boost trade activities and generate profits (Byerlee, et al. 2013; Adenle et al. 2017). Large-scale land acquisitions in Africa epitomize these processes as private-sector investors seek to expand their spheres of influence and engage in lucrative business ventures.

Critical development scholars, in turn, are sceptical about modernization narratives and market-liberalism. Informed by derivatives of dependency theory, neo-Marxism, post-development thinking and indigenous worldviews, critical development approaches seek to expose the shortcomings and contradictions of the mainstream orthodoxy (Veltmeyer and Bowles 2017). According to this view, the corporate farming model hinders sustainable development efforts as it results in land disputes, environmental degradation and a loss of rural livelihoods (Anseeuw et al. 2013; Hamann 2020). These perspectives highlight the negative impacts of large-scale land acquisitions, claiming they serve extractive purposes and exacerbate economic and social inequalities. Critical scholarship considers the contentious interplay and politics of ideas, institutions, and power relations in change processes (Sneyd 2019). It raises questions about land ownership, control, and the distribution of economic benefits among affected stakeholders. It has inspired forms of resistance against large-scale land acquisitions, such as the international peasant movement *La Vía Campesina*, which was formed in opposition to corporate-driven agriculture (Vía Campesina 2019). This study of Cameroon, therefore, introduces cases of land acquisitions from a perspective that centres largely around the impacts they have on rural communities and the resistance movements they have elicited.

Methods

The quantitative data used for this chapter was obtained from the Land Matrix in November 2019 (Land Matrix 2019). The information was compiled by the Cameroon National Land Observatory, which is hosted by two civil society organizations, the Centre pour le Développement et l'Environnement (CED) and the Mbororo Social and Cultural Association (MBoscuda). For each land deal listed in the database, the authors followed up and verified the current status wherever possible, based on publicly available data. If updates were found or gaps could be filled, the Land Matrix support staff was notified. This information was derived from a literature review involving media and civil society reports relating to the deals in question, relevant corporate publications, and legal frameworks. In addition, qualitative data was collected during three field trip missions between 2014 and 2017. The authors conducted more than 100 semi-structured and informal interviews with policymakers, corporate executives, researchers, journalists, CSO representatives, and farm workers in the agro-industrial sector to investigate the impacts of corporate investment projects in rural Cameroon.

Data accessibility for land deals in Cameroon is a serious challenge, as contracts concerning large-scale agriculture are not posted publicly by the government or corporate actors. Unless they are obtained and 'leaked' by civil society actors, information about the extent of land transactions largely relies on secondary reports and the input of key informants. While these limitations must be acknowledged, we are confident that the material collected for the Cameroonian case is representative of the overarching trends in the country.

The Land Matrix defines a land deal as 'any intended, concluded, or failed attempt to acquire land through purchase, lease, or concession (…) in low- and middle-income countries' (Land Matrix 2019). According to the criteria set up for the database, deals are usually recorded when they entail a transfer of rights to use, control, or ownership of a land area encompassing 200 ha or more. However, '[i]n some cases, regional and national criteria may differ from the global set if agreed to by the organization(s) coordinating it, for example, the amount of area covered' (Land Matrix 2019). This is the case in Cameroon, where seven deals fall below the 200-ha threshold. The analysis below focuses on agricultural projects. Mining and logging deals are not treated in significant depth due to the fact that these activities involve concessions that do not imply legal land possession but merely provide permit holders with a limited right to operate on the land. Only one agricultural deal currently listed in the Land Matrix was excluded from this analysis (deal #6000, involving Telcar Cocoa Ltd.) because it refers to an outgrower scheme and was listed with a deal size of 0 ha.

Legal, Policy, and Regulatory Context

The infamous 'Herakles Debacle,' which had made waves both nationally and in the international press, prompted an extraordinary move from the Cameroonian Prime Minster in 2014. The high-ranking official felt obliged to issue a special memo addressed to all federal ministries, stating:

> Some administrations undertake land commitments in violation of the laws and regulations in force in Cameroon (...). While reaffirming the willingness and availability of the Government of Cameroon to facilitate access to land for investors in our country, it is important to ensure that the laws and regulations are respected in this area. It therefore seems necessary to recall the procedures to be followed by domestic and foreign investors for access to land. (Government of Cameroon 2014)

This was followed by a seven-page summary of the complex regulatory framework that governs land transactions in the country. Given the fact that even policymakers and bureaucrats in the Cameroonian government required a refresher, this section will briefly outline the strategic guidelines and concrete laws that shape land-based policies and decisions concerning land deals in Cameroon. Central policies affecting land acquisitions in Cameroon include overarching economic framework such as the investment promotion policy and, more importantly, the land code itself.

Vision 2035 and Investment Code Reform

In the late 2000s, senior government officials in the Cameroonian administration started campaigning vigorously to attract private-sector investors. In its national strategy paper titled 'Cameroon Vision 2035,' the government boldly declared its ambition to become an emerging country by the year 2035 (Government of Cameroon 2009). A ten-year development plan called the *Growth and Employment Strategy Paper*—derived from the objectives spelled out in the 'Vision'—emphasized the state's desire to pursue modernization and industrialization in the agricultural sector in order to increase economic performance (MINEPAT 2009). The dominant strategic direction was devised by a generation of policymakers and bureaucrats who had been brought up and trained in the era of structural adjustment; many of them stout believers in neoliberal principles. These high-level figures advocate for a market fundamentalist perspective in the development of the agri-food sector (Sneyd 2014).

In line with this strategic orientation, the government overhauled its investment law and established the Investment Promotion Agency to offer generous economic incentives to potential investors—including low land rents, generous tax breaks, and a flexible labour code. The new investment code (Law No. 2013/004 of 18 April 2013) does not discriminate between local and foreign investors and contains no legal provisions for minimum investment requirements.

According to the new law, investors can benefit from substantial administrative and fiscal advantages during an initial five-year 'business establishment phase' and for the first ten years of the 'operational phase,' as long as they meet at least one of the following performance requirements: (1) Employ at least one Cameroonian for every 5–25 million XAF of projected investments; (2) Carry out annual export activity of at least 10% of total turnover excluding taxes; (3) Use national resources to the extent of 10–25% of the value of inputs; (4) Contribute to national value added to the tune of 10–30% of turnover.

Overall, the law is very lenient in comparison to most African investment codes. Even if a company fulfils only *one* of the stipulated conditions, it legally qualifies for a total of 15 years of substantial tax benefits across the board. According to statistical data obtained from the Investment Promotion Agency, 269 companies in various sectors of the Cameroonian economy had applied for the investment benefits between 2013 and mid-2016. Eighty-five of those applications had been approved—albeit, not all of them required substantial land areas for their proposed activities. Projected investments for the approved operations total more than $US1.7 billion, and the IPA expects that 33,765 jobs will be created for Cameroonians. Whether or not these optimistic predictions will in fact materialize can only be assessed on the ground once these business plans are put into operation.

Unlike the investment code, Cameroon's land code has not undergone a reform recently. This is perplexing, considering that it has been an official goal for almost a decade. In January 2011, President Paul Biya publicly declared land reform a matter of urgency and announced that it was to be completed within a span of six months (Nguiffo and Sonkoue 2015, 13). Yet, policymakers have been dragging their feet. Jacqueline Koung à Bessiké, head of the Ministry of State Property and Land Tenure since 2011, was ousted in January 2019 and criminally investigated due to allegations of corruption. As a result of failed efforts to reform, Cameroon's current land tenure regulations date back to the 1970s.

Cameroon's Land Code

Land tenure procedures in Cameroon are riddled with problems, ranging from a lack of transparency and corrupt allocation practices to their inherent gender blindness. The most recent fundamental land rights reform in Cameroon took place from 1974 to 1976, with the passing of the Land Tenure Ordinances that remain valid today. According to the 1974 decrees, all land in Cameroon is placed under the authority of the state. Article 1 (2) of Ordinance No. 74-1 of 6 July 1974 specifies: 'The State shall be the guardian of all lands. It may in this capacity intervene to ensure rational use of land or in the imperative interest of defence or the economic policies of the Nation.' The law decrees that all land which is to be characterized as 'private land' must be registered and titled—making registration the sole means of acquiring official land ownership.

All unregistered land is deemed to be either public or national land—the latter can be made available by the government for foreign or domestic investments. More precisely, the three categories for land management established in 1974 are distinguished as follows (Belaunde et al. 2010; Javelle 2013):

Private Domain: Includes lands for which an official title has been granted to a landholder by means of land registration. Private lands can be owned by individuals, corporate entities, or by the state. Private state lands are used, for example, to house public buildings.

Public Domain: Refers to land held by the state on behalf of the public and for collective use by the people of Cameroon; it is inalienable and includes land used for roads, waterways, and maritime areas.

National Domain: Encompasses all remaining land areas, which constitute the vast majority. The national domain is administered by the state 'for the public good' and is made up of land that is neither in the private nor in the public domain. It is considered a land reserve and includes most unoccupied land, grazing land, and all untitled land occupied and used by rural communities under customary law.

The legal implications of this ordinance are hotly contested (Alden Wily 2011; Kenfack et al. 2016). In the perception of the administration, the ordinance stipulates that private ownership of national land can merely be granted in terms of access rights, since the land belongs to the state. Civil society advocates, in turn, claim that the law does not grant ownership over untitled land to the government. According to this view, the national land domain belongs to the entire Cameroonian Nation (Assembe-Mvondo et al. 2014). As in most post-colonial African countries, Cameroon's contested land tenure system combines the modern (state-based) law with customary land rights. Customary law generally entails unwritten rules and procedures that regulate land relations at the community level (Alden Wily 2011). The axe-right—the right to usage of land, created through the clearing of wild vegetation and the planting of perennial crops—remains the most important form of designating customary land use rights. Community members recognize this form of law by respecting the physical boundaries of cleared territory that was put to productive use by one of their neighbours; traditional chiefs arbitrate in cases of disputes.

As members of 'Land Consultative Committees,' (LCCs) traditional chiefs are also consulted for official land registration procedures. Land Consultative Committees are established at the district level and include the Divisional Officer, local ministerial officials, and three community dignitaries (Decree 76/166 of 27 April 1976, Article 12). They serve as advisory boards to the Ministry of Land Tenure and—although the government can bypass their recommendations by a special decree—the board's deliberations play an important role in title allocation processes (Javelle 2013). The 1974 Ordinance established different sets of rules for titling lands in the national domain that are deemed 'occupied effectively' and for those deemed 'vacant lands.' To gain access to land that is deemed vacant or which was occupied after 1974, land investors must apply for a preliminary five-year concession. After a review by the local LCC, the concession can be granted either by ministerial decree (for plots that are smaller than fifty hectares) or by presidential decree (for larger plots). If, after five years, the LCC finds that the land has been effectively developed, the Senior Divisional Officer can transform it into a permanent concession, which confers a right to (a) title the land if the purchaser is Cameroonian; or (b) a long-term lease if the purchaser is from abroad (Belaunde et al. 2010; Javelle 2013). During the application process, a memorandum of understanding ('*cahier des charges*') must be submitted to the Ministry, which stipulates the rights and obligations of the investor and the state, respectively (Decree 76/166 of 27 April 1976, Article 7). Specifically, it sets out the obligations of the state and the developer, 'in particular with regard to the guarantee of a living space and the improvement of the living conditions for local populations' (Government of Cameroon 2014). There is no formal legal requirement for the free, prior informed consent of affected populations.

Information on the number of official land registrations in Cameroon is hard to obtain and inconsistent. In 2009, the Ministry of State Property estimated the total number of land certificates to be 150,000, while a study on the National Cadastral Survey Project estimated that there were already 2,600,000 plots in the year 2000 (African Development Bank 2009, 11). Legal procedures are complex and out of reach for many. Kenfack et al. (2016, 1) criticize that communities seeking recourse for a decision concerning a land concession 'have to go through the administrative courts, but this can be a lengthy and expensive process. And although each region now has an administrative court (thanks to the recent decentralisation of the judicial system), access to justice is still physically and financially beyond the reach of most local people.'

Influential community members, on the other hand, can benefit personally from such deals. Powerful chiefs and dignitaries represented on the LCCs can delay or accelerate the process of endorsing a land transaction (Teyssier 2004; Tadjudje 2005). Without clearly defined rules of conduct, their decisions can be arbitrary and subject to corrupt practices. Reports about illegal payments or acts of bribery to facilitate land deals emerge frequently in the Cameroonian context (Fotsing 1995; Mope Simo 2009; Dupuy and Achankap Bakia 2013; Fonjong 2019). Fonjong (2019) demonstrates that land deals tend to have the most negative effects on relatively marginalized groups in Cameroon's society, particularly rural women. This is due to women's 'over-reliance on the forest for cultivation, water, exploitation of non-timber forest products (NTFPs) and medicinal plants—resources which they risk losing' (Fonjong 2019, 219). He characterizes the land registration process in Cameroon as patriarchal and chronically gender-blind. There are no specific provisions necessitating gender equity for LCCs, and the vast majority of public officials in positions of power are men (Fonjong 2019, 224). Given the existing structural injustices, there are increasingly loud calls for land reform in Cameroon. The London-based International Institute for Environment and Development (IIED), in collaboration with Cameroonian civil society organizations, has been a major proponent of improved land governance in the country. Through the multi-year LandCam project, the IIED engages key stakeholders to foster inclusive dialogues, strengthen negotiation capacities, and encourage good governance on the path towards a comprehensive land law reform (LandCam 2019).

Findings: The New Rush for Land in Cameroon

When the latest African land rush took off, a new literature tracing investor activities and land ownership in Cameroon evolved. In 2009, the African Development Bank undertook a fact-finding mission and published a diagnostic study about the country's land and surveys sector. It found that most land in Cameroon was held informally in accordance with customary tenure arrangements. Formal land certificates had been issued 'for barely 2% of the territory' (African Development Bank 2009, 9). According to another estimate, only 11% of privately used land in Cameroon was directly registered as private domain (Belaunde et al. 2010). As investor interest increased, researchers and civil society organizations began tracking the ongoing negotiations, particularly in the agro-industrial sector. An explosive report by Hoyle and Levang (2012) surveyed the oil palm plantation sector and described the attempts of six transnational companies seeking to secure a total land area exceeding 1 million hectares in Cameroon's southern regions. Throughout the following years, more reports about land grabbing practices and their impacts on Cameroonian communities and biodiversity emerged (Williams 2013; Maulet and Elong 2015; Salisbury 2016; Greenpeace 2018). At the height of the land grab hype, the Yaoundé-based Center for the Environment and Development (CED), in collaboration with the IIED, reported that more than 1.3 million hectares of land had been sought by investors for agro-industrial purposes between 2005 and 2013 (Nguiffo and Sonkoue 2015). Based on extensive field missions, the authors identified 29 domestic and foreign agro-industry companies that had allegedly requested or already concluded lease contracts for large areas of fertile land in Cameroon.

What has become of these deals by the end of the 2010s? Who acquired land in Cameroon and for what purpose? Have all agro-industrial companies succeeded in securing the massive land concessions they were after? How many lease contracts were granted and how many of the negotiations failed? What role did local communities play in the negotiations between corporate actors and state officials? In responding to these questions, the remainder of this section presents a systematic analysis of the information recorded in the Land Matrix database for Cameroon a decade after the news broke globally about the latest African land rush.

Landscape of Investments Today

As of late November 2019, the Land Matrix has recorded 52 deals in Cameroon. The total land area that has allegedly been subjected to negotiations amounts to 2,771,406 ha, which covers approximately 44.7% of Cameroon's arable land (FAOSTAT 2019). A significant majority (44 deals) are marked as *concluded*; they account for 2,065,998 ha. The existing data shows that land transactions for which a contract was signed are almost exclusively located in Cameroon's fertile tropical zones (Table 2.1). The only outliers in the data set are 72 hectares of land-based transactions registered in Cameroon's semi-arid North Region; these are attributed to two mining ventures operating limestone and marble quarries (Bissou et al. 2014).

The area subjected to land deals in the East Region of Cameroon is almost twice as large as all other deals combined. This may come as a surprise to those familiar with the land grab literature originating in the country, as most of the existing research focuses on controversial projects in Cameroon's western, coastal, southern, and central geographical regions. Figure 2.2 provides an insight into the reasons behind the

Table 2.1 Location of investments by geographical region (aggregate contract size)

Geographical region	*Number of concluded deals*	*Contracted Land (in ha)*
East Region	17	1,319,314
Littoral Region	7	202,769
Centre Region	4	187,308
South Region	5	258,982
Southwest Region	4	85,843
Northwest Region	5	11,710
North Region	2	72

Data source Land Matrix (2019)

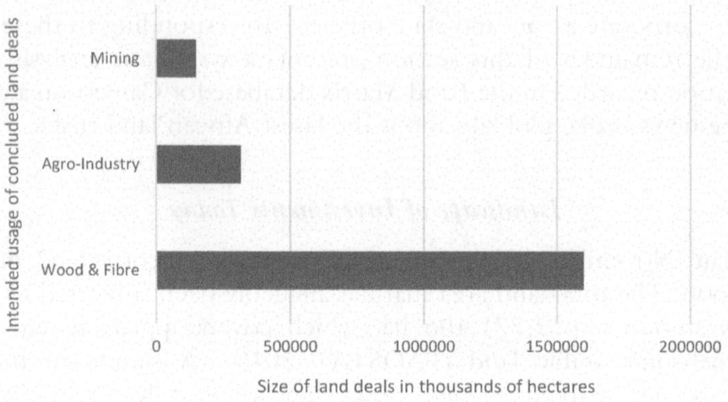

Fig. 2.2 Size of concluded land deals according to sector (*Data source* Land Matrix [2019])

geographical distribution of land claims. The vast majority of land transactions listed for Cameroon—1,600,414 ha in total—were registered in the logging sector and serve the purpose of extracting wood and fibre resources.

Most of the businesses in the wood and fibre sector are based in the forested East, Cameroon's largest and least densely populated region. Cameroon is Africa's largest exporter of tropical hardwood to the European Union, and yet, China has recently become the country's biggest timber buyer (EFI 2019; Mayers et al. 2019). Despite some improvements in the legal and institutional framework (APV Cameroun 2019; ATIBT 2019), the forestry sector contributes to unsustainable land use practices in Cameroon (Cannon 2015; Kahya 2016; Aroundsavath 2019).

East Cameroon is also the site of three metal mining operations: the dormant Cam Iron project owned by Australian investor Sundance (Sonti and Phillips 2010; Mbodiam 2019), the US-based Geovic mine intended for cobalt, nickel and manganese extraction (Reuters 2009; Andzongo 2019), and C&K Mining, a joint venture between Cameroonians and South Koreans that was exposed as a so-called 'pump and dump' scheme in 2014 (Reuters 2011; Mbodiam 2014). Mining accounts for a total of 148,697 ha in the dataset. However, except for the two northern quarries, there are no active industrial-scale mines in the country today. Industrial mining ventures in Cameroon's metal sector have been plagued by scandals implicating members of the political ruling class for corrupt practices

(Freudenthal 2016, 2017). Smaller non-industrial ('semi-mechanized') operations, which boomed in the 2000s and attracted a multitude of east Asian investors (Weng et al. 2015; Kouankap Nono et al. 2017; Jiji 2018), are not captured in the Land Matrix dataset.

Logging and mining concessions in Cameroon convey to the holder a limited right to operate on the land for a specific purpose; they do not entail outright land ownership. For this reason, they are excluded from the analysis below. This chapter instead centres around agro-industrial projects, which entail long-term usage rights and usually cause the greatest land grab controversies because of the effect they have on rural populations relying on farmland. In Cameroon, these deals are predominantly found in the coastal, central, southern, and western regions and make up a total of 316,887 ha in the Land Matrix dataset.

Agriculture Deals: Cases and Controversies

The Land Matrix database listed 20 concluded agricultural deals in late 2019. A total of eight deals have not—or not yet—come to fruition. A closer look at individual cases reveals that some companies' ambitions were significantly reduced or entirely abandoned over the course of their mission to obtain land in Cameroon. The latter category includes the 300,000-ha mega-deal proposed by the Malaysian-based palm oil producer Sime Darby (Brown 2011), a pitch by the Indo-Cameroonian business Justin Sugar Mills (Lewis 2012), and a 50,000-ha oil palm project proposed by US conglomerate Cargill (Reuters 2012), which were all eventually cancelled. Overall, the aggregate size of failed deals exceeds that of agricultural land transactions that have been completed in Cameroon (Fig. 2.3).

The timeline of recent investments is difficult to establish since the government does not make contracts freely available to the public and there is no specific law on freedom of information (Freedom House 2015). Data collected for publication in the Land Matrix is largely derived from painstaking field research, interviews, leaked documents, and secondary reports. One group of actors with a growing interest in the Cameroonian market for agricultural land concessions that is not adequately captured in this piecemeal dataset are national elites. The term 'élites' is used in francophone regions of sub-Saharan Africa to describe individuals in influential positions, including elected public officials, senior civil servants, military officers, or business owners, who exert

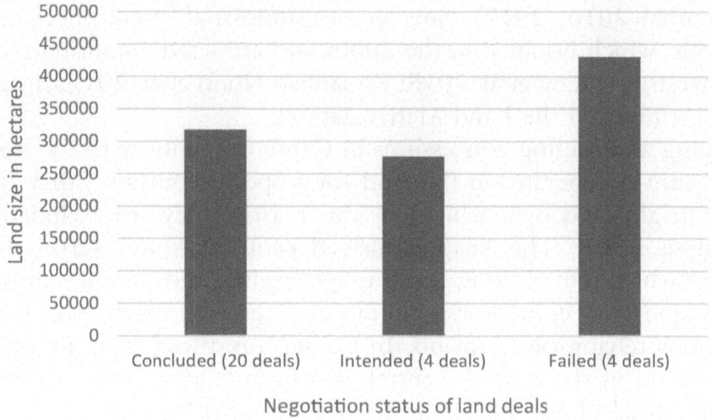

Fig. 2.3 Agricultural land deal size according to negotiation status (*Data source* Land Matrix [2019])

a considerable amount of power and influence in their communities through strategic acts of patronage. They differ from the majority of rural dwellers because they have regular and comparatively high incomes at their disposal. Following structural adjustment and the wave of dismissals in the public administration in the 1990s, numerous former officials sought investment opportunities to diversify their assets and secure their retirement. Some of them invested in agricultural plantations that encompass anything from approximately ten to several hundreds of hectares and often employ a rural labour force (Hamann 2017). Although there are no publicly available statistics regarding the number or extent of these plantations, it is certain that the amount has grown significantly in the past two decades, particularly in the palm oil sector. Research conducted in Cameroon's South Region in 2010, for example, identified ninety-three 'elite plantations' that covered a total surface area of 3,392 ha (Priso and Ndjogui 2011).

Table 2.2 lists the 20 agricultural deals that have been concluded in Cameroon between 2000 and 2019, according to the Land Matrix database. Most investments in Cameroon's agricultural sector involve large-scale concessions for the cultivation of food and biofuel crops, which is highlighted here with a brief discussion of the most prominent cases.

Table 2.2 Concluded agricultural land deals in Cameroon 2000–2019 by deal size

Operating company/parent company	*Origin of parent company*	*Deal size (ha)*	*Primary production sector*
SOCAPALM/SOCFIN	Luxembourg	63,763	Oil palm
HEVECAM/Halcyon	Singapore	59,365	Rubber
SUDCAM/Halcyon	Singapore	45,000	Rubber
Cameroon Development Corporation/Government of Cameroon	Cameroon	41,000	Oil palm
Pamol Plantations PLC/Government of Cameroon	Cameroon	24,300	Oil palm
SG Sustainable Oils Cameroon/Herakles Capital	USA	19,843	Oil palm
Plantations du Haut Penja (PHP)[a]/Compagnie Fruitière	France	17,806	Banana
SAFACAM/SOCFIN	Luxembourg	15,500	Rubber
SOSUCAM/SOMDIAA	France	11,980	Sugar cane
Société des Palmeraies de la Ferme Suisse/SOCFIN	Luxembourg	5700	Oil palm
Ndamware Highland Tea Estate/Baba Ahmadou Group	Cameroon	5000	Tea
Palm Resources Cameroon/Biopalm Energy	Singapore	3348	Oil palm
Upper North Valley Development Authority (UNVDA)	Cameroon	3000	Rice
Boh Plantations Limited (BPL)	Cameroon	700	Banana
West End Farms/Phatisa	Mauritius	350	Poultry
Sino-Cam Iko Ltd./Shaanxi Overseas	China	120	Rice
Orient's Sugar and Industry (OSI)	USA	100	Maize
Unknown/Smart Globe International	USA	12	Cacao, coffee

[a]Three separate deals are registered for this investor, accounting for 12,506 ha, 4,500 ha and 800 ha, respectively

Data source Land Matrix (2019)

Several of the major agricultural deals took place during the structural adjustment era, starting in the late 1980s. The state-owned fruit-producing Plantations du Haut Penja (PHP) was sold to the French Compagnie Fruitière in 1987, and its subsequent growth has given rise to a deeply conflictual relationship with local communities (Bieleu 2011; Transparency International 2014). In 1996, the public rubber plantation HEVECAM was sold to Singapore-listed Halcyon Agri (formerly GMG Global), a subsidiary of the Chinese Sinochem Group. In 2008, the investor expanded with the establishment of a second operation known as SUDCAM. The gigantic rubber business has come under fire for unsustainable environmental practices, community displacement, and poor labour conditions (Greenpeace 2018; Fritts 2019; Mayers et al. 2019). The state-owned sugar producer CAMSUCO was taken over by the French SOMDIAA group in 1998, then integrated into the existing private SOSUCAM operation, and expanded significantly in 2006 (Hamann, forthcoming-a). In 2000, the government ceded the majority of its shares for the oil palm plantation SOCAPALM to the SOCFIN group, which is controlled by the Belgian Fabri and the French Bolloré families. SOCFIN also eventually acquired the SAFACAM and the Ferme Suisse plantations and started expanding its plantations, emerging as the dominant agro-industrial palm oil producer in the francophone part of the country today (Schneider 2015; Hamann 2017). In the anglophone Southwest region, the government operates two major parastatal plantation businesses, the Cameroon Development Corporation (CDC) and PAMOL Plantations. Although privatization has been on the official agenda for decades, it is doubtful whether it is the true intent of those in power, because this step would lead to a significant loss of central government control in this strategically important region, that has been the site of secessionist tensions for years.

The most recent land rush wave saw several spectacular deals that gave rise to significant scrutiny and local resistance movements. Biopalm Energy, a subsidiary of the Singaporean SIVA group, established a new concession in the South region. While initial reports suggested that it targeted a land area of 200,000 ha (Cameroon News 2011), it was eventually granted 3,348 ha via temporary lease in 2012. By presidential decree, Paul Biya authorized the signing of an emphyteutic lease covering 18,365 ha in December 2018; local indigenous communities and civil society organizations are contesting the decision vigorously

(Forest Peoples Programme 2019a, b). The most infamous case of agricultural land grabbing in Cameroon was the establishment of Sithe Global Sustainable Oils Cameroon (SGSOC), better known as Herakles Farms. It gained attention in 2012, when a US-based venture capital firm claimed to have obtained a 99-year lease for a 73,000-ha concession in Cameroon's Southwest region. A memorandum of understanding between the investor and the government initially provided for an annual rent of 1.00 USD per hectare for developed land and 0.50 USD for undeveloped land, with an annual rate increase of 2% (Government of Cameroon and Herakles Farms 2009). Demarcation and clearing operations started in 2010 in spite of the fact that the required presidential decree was not issued until 2013; and rather than fulfilling lofty promises relating to infrastructure development and employment creation, SGSOC engaged in corrupt business practices and illegal logging activities to finance its operations (Mousseau 2013; Greenpeace 2013). The activities were met with fierce opposition by local residents and the actual land concession granted was eventually reduced to less than 20,000 ha. The 'Herakles Debacle' exposed disastrous deficiencies in Cameroon's land allocation system and generated a wealth of research (Nguiffo and Schwartz 2012; Dupuy and Achankap Bakia 2013; Greenpeace Africa 2016; Ndi 2018; Wanki and Ndi 2019).

Apart from prominent transnational deals, a number of private Cameroonian investors have acquired smaller land areas for the cultivation of lucrative crops. This includes Baba Ahmadou Danpullo's tea estates and the Boh Plantations banana business (Trustfull 2017; Mbodiam 2017). One case that has raised serious contentions is the Greenfil/Azur oil palm plantation, an investment in the Littoral region by business magnate Nana Bouba Djoda. The site is located in close proximity to the Ebo Forest, home to endangered species (Mowbray 2017). Though listed as an 'intended' agricultural deal, site visits revealed that planting activities have begun even before an official land lease was obtained (Mbadi 2016; Earthsight 2018; Osuna Orozco and Salber 2019; Hamann, forthcoming-b).

Conclusion and Discussion

This chapter employed a critical development perspective to expose the drivers and impacts of the land rush in Cameroon and highlighted contesting ideas, institutions, and power relations among relevant stakeholders. Three key insights can be gleaned from studying the recent history of agricultural land acquisitions in Cameroon. Firstly, the land rush in the Central African country did not happen suddenly, and neither was it principally a result of the commodity price hike. Secondly, weak regulations play a significant role in the perpetuation of conflictual land relations in Cameroon. Thirdly, domestic actors and processes, not foreign corporations, are at the core of the rush for land in the country's agricultural sector.

The bulk of the land grab in Cameroon took place during the colonial era, when imperial powers asserted controlling rights over African land areas and European businesses established their exploitative plantation economy in Cameroon's most fertile regions. The overarching structure of the rural economy has not been subjected to any major disruptions since decolonization, leaving large-scale agriculture in place as the dominant producer of cash and food crops such as palm oil, rubber, tobacco, and bananas. Recent land acquisitions in Cameroon were not the result of an outright land rush perpetuated by foreign actors, but to a large degree the effect of colonial legacies and government policy. The surge in long-term leases for large-scale concessions around the turn of the twenty-first century was not primarily an outright rush for land by foreign companies, but to a large degree the effect of neoliberal restructuring. The privatization of publicly-owned operations was the driver behind key acquisitions such as the SOCAPALM palm oil plantations, the HEVECAM rubber plantations, the PHP banana plantations, and the CAMSUCO sugar cane plantations. Rather than entailing a complete restructuring of the rural landscape, these deals involved the transfer of majority shares over existing production infrastructure from the Cameroonian government to private investors. In most cases, the investors subsequently proceeded to acquire additional land resources in the vicinity of the existing production sites, once they had taken ownership of key assets. A close look at the Cameroonian data therefore shows that private-sector involvement in large-scale land deals started years before the 'land grab hype.' Although the commodity price hike did give rise to speculative investment ventures, the scale of the phenomenon in Cameroon was smaller than originally anticipated. Around the time that interest in transnational land acquisitions peaked, Nguiffo and Sonkue (2015) identified 29 agro-industry investors seeking land tracts in Cameroon, whose demands added up to more than 1.3 million ha. The Land Matrix data of 2019 shows that the agricultural sector in fact accounts for a total of 316,887 ha of land deals concluded after the turn of the millennium. The largest and most spectacular deals did not come to fruition as once envisioned. This includes the oil palm mega-deals proposed by Sime Darby, Herakles Capital, and Cargill. Their failure or curtailment may well be a result of the close scrutiny to which they were subjected by civil society organizations.

The second major conclusion from the Cameroonian case study is that weak and ineffective regulations are at the centre of Cameroon's land-related disputes. Although domestic policies play a significant role in driving land ownership trends in the country, the existing governance frameworks are primarily designed to incentivize investment activities. Regulations designed to mitigate harmful behaviours, such as environmental destruction or rent seeking, are feeble or outdated. For almost a decade, Cameroonian constituents have waited in vain for an update of the land and tenure laws. The state is the bearer of sovereign power and the only formal institutions that can officially sanction illegal activities through legislative and judicial processes. With a land code that dates back to the 1970s and administrative processes that lack transparency, Cameroonians are adversely affected by their uncertain policy environment. Land tenure is subjected to a complex duality that combines written legal acts and customary rights. Significant power is granted to Land Consultative Committees, with insufficient oversight or accountability regarding corrupt or avaricious activities. Women tend to be marginalized in land transactions as a result of dominant patriarchal structures and the gender blindness of existing regulatory frameworks. Without a formal legal requirement for free, prior, and informed consent or the equitable sharing of benefits, rural communities are easily subjected to exploitation and dispossessed of their livelihood resources. Agro-industrial land transactions remain obscure, although there has been some progress on the transparency of deals in the forest and mining sectors in recent years. To develop a system of control and verification of legal timber exports, Cameroon signed a Voluntary Partnership Agreement with the European Union's Forest Law Enforcement, Governance and Trade Facility (VPA-FLEGT) in 2010 (EFI 2019). The Ministry of Forests and Wildlife has published a list of valid forestry titles on the government's official VPA website (APV Cameroun 2019). Nevertheless, the forestry sector is falling short. The VPA is not currently operational (ATIBT 2019). The official VPA website suffers from frequent outages and information on the volume of timber production and export remain inaccessible, preventing proper traceability. In the Cameroonian mining sector, monitoring and operational capacities of the Ministry of Mines have been enhanced thanks to an advanced geo-mapping system for the Cameroonian mining cadastre. In 2016, a contract was awarded to the Vancouver-based company Spatial Dimensions, which created a digital web portal that publishes mining- and cadastre-related data (Feast 2016; FlexiCadastre 2017). Similar innovations must be implemented in the agricultural sector.

The third and final takeaway from studying Cameroon is that the land rush was not perpetuated solely by foreign investors, but that domestic actors play a decisive role in the context of land transactions. This echoes the impressions from several other chapters in this volume. The spike in agricultural deals in Cameroon was a direct result of government policies, and the state continues to offer significant incentives to attract potential investors. At the same time, the government has a solid hold on large-scale plantations in strategically selected locations, namely in the conflict-ridden western provinces. In contrast to the wave of privatizations that was initiated in the francophone parts of the country, the Cameroon Development Corporation and PAMOL Plantations—two of the largest employers in anglophone Cameroon—have retained their status as state-owned companies throughout this period. Revenues have plummeted lately, as a result of the violent clashes between anglophone separatists and government forces that started shaking the region in 2016 (Mbodiam 2020). Aside from the Cameroonian government, other national investors also play a more important role than foreseen during the 'hype.' Wealthy nationals are the driving force behind a number of notable investment projects in the agricultural sector. Finally, although the scale of the 'land grab' in Cameroon is smaller than originally expected, there are a number of foreign-initiated ventures that gave rise to concern due to their harmful impacts on local populations and the environment, including Herakles Farms, SUDCAM and Biopalm Energy. These and other controversial deals have been under close scrutiny by civil society organizations and gave rise to evolving forms of local resistance. Contentious social movements and the mobilization of affected communities led to a significant reduction or outright abandonment of several mega-deals, revealing that Cameroonian nationals have the power and agency to disrupt land grabbing practices.

References

Adenle, Ademola, Louise Manning, and Hossein Azadi. 2017. Agribusiness innovation: A pathway to sustainable economic growth in Africa. *Trends in Food Science & Technology* 59: 88–104.

African Development Bank. 2002. Cameroon structural adjustment programme II project performance evaluation report. Operations Evaluation Department.

African Development Bank. 2009. Cameroon—Diagnostic study for modernization of the lands and survey sectors. Country Regional Department Center.

African Development Fund. 2005. Republic of Cameroon: Third structural adjustment programme completion report.

Alden Wily, Liz. 2011. *Whose land is it? The status of customary land tenure in Cameroon*. Yaoundé: Center for Environment and Development, FERN, the Rainforest Foundation UK.

Andzongo, Sylvain. 2019. American Geovic promises XAF235 bln of investment in its nickel-cobalt-manganese project in Cameroon. *Business in Cameroon*, July 29.

Anseeuw, Ward, Lorenzo Cotula, and Mike Taylor. 2013. Expectations and implications of the rush for land: Understanding the opportunities and risks at stake in Africa. In *Handbook of land and water grabs in Africa: Foreign direct investment and food and water security*, ed. Tony Allan, Martin Keulertz, Suvi Sojamo, and Jeroen Warner, 421–435. New York, NY: Routledge.

APV Cameroun. 2019. Accord de partenariat volontaire. Accessed November 27, 2019: https://www.apvcameroun.com/.

Aroundsavath, Frida. 2019. *Undercutting rights: Human rights and environmental due diligence in the tropical forestry sector*. Stockholm, Sweden: Swedwatch.

Assembe-Mvondo, Samuel, Carol Colfer, Maria Brockhaus, and Raphael Tsanga. 2014. Review of the legal ownership status of national lands in Cameroon: A more nuanced view. *Development Studies Research* 1 (1): 148–160.

ATIBT. 2019. Challenges and recommendations identified to relaunch Cameroon FLEGT VPA. Accessed November 27, 2019: https://www.atibt.org/en/challenges-and-recommendations-identified-to-relaunch-cameroon-flegt-vpa/.

Belaunde, Sandra, Maria Cortes, Jonathan Hogstad, Enrique Ku, Kode Nascimento, and Leah Trzcinski. 2010. *Land, legitimacy and governance in Cameroon*. Research Report. New York, NY: Columbia University and Institute for Research and Debate on Governance.

Bieleu, Frank. 2011. *The Big Banana*. Directed by Franck Bileu. Produced by ArtMattan.

Bieleu, Frank. 2012. *The Herakles Debacle*. Directed by Franck Bieleu. Produced by Oakland Institute, Center for Environment and Development.

Bissou, Michel, Jaff Bamenjo, and Apollin Koagne. 2014. *EITI and mining governance in Cameroon: Between rhetoric and reality*. Yaoundé: RELUFA and Natural Resource Governance Institute.

Brown, Kevin. 2011. Sime Darby eyes palm oil expansion in Africa. *Financial Times*, February 27.

Byerlee, Derek, Andres Garcia, Åsa Giertz, and Vincent Palmade. 2013. *Growing Africa: Unlocking the potential of agribusiness*. Washington, DC: The World Bank.

Cameroon News. 2011. SIVA group, BioPalm Energy Limited: FCFA 900 billion oil palm project launched in Kribi, Cameroon. Cameroon Today, August 25. Yaoundé.

Cannon, John. 2015. Illegal logging still a big issue in Cameroon. Mongabay.

Cotula, Lorenzo. 2013. *The great African land grab? Agricultural investments and the global food system*. Zed Books: New York, NY.

Dupuy, Julien, and Mor Achankap Bakia. 2013. Fact finding mission on Herakles Farms (SGSOC) oil palm plantation project. Ministry of Forestry and Wildlife, Programme for the Sustainable Management of Natural Resources.

Earthsight. 2018. *The coming storm*. London, UK: Earthsight.

EFI. 2019. Cameroon. European Forest Institute. Accessed November 27, 2019: https://www.euflegt.efi.int/cameroon.

Epale, Simon. 1985. *Plantations and development in western Cameroon, 1885–1975: A study in agrarian capitalism*. New York: Vantage Press.

Ewangue, Jean-Lucien. 2007. L'économie de plantation et son impact au Cameroun sous administration française, 1916–1960. Doctoral thesis, Université Paris Diderot, Paris, France, March 20.

FAOSTAT. 2019. Land use. Accessed November 20, 2019: https://www.fao.org/faostat/en/#data/RL.

Feast, Bill. 2016. Spatial dimension. Cameroon adopts FlexiCadastre to drive mining sector governance and growth, May 13. Accessed October 10, 2016: https://www.spatialdimension.com/News/News/ArticleID/290/Cameroon-adopts-FlexiCadastre-to-drive-mining-sector-governance-and-growth#prettyPhoto.

FlexiCadastre. 2017. Cameroon mining cadastre portal. Accessed November 27, 2019: https://portals.flexicadastre.com/cameroon/en/.

Fonjong, Lotsmart. 2019. Mainstreaming gender in the process of large-scale land acquisitions for agro-investments in Cameroon. In *Natural resource endowment and the fallacy of development in Cameroon*, ed. Lotsmart Fonjong, 215–244. Bamenda: Langaa.

Forest Peoples Programme. 2019a. Cameroon: The Bagyeli women strongly opposing Biopalm.

Forest Peoples Programme. 2019b. Declaration by NGOs & associations on land grabbing by the government & Biopalm Energy Ltd.

Fotsing, Jean-Marie. 1995. Compétition foncière et stratégies d'occupation des terres en pays Bamiléké. In *Terre, terroir, territoire: Les tensions foncières*, ed. Chantal Blanc-Pamard and Luc Cambrézy, 131–148. Paris: ORSTOM.

Freedom House. 2015. Freedom of the press report. Freedom House.

Freudenthal, Emmanuel. 2016. Virtual mining in Cameroon: how to make a fortune by failing. African Arguments, March 14.

Freudenthal, Emmanuel. 2017. Au Cameroun, des fortunes se font et se défont sur une mine de fer qui n'a jamais produit. *Le Monde*, September 24.

Fritts, Rachel. 2019. Huge rubber plantation in Cameroon hals deforestation following rebuke. Mongabay.

Gerber, Julien-François. 2008. *Résistances contre deux géantsindustriels en forêt tropicale*. Montevideo: World Rainforest Movement.

Government of Cameroon. 2009. *Cameroon Vision 2035*. Yaoundé: Ministry of Economy, Planning and Regional Development.

Government of Cameroon. 2014. Circulaire relative aux dispositions applicables aux investisseurs pour l'accès à la terre au Cameroun. Circulaire No 001/CAB/PM, Yaoundé. Cameroon: Prime Minister's Office.

Government of Cameroon and Herakles Farms. 2009. Establishment convention by and between the Republic of Cameroon and SG Sustainable Oils Cameroon, September 17.

Greenpeace. 2013. *Herakles farms in Cameroon: A showcase in bad palm oil production*. Washington, DC: Greenpeace USA.

Greenpeace. 2018. Halcyon Agri's ruinous rubber. Greenpeace Africa.

Greenpeace Africa. 2016. Herakles Farms/SGSOC: The chaotic history of a destructive palm oil project. Randburg, South Africa.

Hamann, Steffi. 2017. Sustainability and governance of palm oil development in sub-Saharan Africa: Evidence from Cameroon. Doctoral Thesis, University of Guelph, Guelph, ON.

Hamann, Steffi. 2020. The global food system, agro-industrialization and governance: Alternative conceptions for sub-Saharan Africa. *Globalizations* 17 (8): 1405–1420.

Hamann, Steffi. forthcoming-a. Greasy business: Perceptions of responsibility in Cameroon's palm oil sector. In *Commodity politics: Contesting responsibility in Cameroon*, Adam Sneyd, Steffi Hamann, Charis Enns, and Lauren Sneyd (co-authors). Montreal, QC and Kingston, ON: McGill-Queen's University Press.

Hamann, Steffi. forthcoming-b. Sugaring up responsibility: Sugar and formal corporate social responsibility in Cameroon. In *Commodity politics: Contesting responsibility in Cameroon*, Adam Sneyd, Steffi Hamann, Charis Enns, and Lauren Sneyd (co-authors). Montreal, QC and Kingston, ON: McGill-Queen's University Press.

Haupt, Werner. 1984. *Deutschlands Schutzgebiete in Übersee 1884–1918*. Friedberg: Podzun-Pallas Verlag.

Hausen, Karin. 1970. *Deutsche Kolonialherrschaft in Afrika: Wirtschaftsinteressen und Kolonialverwaltung in Kamerun vor 1914*. Zurich and Freiburg: Atlantis.

Hoyle, David, and Patrice Levang. 2012. *Oil palm development in Cameroon*. Yaoundé: WWF, IRD, CIFOR.

Javelle, Anne-Gaelle. 2013. Land registration in Cameroon. Focus on Land in Africa Brief, World Resources Institute and Landesa.

Jiji. 2018. Chinese gold mining in Cameroon tied to killings, corruption and land grabs. *The Japanese Times*, April 23.

Kahya, Damian. 2016. Investigation: How illegal timber from Cameroon's rainforest could be landing in China's ports. Greenpeace.

Kenfack, Pierre-Etienne, Samuel Nguiffo, and Téodyl Nkuintchua. 2016. *Land investments, accountability and the law: Lessons from Cameroon*. London: International Institute for Environment and Development (IIED).

Konings, Piet. 2011. *Crisis and neoliberal reforms in Africa*. Bamenda: Langaa Research and Publishing Common Initiative Group.

Kouankap Nono, Gus Djibril, Cliford Tah Bong, Pierre Wotchoko, Alice Magha, Japhet Kuma Chianebeng, and Joëlle Flore Tene Djoukam. 2017. Artisanal gold mining in Batouri area, East Cameroon: Impacts on the mining popluation and their environment. *Journal of Geology and Mining Research* 9 (1): 1–8.

Kugelman, Michael. 2013. Introduction. In *The global farms race: Land grabs, agricultural investment, and the scramble for food security*, ed. Michael Kugelman and Susan Levenstein, 1–20. Washington, DC: Island Press.

LandCam. 2019. About us. Accessed November 30, 2019: https://www.landcam.org/en/about-us.

Land Matrix. 2019. Cameroon. Accessed November 30, 2019: https://landmatrix.org/data/?country=120.

Lewis, David. 2012. Cameroon, Indian investors target $113 million sugar plant, August 14. Accessed November 13, 2019: https://www.reuters.com/article/cameroon-india-sugar/cameroon-indian-investors-target-113-mln-sugar-plant-idUSL6E8JEB8020120814.

Maulet, Eloise, and Emmanuel Elong. 2015. Global resistance to land grabs by Bolloré and Socfin. GRAIN.

Mayers, James, Samuel Nguiffo, and Samuel Assembe-Mvondo. 2019. *China in Cameroon's forests: A review of issues and progess for livelihoods and sustainability*. London: International Institute for Environment and Development (IIED).

Mbadi, Omer. 2016. Agro-industrie: au Cameroun, Nana Bouba Djoda prépare la relève. *Jeune Afrique*, May 25.

Mbodiam, Brice. 2014. C&K Mining sells assets in Mobilong diamond mining to Chinese-American investor. *Business in Cameroon*, November 24.

Mbodiam, Brice. 2017. Boh Plantations, the minnow in the banana market in Cameroon, boosts national exports at end May 2017. *Business in Cameroon*, June 22.

Mbodiam, Brice. 2019. Sundance Resources expects a new agreement on Mbalam iron project before end June 2020. *Business in Cameroon*, October 22.

Mbodiam, Brice. 2020. Pamol and CDC's turnover plummeted by 83.4% and 60.9% respectively in 2016–2018, due to separatists crisis. *Business in Cameroon*, January 24.

MINEPAT. 2009. Growth and employment strategy paper: Reference framework for government action over the period 2010–2020. Yaoundé: Ministry of Economy, Planning and Regional Development.

Mope Simo, John. 2009. Challenges to chieftaincy today. In Les mutations en Afrique, ed. Elizabeth Tamajong, 159–193. Yaoundé: Presses d'UCCAC.

Mousseau, Frederic. 2013. *Herakles exposed: The truth behind Herakles farms. False promises in Cameroon*. Oakland, CA: Oakland Institute and Greenpeace International.

Mowbray, Sean. 2017. Ebo forest great apes threatened by stalled Cameroon national park. Mongabay, April 3. Accessed February 13, 2020: https://news.mongabay.com/2017/04/ebo-forest-great-apes-threatened-by-stalled-cameroon-national-park/.

Ndi, Frankline. 2018. Land grabbing, gender and access to land: Implications for local food production and rural livelihoods in Nguti sub-division, South West Cameroon. *Canadian Journal of African Studies* 53 (1): 131–154.

Nguiffo, Samuel, and Brendan Schwartz. 2012. *Herakles' 13th labour? A study of SGSOC's land concession in South-West Cameroon*. Yaoundé: Centre Pour l'Environnement et le Développement.

Nguiffo, Samuel, and Michelle Sonkoue. 2015. *Agro-industrial investments in Cameroon: Large-scale land acquisitions since 2005*. London, UK: International Institute for Environment and Development.

Osuna Orozco, Ana, and Maud Salber. 2019. Palmed off. Rainforest Foundation.

Priso, D. Dickens, and Thomas Eric Ndjogui. 2011. Élites urbaines dans la région du Sud (Cameroun): Analyse des spéculations et des superficies des exploitations. In *L'Elite Urbaine dans l'Espace Agricole Africain*, ed. Joseph Gabriel Elong, 175–196. Paris: L'Harmattan..

Reuters. 2009. Geovic determined on Cameroon cobalt mine. Thomson Reuters.

Reuters. 2011. C&K wins license for Cameroon diamond mine. Thomson Reuters.

Reuters. 2012. Cameroon says Cargill eyes 50,000-ha oil palm project, May 22. Accessed November 13, 2019: https://www.reuters.com/article/cargill-cameroon-palm-idAFL5E8GMFNE20120522.

Rostow, Walt. 1960. *The stages of economic growth: A non-communist manifesto.* Cambridge, MA: Cambridge University Press.

Salisbury, Claire. 2016. Palm oil's new frontier: Averting a Great Ape catastrophe in Cameroon. Mongabay.

Schneider, Victoria. 2015. The palm oil company at the centre of a bitter land rights struggle in Cameroon. *The Guardian*, July 27.

Sneyd, Adam. 2014. Cameroon: Perspectives on food security and the emerging power footprint. *Sustainability* 6 (4): 1868–1895.

Sneyd, Adam. 2019. *Politics rules: Power, globalization and development*. Black Point, NS: Fernwood.

Sonti, Chalpat, and Liam Phillips. No survivors in plane crash. *Sydney Morning Herald*, June 20.

Tadjudje, Willy. 2005. La déconcentration de la gestion foncière au Cameroun: une analyse du décret n°2005/481 du 16 décembre 2005. DEA thesis, Université de Yaoundé II, Yaoundé.

Teyssier, André. 2004. La régulation foncière au Cameroun : Entre régimes communautaires et aspirations citoyennes. *Cahiers Agricultures* 13: 522–527.

Transparency International. 2014. *Banana report: The bone of contention and its acidic political taste*. Yaoundé: Transparency International Cameroon.

Trustfull, Paul. 2017. Baba Ahmadou Danpullo: Africa's discreet business magnate. *World Finance*, February 1.

Veltmeyer, Henry, and Paul Bowles. 2017. *The essential guide to critical development studies*. London: Routledge.

Vía Campesina. 2019. The international peasant's voice. Accessed November 19, 2019: https://viacampesina.org/en/international-peasants-voice/.

Wanki, James, and Frankline Ndi. 2019. Land grabbing in south-western Cameroon: Deconstructing the complexity of local responses. In *Natural resource endowment and the fallacy of development in Cameroon*, ed. Lotsmart Fonjong, 111–146. Bamenda: Langaa.

Weng, Lingfei, Dominique Endamana, Agni Klintuni Boedhihartono, Patrice Levang, Chris Margules, and Jeffrey Sayer. 2015. Asian investment at artisanal and small-scale mines in rural Cameroon. *The Extractive Industries and Society* 2 (1): 64–72.

Williams, Laila. 2013. Herakles Cameroon palm oil project starts to run off the rails. Greenpeace.

World Bank. 1989. *Memorandum and recommendation of the president of the International Bank for Reconstruction and Development to the executive directors on a proposed loan of US$150 million equivalent to the Republic of Cameroon for a structural adjustment program*. Washington, DC: International Bank for Reconstruction and Development.

CHAPTER 3

The Faltering Land Rush and the Limits to Extractive Capitalism in Senegal

Marie Gagné and Ashley Fent

Introduction

Since the 2000s, the Senegalese government has emphasized agriculture and mining as strategic priorities for economic development. The promotion of large-scale agro-industrial projects and the awarding of mining licences reflect a strong embrace of extractive capitalism, wherein the state relies on the production, extraction, and export of agricultural produce and natural resources as the basis for economic growth. These domestic priorities have aligned with broader transformations in the international economic environment, particularly the spatial relocation of capitalistic investments to the Global South, including Senegal.

M. Gagné (✉)
Concordia University, Montreal, QC, Canada
e-mail: marie.gagne@mail.concordia.ca

A. Fent
Vassar College, Poughkeepsie, NY, USA

L. Cochrane and N. Andrews (eds.), *The Transnational Land Rush in Africa*, International Political Economy Series,
https://doi.org/10.1007/978-3-030-60789-0_3

Despite the Senegalese government's commitment to extractive capitalism and a higher global demand for food and mineral commodities, several high-profile projects in the agricultural and mining sectors have not materialized due to project failure, delay, or abandonment. Although the lack of accessible and accurate information makes it difficult to assess the magnitude of the land rush in Senegal, we conclude based on an original dataset that the number of new land-based projects gradually diminished after peaking in 2008. Several announced investments have also fallen through, particularly in the biofuel sector and to a lesser extent in the agricultural and mining sectors.

What accounts for the discrepancy between stated goals and realized investments? In this chapter, we analyse why external investors have been unable to acquire land or fully cultivate acquired land, have yielded substandard crop outputs, have failed to meet project schedules, and/or have cancelled projects completely.[1] We identify three main factors that account for the faltering land rush and the limits to extractive capitalism in Senegal: (1) the effectiveness of social resistance to land investments, (2) the contradictory behaviour and motivations of the Senegalese state, and (3) the managerial deficiencies of companies in charge of these projects. We argue that the abandonment, delay, or cancellation of most projects are attributable to some combination of these factors.

Agricultural and mining projects—whether ongoing, delayed, or failed—may have detrimental impacts on local populations and ecological systems. Many communities in Senegal have been unjustly dispossessed of their land and have often been unable to either recover land that investors do not farm or force companies to respect their unfilled promises (GRAIN 2018). Some companies also deforested vast swathes of land that were ultimately left uncultivated, thereby aggravating soil erosion and depriving communities of access to food, pastures, and ecosystem services.

In this chapter, we first introduce our theoretical framework and then describe our methods. Next, we appraise the characteristics of the land rush in Senegal, followed by an analysis of the reasons for a low level of project implementation. We conclude with a discussion about the future of extractive capitalism and land deals in Senegal.

[1] By external investors, we mean both domestic and foreign investors who are outsiders to the community where they seek land.

Contemporary Land Deals as Extractive Capitalism

The rapid growth of land deals worldwide in the early 2000s was triggered by dramatic increases in global food prices and high demand for biofuels, amid concerns about the viability and price volatility of conventional energy sources. Land deals also served as an important outlet for speculative capital in the aftermath of the global financial crisis of 2008–2009 (Anseeuw et al. 2012; Knuth 2015). Pressures on land were further heightened by a surge of investments in tree plantations, onshore petroleum drilling, and open-pit mining (Cotula 2012), indicating the frequent co-occurrence of agricultural land deals with other forms of primary commodity extraction (Hamann and Sneyd, this volume). Urbanization, infrastructure development, and large tourist complexes are also important factors in the increased demand for land but are beyond the scope of this chapter.

We examine project delays and contestations over agricultural and mining deals through the lens of extractive capitalism, while also offering some correctives to this analytical approach. Extractivism is a model of economic growth that is highly dependent on the production, extraction, and exportation of natural resources, including minerals, oil, timber, and cash crops (Veltmeyer 2013). The theorization of extractive capitalism goes further, suggesting that natural resource exploitation played a central role in the historical development of colonialism and global capitalism. As Wolfgang Sachs (2010, xi) states, '[t]here would have been no industrial society without the mobilization of resources from both the expanse of geographical space and the depth of geological time.' These processes of commodification continue to channel agricultural, mineral, and hydrocarbon resources into commercial circuits that primarily serve the capitalist interests of a global elite concentrated in a handful of countries, as opposed to local communities.

However, capitalism is perpetually plagued by two key contradictions. David Harvey (2003) describes the first contradiction: expanded reproduction generates overaccumulation crises. These crises are temporarily resolved through spatial fixes that create new investment opportunities. Capitalism requires the continual production of new, high-profit spaces for investment; as private ventures become concentrated in these areas, capital experiences diminishing returns and must seek opportunities in places that have experienced disinvestment or that have not yet been commodified (Smith 2008 [1990]). This process often involves accumulation by dispossession, that is, the use of extra-economic measures such as coercion, violence, or legal action to free up land and resources (Harvey 2003). The second contradiction hinges upon capitalism's dependence on and depletion of finite resources; in so doing, capitalism continually undermines the ecological basis of its own reproduction (Foster 2002). As a result of these two contradictions, new kinds of natural resource commodities are produced and exploited in new places. This creates new capitalist frontiers, where resource extraction often displaces existing users of land, replaces forms of crop production, and disrupts social and ecological processes.

Analyses of extractive capitalism and uneven development are helpful in generating broad theorizations of global political economy. However, they tend to overlook the numerous contestations and obstacles that investors confront in new locales. Projects frequently encounter "friction" (Tsing 2005) when interacting with local systems of knowledge, social practices, and political interests. Although many African governments have in recent years adopted extractivism as a developmental paradigm and attempted to reform their business environment to "make room" for private investors, this strategy is an unfinished and incoherent process (Baglioni and Gibbon 2013). Thus, investors may be unable to implement and maintain projects in places with little existing capital investment, infrastructure, or market opportunities.

Foreign capital does not enter areas that are blank slates. New relationships between investors, local populations, and the state in regard to land ownership create and reproduce complex opportunities for dispossession and enrichment—not only by foreign firms seeking to extract resources and generate profit, but also by local elites and state actors. Early media and academic reports on land grabs focused largely on the role of external actors and the "foreignisation of space" (Zoomers 2010); however, national elites, parastatals, and regional investors take part in land transactions both as brokers and acquirers (Anseeuw et al. 2012; Faye et al. 2011; Hall 2011). States also have their own objectives in facilitating land expropriation and/or increased commercialization of farming—processes which do not exclusively serve the imperatives of capital but also benefit domestic elites. For example, national actors may secure land through "indirect dispossession," sometimes for personal interests (Fairbairn 2013). Some state agents may on the contrary refuse to succumb to the pressures of external investors, choosing instead to protect local populations from destitution and displacement.

Although the land grab literature understands land deals as an outlet for restless capital, many projects fail to materialize either in the course of negotiations or when confronted with the financial and managerial challenges arising from large-scale operations (Anseeuw et al. 2012; Cotula 2012; Deininger 2011; Schönweger and Messerli 2015). When projects are in fact implemented, they often begin at a much smaller scale than initially publicized (Cotula 2012). It might have been expected that low levels of implementation early in the land rush would improve over time as companies gradually entered the production stage. However, it seems that implementation rates are stagnating or decreasing. This demonstrates that global extractivist ventures unfold in variegated and complicated ways, defying facile depictions of unrestrained capitalist expansion. The literatures on extractive capitalism and on land deals have not yet fully identified the broader causes and implications of failed investments. This chapter offers some answers in the context of Senegal.

Methods

The chapter builds on three empirical case studies that involved sustained field research by the two authors: two agribusiness projects (Jatropha Technology Farm and Senhuile) and one mining venture (the Niafarang Project) (see Fig. 3.1).[2] Both authors also drew upon desk studies of mining and agricultural land deals in Senegal to complete the analysis.

Marie Gagné conducted extensive fieldwork for a total of two years, investigating the determinants of corporate land control through a combination of documentary analysis, more than 300 qualitative interviews, and field observations. She examined seven cases of large-scale land acquisitions, with a particular focus on the two most ambitious biofuel projects initiated to-date in Senegal. The first case study is Jatropha Technology Farm (JTF), a 50,000-hectare (ha) project launched in 2009 in eastern Senegal for the production of biofuels. The investor was forced to cease operations after only two years due to the revocation of their forestry permit and, by extension, their land concession. The second project is Senhuile, a 20,0000-ha land deal halted in October 2011 due to the vehement opposition of municipal councillors, villagers, and Dakar-based elites. The conflict over Senhuile resulted in fatalities, leading President

[2] Senhuile now operates as Les Fermes de la Teranga. In this chapter, we use Senhuile, the investor's most widely known name by the broader public.

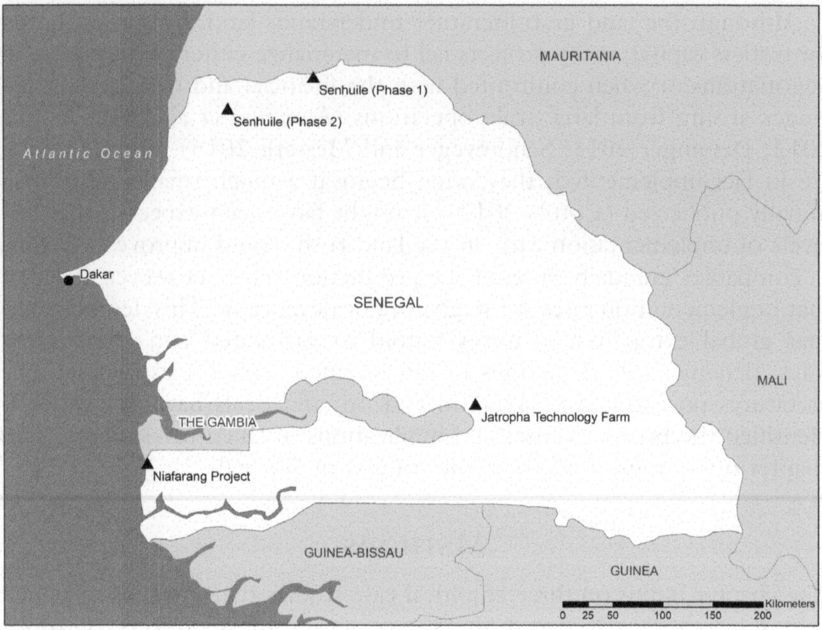

Fig. 3.1 Case Study Locations (map by Ashley Fent)

Abdoulaye Wade to relocate the investment to the Senegal River delta to avoid further controversy. The project started as a biofuel venture but eventually converted to agribusiness. In addition to these case studies, Gagné compiled a comprehensive original inventory of agricultural and mining projects initiated in Senegal since the 1890s, with contributions from the second author. She collected data using newspaper articles, grey literature, institutional reports, fieldwork materials, and existing inventories.

Ashley Fent conducted ethnographic research on the Niafarang Project, a controversial stalled zircon and titanium sands mining project in Casamance, over fourteen months between 2014 and 2015–2016, with return visits in 2017 and 2019. Her field research included sustained participation in daily community life; attendance at public forums, village assemblies, and meetings of activist groups in opposition to the mining project; and building relationships with state actors and local residents in affected villages. She also conducted 80 interviews with residents, activists, members of the separatist Movement of Democratic Forces of Casamance (*Mouvement des forces démocratiques de la Casamance*), appointed state agents at multiple levels of government, elected local officials, officials in the regional and national offices of the Ministry of Industry and Mines and the Ministry of Environment and Sustainable Development, and consultants for the mining project. In 2014, she also conducted a series of interviews with local residents affected by Grande Côte Operations, an operational zircon and titanium sands in northern Senegal.

Country Background and Legal Frameworks

Political Situation in Senegal

Senegal's strong and pluralist civil society has been instrumental in shaping the country's political trajectory since independence in 1960 (Diop and Diouf 1990). Senegal is widely regarded as a stable democracy, with a history of peaceful transitions of power and changes in ruling parties—most notably, from the Socialist Party to the Senegalese Democratic Party with Abdoulaye Wade's election in 2000. In 2012, another smooth transfer of power occurred with the election of Wade's former Prime Minister, Macky Sall, who represented the Alliance for the Republic and the coalition party Benno Bokk Yakaar. Despite its strong democratic reputation, Senegal still suffers from issues of corruption (particularly under the Wade administration), the suppression of political opposition, and weak governmental capacity (Shipley 2018). Nevertheless, the fact that protests and active civil society participation are legal in Senegal has provided opportunities for successful action against recent land deals.

Senegal has also been ideologically and legally committed to a process of decentralization since independence, including in the realm of natural resource management. The Senegalese state rolled out administrative reforms in this regard shortly after independence, in 1964 and 1972. The 1972 reforms established rural councils while retaining the central appointment of prefects and sub-prefects who assumed a "supervisory" role over local leadership (Faye 2008). These rural councils served as the local government for rural communities (*communautés rurales*), which were comprised of several villages. In 1996, Senegal passed a decentralization law that shifted more power and decision-making authority to local governments in the governance of land (Faye 2008). In theory, decentralization entailed increased public involvement and localized decision-making. However, decentralization rarely resulted in more equitable access for community members; instead, new opportunities for elite rent-seeking and corruption emerged (Ribot 1999). In 2013, an institutional reform commonly referred to as Decentralization Act III further reorganized the territorial distribution of decision-making power and converted rural communities into *communes* (République du Sénégal 2013).

Land Tenure in Senegal

Surface land acquisition by corporations occurs in one of three ways in Senegal, depending on the relevant jurisdiction. Investors can obtain (1) an "excerpt of minutes" on land belonging to the **national domain**; (2) a long-term lease for land located in the **state domain**; and (3) a property title on land in the **private domain.**[3]

The national domain comprises all land that has not been registered as part of the private or state domain, which covered approximately 95% of the territory when the National Domain Law was enacted in 1964. Municipal councils administer rural zones of the national domain and issue "excerpts of minutes" to land claimants whose requests have been approved (République du Sénégal 1964). Excerpts of minutes do not confer permanent ownership rights; claimants only receive revocable use rights conditional on farming the land. Most agricultural entrepreneurs seek excerpts of minutes.

The state domain is divided into two categories: public and private. The state can partition and sell land or buildings belonging to its private domain. It can also grant long-term leases of up to 50 years with a possibility of renewal (République du Sénégal 1976). Long-term leases confer on their beneficiaries a substantive land right subject to mortgage, but not the right to alienate land. These leases also involve the obligation to put land to productive use, pay rent, and cover property expenses. Long-term leases are not an overly common mechanism of land acquisition in Senegal, although they are on the rise.

The private domain refers to land officially registered in the cadastre (*Livre foncier*) and owned by natural or legal persons, principally in urban

[3] Some investors also informally rent land from local users.

areas (République du Sénégal 2011). In principle, private property offers the most durable form of land control, but it is not very common in Senegal. Studies suggest that only 20,000 written property titles existed in 1960 (Hesseling 2009, 269). By 2015, this number had reached 152,000 titles (Agence de presse sénégalaise 2015a) in a total population of approximately 15 million people.

The National Domain Law and subsequent laws assumed that land users in rural areas were local farmers, not external investors. The legislative goal was to confirm customary land rights and allow previously excluded peoples, such as the descendants of slaves, to access land (Hesseling 2009). As a result, the law does not require municipal councils to carry out public consultations when approached by land-seeking investors. The capacity of local populations to negotiate fair deals with external parties and achieve intra-community consensus thus varies considerably. In addition, most people in rural areas still hold land under customary arrangements, as the state never fully enforced the National Domain Law. Whereas other African countries have since the 1990s introduced reforms to protect customary land rights (Amanor 2008), Senegal does not formally recognize traditional land rights that are unregistered with the state. Additionally, although the Environmental Code stipulates that environmental impact assessments must include public hearings (République du Sénégal 2001), several companies fail to fulfil these obligations. Even when they do, populations cannot veto projects, and the government does not have the capacity to monitor company compliance with agreed-upon mitigation measures.

The laws and regulations of the mining sector are somewhat different than those pertaining to land and agriculture. Like most countries, Senegal considers subsurface resources to be the exclusive property of the nation. The central state is the only entity that is legally able to negotiate and approve exploration and mining licences (Diallo 2017). As exploration licences are legally accorded without any consultation of the public, the only opportunity for public comment and involvement in negotiations occurs during environmental and social impact assessments, prior to the granting of a mining licence. Local people and elected municipal governments, although entitled to participate in the public hearings mentioned above, possess very limited power in blocking or amending proposed projects. However, there are usually community- or individual-level negotiations between investors and affected populations about compensation following the state's approval of mining licences.

These various legal lacunas have facilitated land acquisitions by external investors in the agricultural and mining sectors. In some cases, the lack of prior consultation has compelled aggrieved populations to engage in vigorous anti-land grab campaigns, as we discuss later in this chapter.

The Senegalese Land Rush

Large-scale land deals for agribusiness and mining in Senegal are not new. The French colonial government set up experimental farms and irrigation schemes in the Senegal River Valley from the early nineteenth century until the eve of independence (Seck 1991). Concessionary companies also established a few sisal, rubber, and manioc plantations, mostly in Eastern Senegal and Casamance. However, these colonial experiments were for the most part unsuccessful and short-lived, partially due to labour shortages and resistance to forced labour (Touré 1984). The agricultural sector in Senegal remained primarily dominated by smallholders cultivating food and export crops independently or under the leadership of religious *marabouts*, especially Mourides.[4]

In post-colonial Senegal, examples of large-scale agricultural schemes include: the attribution of thousands of hectares to powerful *marabouts* in keeping with colonial practices; the creation in 1970 of the Compagnie sucrière sénégalaise that now covers more than 12,000 ha; a domestic elite-driven land grab for rice farming in the Senegal River Valley in the 1990s; and the gradual allocation of 20,000 ha to a Saudi company for the production of Arabic gum in the Peanut Basin starting in 1999. While the colonial and early post-colonial economies were based on groundnut production, international donors encouraged a re-orientation towards horticultural exports in the late 1970s. Most exporters in this sector were Senegalese businesspeople who initially sourced agricultural produce through contract farming. The introduction of more stringent food safety and quality standards in European markets from the mid-1990s onwards led many Senegalese exporters to vertically integrate and switch, at least partially, to "estate farming" over vast areas of land (Baglioni 2015, 23).

[4] The Mouride brotherhood is a Muslim Sufi order, whose organization is based on the unpaid labour of disciples who cultivate the land of their spiritual guide (*marabout*), in exchange for which they eventually receive a plot of land of their own.

Although land acquisitions in Senegal since the 2000s have occurred in the context of longer histories of land expropriation, commercialization, and conversion, they are distinguished from earlier processes of dispossession by their scale, intensity, and purposes (Anseeuw et al. 2012; Cotula et al. 2014). According to our data, the number of land deals in Senegal sharply accelerated in the mid-2000s during the administration of President Abdoulaye Wade (2000–2012), who promulgated various agricultural and biofuel programmes. For example, President Wade put in place the REVA Plan (*Plan Retour vers l'agriculture*) and the Grand Agricultural Offensive for Food and Abundance (*Grande offensive agricole pour la nourriture et l'abondance*), which both explicitly invited the private sector to invest in agriculture. Under Wade's presidency, attempted or concluded land deals occurred on an unprecedented scale. Many Senegalese individuals, who might not have otherwise become involved in agriculture, seized the opportunity and responded to President Wade's invitation. Companies from countries as diverse as Italy, France, Great Britain, Norway, Romania, Israel, India, Saudi Arabia, and Nigeria also became involved in Senegal's agribusiness sector.

Senegal's current President Macky Sall, elected in 2012 and re-elected in 2019, does not fundamentally depart from the objectives and policies of his predecessor. President Sall has continued existing programmes such as the Programme for National Rice Self-Sufficiency and has realized projects initially conceived by the Wade administration, such as the creation of investment funds to finance small and medium enterprises in the agricultural sector. However, the number of new land deals since Sall's ascension to power has significantly diminished; the Senegalese state under President Sall even interrupted some high-profile investments it previously supported.

Under both Wade and Sall, new investors have targeted areas with existing infrastructure near urban centres. Many of the recorded deals in our database involve horticultural export companies located in the Senegal River delta, particularly the departments of Dagana and Saint-Louis (see Fig. 3.2). Approximately 20 horticultural farms are also located in the Niayes, a fertile farming region along the coast that stretches from the Rufisque Department to the Louga Department. The Department of Mbour is also a popular destination for mining projects.

Contemporary land deals in the mining sector also build on colonial and post-colonial histories of extractivism. For example, the European Compagnie des Mines de Falémé-Gambie, founded in 1911, dredged for

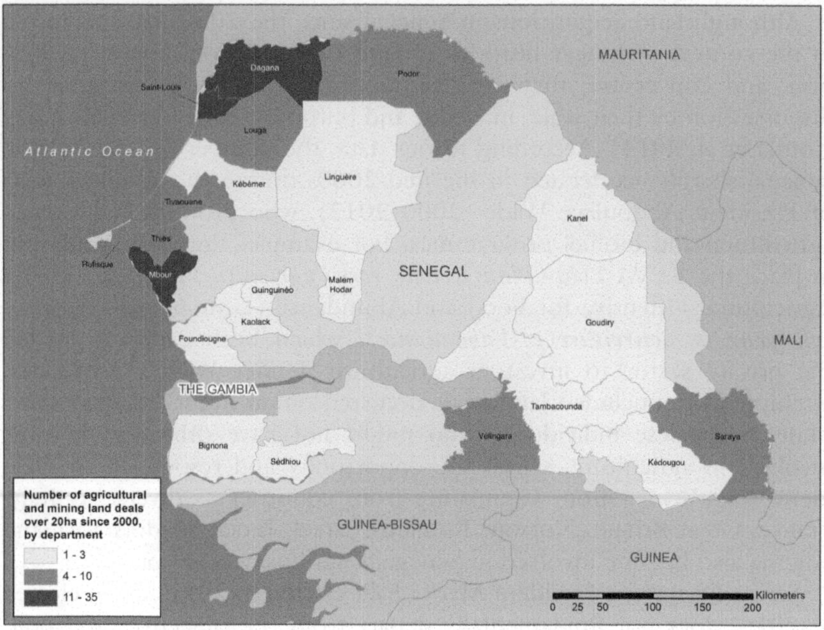

Fig. 3.2 Number of agricultural land deals over 20 ha and mining concessions by department, 2000–2020 (map by Ashley Fent). Our dataset includes mining concessions over 20 ha recorded by the Extractive Industries Transparency Initiative (EITI), as well as other deals over 20 ha for which we acquired data. It does not include land deals which lack information on the specific department; corporate small mine licences; artisanal mines (which are limited to concessions under 50 ha); or rock and sand quarries over 20 ha

gold in eastern Senegal (d'Avignon 2018). The exploitation of phosphates started in the 1950s in the Thiès region and has gradually expanded until the present. Heavy mineral sands (zircon and titanium) were also mined in Sangomar and Djifer in the Sine-Saloum until 1965 (Bureau of Mines 1967).

All of Senegal's presidents since independence have focused on mining exploration and development as a strategy for economic growth, but efforts have ramped up since the 1980s. The administrations of Léopold Sédar Senghor (1960–1980) and Abdou Diouf (1981–2000) conducted extensive research on the gold deposits in eastern Senegal, in addition to the continued mining of phosphates and limestone (for fertilizers and cement production, respectively). The neoliberalization of the mining code in the 1980s and growing interest from foreign investors resulted in the granting of 28 exploration permits by 1997 (d'Avignon 2018, 120). Under the Wade administration, the Canadian company Teranga Gold received a mining permit in 2005 and produced the first gold bar in 2009 at its Sabodala Mine (Diallo 2009). Two additional corporations, Toro Gold Ltd. and Bassari Resources, have since obtained mining permits, and even more sites are under exploration and development (d'Avignon 2018).

The Sall administration has also encouraged increased activity in various types of mining. Sall's economic growth platform, the Emerging Senegal Programme (*Plan Sénégal Émergent, PSE*), envisions a key role for mining in the industrial and infrastructural development of the country (PSE 2014, 73). In addition to promoting investments in the gold and hydrocarbon sectors, the current government aims to make Senegal one of the top global producers of phosphates. While the Wade administration expressed initial interest in several projects and granted some exploration licences, many of these proposed projects have ultimately come to fruition under Sall's government. For example, Grande Côte Operations, a large-scale heavy mineral sands project north of Dakar, entered into operations in 2014 after several years of exploration and three years of negotiations and project planning (Staff, n.d.).

The Senegalese government's emphasis on agribusiness and mining illustrates the broader tendency of extractive capitalism to become imbricated with national political economy, as a means for ruling governments to performatively enact domestic priorities around development, economic growth, or self-sufficiency (see Matondi and Rutherford, this volume).

Documenting the Faltering Land Rush in Senegal

Accurately determining the extent of concluded and operational land deals in Senegal, as elsewhere, is extremely difficult (Cotula et al. 2014). According to some critics, this exercise is also beside the point since it neglects other non-hectare-centric measures and processes that are more important to the transformations of social relations and local environments (Edelman 2013; Oya 2013; Scoones et al. 2013). Estimates published by the Land Matrix and other databases rely heavily on crowd-sourced information and reported deals, which in many cases have been exaggerated, unconfirmed, or cancelled and thus cannot be treated as facts (Oya 2013; Cotula et al. 2014).

The multiplicity of selection criteria used by different data inventories further obfuscates the picture of land transfers in Senegal. For example, the Land Matrix groups projects that potentially generate dispossession, such as mining and agricultural land acquisitions, with projects that do not involve population displacements, such as mangrove reforestation programmes and contract farming schemes. One Senegalese inventory also includes a US aid project aimed at developing irrigation infrastructure and formalizing land rights for local populations, as well as a case wherein state domain land was privatized for the benefit of investors. Additionally, some lists comprise mining projects, while others do not. Inconsistencies also arise from the inclusion of incorrect information, despite recent efforts at cleaning up data. For instance, two of the 19 land deals categorized as operational by the Land Matrix in 2016 were erroneous, one was smaller than indicated, three had been interrupted, and one was unverified (Niang 2017).

Beyond the difficulties of acquiring accurate and systematic data, the business of gathering evidence on the land rush is eminently political (Dieng 2017; Edelman 2013). At the beginning of the land rush, civil society organizations (CSOs) opposed to land grabs had a strategic incentive to report the highest estimates available as a means to dramatize the situation (Ba et al. 2013). Early figures on the extent of the land rush in Senegal have been repeated ad nauseam over many years, acquiring a life of their own without being carefully cross-checked. Noting that many investors failed to cultivate their land as proposed, CSOs have since adapted their discourse to highlight instead the inefficacy of agribusiness in comparison to smallholder agriculture (Enda Pronat 2017).

The land grab literature has largely moved away from focusing on the sheer size and cumulative extent of land deals towards examining the social and political processes of land acquisition. Without falling prey to a "fetichisation" of numbers (Edelman 2013), it remains important to analyse concrete data on the scale of the land rush to document wider patterns of agrarian change and the expansion of extractive resource frontiers. In particular, it is essential to establish a ratio of failed deals to operational ones, albeit imperfectly, as it speaks to frictions of capitalist

Table 3.1 Agricultural and mining deals in Senegal by implementation status, 2000–2020

	Number	%
Operational	58	35
Aborted	16	9.6
Inoperative/terminated	41	24.7
Unclear	51	30.7
Total	166	100

accumulation in the African countryside that may prevent or block investments. Our dataset highlights these elements, although the collected data almost certainly underestimate the number of land investments and, to an even greater degree, the number of failed projects, since these are more likely to lack reliable information.[5] Based on available data, we find that only slightly over a third (58) of the 166 investors involved in publicized agricultural and mining deals in Senegal since 2000 are confirmed to be operational, as displayed in Table 3.1.

In comparison, 57 land projects (34%) announced since 2000 were cancelled either before a deal was sealed or after operations began. No information could be found on the status of the remaining land deals, meaning that more than two thirds of all tentative or actual land-based investments appear to have failed. Our data also indicate a steady decline in the number of land deals since 2012 (see Fig. 3.3). The surge in the hectarage acquired in 2015 is due to the attribution of a 130,000 ha mining concession to be operated by the Turkish company Tosyali in partnership with the Senegalese government (Africa Intelligence 2020).[6]

Disappointment has been particularly pronounced in the biofuel sector, which was enthusiastically promoted by the Senegalese government under Wade. From 2007 to 2010, at least nine biofuel projects supposed to cover a total of 90,000 ha of land were accredited (APIX 2010). By

[5] It is important to note that we could not verify the status of every single land allocation, in part because there exists no central cadastre of excerpts of minutes—the main avenue through which investors secure land in Senegal. Data on mining deals are more complete and reliable. With Senegal's adhesion to the Extractive Industries Transparency Initiative in October 2013, the government now publishes a repertory of mining projects, which we have used for our database.

[6] This mining concession was previously awarded to ArcelorMittal in 2007, after the Senegalese government rescinded its contract with Kumba Resources over the same concession.

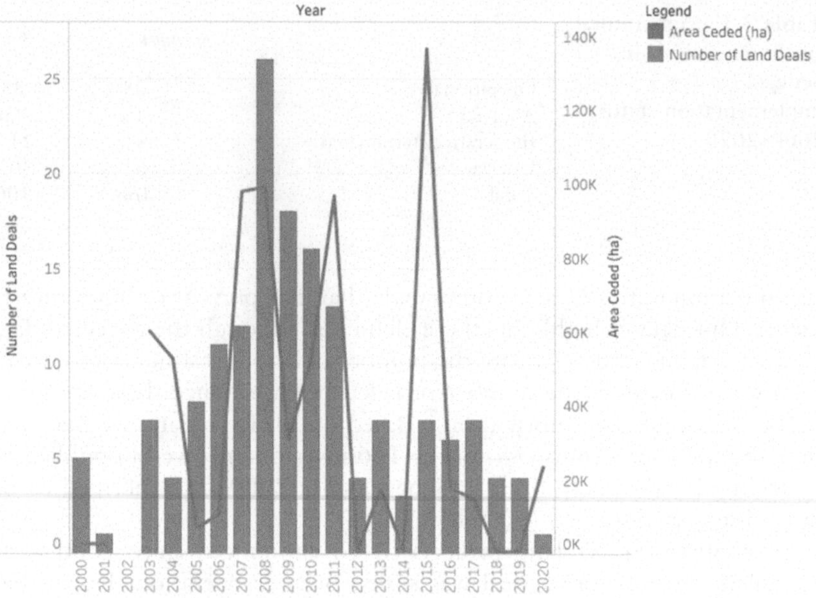

Fig. 3.3 Agricultural land deals over 20 ha and mining concessions in Senegal, 2000–2020 (Compiled by Marie Gagné)

2010, however, only approximately 3000 ha of land were planted with the biofuel crop *Jatropha curcas* (jatropha) (Sarr et al. 2010, 64). By 2012, jatropha still only covered an area of 15,000 ha, according to the most generous government estimates (Ciss 2012).[7] Less than five per cent of the initial government objective, set at 321,000 ha, had thus been fulfilled. Abandoned jatropha and other biofuel projects make up a disproportionate share of failed deals; they account for more than 524,030 ha of all land deals in our database. The collapse of the biofuel sector in Senegal illustrates how overly optimistic market projections may fall short when they come up against the social, political, and economic difficulties involved in implementation.

Foreign investment in the mining sector, although a priority for the Senegalese government, has also encountered severe setbacks. For

[7] Native to Central America, the jatropha plant produces seeds whose oil can be processed into biodiesel.

instance, the Niafarang Project has experienced protracted negotiations and delays, as we discuss below. The Sall administration has also withdrawn the mining concessions of non-operational companies like the Société Sénégalaise des Industries and the multinational giant ArcelorMittal (Dakaractu 2015; Reuters 2013). In sum, mining projects have been important contributors to the land rush in Senegal, but are frequently mired in disputes and obstructions.

Reasons for Project Cancellation and Delays

Community-Level and Civil Society Opposition

Land deals in Senegal have been a source of controversy and conflict at the local, regional, and national levels. Concerted resistance has contributed to the deferral or cancellation of several intended projects. In this section, we assess the reasons underlying opposition, the strategies employed by project opponents, and the effectiveness of these campaigns.

Many national civil society organizations and local groups have objected land deals due to inadequate or non-existent processes of consultation prior to the granting of agricultural and mining concessions. Information about proposed land deals is often intentionally withheld, vague, or not communicated in advance to people whose land and livelihoods may be affected. Local stakeholders are frequently prevented from participating in negotiations or from fully understanding the implications of these investments, raising after-the-fact concerns. In northern Senegal, for example, opposition to the massive Grande Côte Operations mine occurred later in the implementation process, as some local people who had initially consented to the project grew unhappy with the amount of compensation received for their land in comparison to other displaced residents (Agence de presse sénégalaise 2015b). A similar pattern emerged in the case of a biofuel venture in Ourour, where villagers agreed to cede their land but subsequently became dissatisfied with the terms of the project (Ahne 2015). Furthermore, even when investors and state authorities have been careful to communicate clear information beforehand, customary landowners have in several cases refused to surrender their land, due to the political and cultural meanings attached to land and its critical role as a productive asset for rural families.

Communities have employed both legal and extra-legal strategies in opposition to land acquisitions in Senegal. In an increasing number of cases, people have successfully gone to court to demand the cancellation of non-consensual land allocations to external investors (e.g. Afripartners, Senegindia). In other cases, sabotage has been used to challenge controversial land deals. For instance, 12 individuals were arrested for cutting fences and trespassing on land appropriated by an unknown investor presumed to be President Wade (Agence de presse sénégalaise 2013). Villagers were able to reclaim their land after President Wade lost the 2012 presidential elections. Local opponents of the Grande Côte Opérations mine responded similarly to the seizure of their land by setting fire to mine equipment during the construction phase; three protestors were subsequently sentenced to jail time for their roles in the arson.[8]

The capacity of aggrieved populations to halt land deals or, in certain cases, to obtain adequate compensation is determined by the intensity, coherence, and timing of their campaigns, as well as the support received from national and international civil society organizations. Transnational advocacy has often been successful in amplifying the demands of local movements and putting additional pressure on corporate actors (Bush 2011; Keck and Sikkink 1998; Kirsch 2014). These dynamics are visible in Senegal, where international CSOs have assisted local populations in their struggles against external investors (Gagné 2019; Prause 2019).

In some cases, public protest without significant support from CSOs has also succeeded in ending land projects, as exemplified by the case of Senhuile in the rural community of Fanaye. The Senhuile project was derailed due to intense factional rivalry and social polarization. Tensions came to a head in 2011, when violent confrontations resulted in two people dead and 20 injured. The deadly skirmishes reflected poorly on the government and undermined its legitimacy as the contentious 2012 presidential elections approached. In this context, President Wade paused the project and arranged an alternate concession in the Special Avifauna Reserve of Ndiaël. There too, tensions arose in the villages impacted by the investment. The actions of local, national, and international opponents led to an informal decision by the state to diminish the size of the plantation to 10,000 ha, damaged Senhuile's ability to cultivate peacefully, and forced the investor to make concessions to neighbouring populations. However, opponents have not succeeded in completely expelling the company, which has managed to hang on to its

[8] Interviews by Ashley Fent, 6 September 2014; see also Dakaractu (2013).

land despite its disappointing track record. The case of Senhuile represents an intriguing exception, as other campaigns with less intense or similar levels of opposition have succeeded in cancelling agricultural projects.

Although it seems that resistance to mining ventures has been less vehement and successful in halting projects than movements against agricultural projects (Diallo 2017; Prause 2019), some opposition campaigns have hampered disputed mining-related land deals. These campaigns have been most effective when targeting the approval phase of these deals. The mobilization of large numbers of people prior to any commencement of work reflects what Stuart Kirsch (2014) calls the "politics of time." The Niafarang Project in the Ziguinchor region of Casamance has been in negotiation for nearly a decade, in part due to local organizing against the project. A member of a local activist group formed to oppose the mining project, the International Committee Against Zircon Mining in Casamance (hereafter referred to as "the Committee"), explained that it took his organization a number of years to convince the wider population that the environmental effects of the mine could affect residents who lived beyond the actual mine site.[9]

After a difficult start, the Committee successfully rallied people in opposition to the project, before the company could secure a mining licence or begin operations. The Committee deployed tactics such as holding large demonstrations and encouraging widespread attendance at public forums as part of the Environmental and Social Impact Study conducted for the project. As a result of this organizing, the Committee attracted a wide local audience and a broad base of stakeholders who rejected the study in two separate public forums in 2011 and 2014. They also gained the support of two national politicians, as well as European and American academics, lawyers, and activists who engaged in information sharing, helped guide strategy, and increased the visibility of the case. Together, these factors succeeded in stalling the project for many years. A small mine licence was signed in 2017, but construction has still not begun amid public pressure, changing governmental priorities, and project financing issues. The successful mobilization of the Committee is but one example of the numerous community-led campaigns that have slowed down the pace of the land rush in Senegal.

[9] Interview by Ashley Fent, 26 August 2014.

Although local resistance to land deals in the mining and agro-industrial sectors of Senegal has resulted in many project cancellations, there are a number of caveats. First, there are a range of responses to land deals, from popular rejection to acquiescence to proposed arrangements in exchange for compensation (Hall et al. 2015; Ndi and Batterbury 2017). Champions of land investments can more easily discredit an opposition movement as "unrepresentative" when there are disagreements among community members. In both the Niafarang Project and Senhuile cases, we observed that state and corporate co-optation of certain villages and community members has led to inter- and intra-village conflict. Opposition campaigns are also susceptible to various manoeuvres by state officials to circumvent community consultation requirements, often by seeking the approval of municipal councils or local elites.

Second, the opacity of project ownership and the multiplicity of investment streams in contemporary land deals can hinder the engagement and effectiveness of transnational advocacy organizations and local groups (Temper 2019). For example, the Barcelona-based international CSO GRAIN claims it had to conduct a six-month-long investigation into the ownership structure of the Senhuile project, ultimately paying bribes to access information (CRAFS et al. 2013). The plurality of investors, frequent corporate mergers, and common transfer of land leases to other parties make it difficult for project opponents to identify and target corporate actors (Hall 2011). This opacity, combined with the central role of state actors in securing land for private investment, has led many anti-land grab movements in Senegal and elsewhere to direct their actions against the state (Levien 2013).

State Ambivalence and Changing Policy Priorities

Both the Wade and Sall administrations have strongly encouraged private investment in agribusiness while also claiming—perhaps incongruously—a commitment to family-based agriculture (Baglioni 2015; Oya and Ba 2012). The ambivalence of the Senegalese state and its responsiveness to community opposition resulted in the annulment of some high-profile land deals previously supported by the government, including the projects of Senhuile, Afripartners, and Senegindia.

An examination of the biofuel sector also illustrates how the unstable policy framework contributed to project delays—even before global markets' interest in biofuels faded due to concerns about the conversion of farmland to non-food crops and declining oil prices. President Wade created the Ministry of Biofuels in 2007, instituted a special programme for biofuel production between 2007 and 2012, adopted a law on biofuels in 2010, and established a National Committee for Biofuels (Gatete and Dabat 2017). The bylaws discussions stalled, however, causing the implementation of the law on biofuels to lag behind private investors' demands for land, processing facilities, and markets (Dafrallah and Ackom 2016). The institutional context was also unstable, with the Directorate of Biofuels being moved under the aegis of several different ministries (Dafrallah and Ackom 2016). In sum, concrete government support for the production, processing, and commercialization of biofuels was lacking, in spite of legislative commitments (Dia et al. 2009).

The government's diminished interest in biofuels further eroded the sector. Under President Sall, efforts to develop biofuels have withered away, with the exception of research institutes that continue to promote the cultivation of jatropha for local needs. In 2012, the government abolished the Ministry of Biofuels, and the special programme on biofuels was not renewed after its expiration in 2012. In brief, the Senegalese government has moved away from biofuels as a solution to problems of energy provision.

While interest in biofuels has decreased, the state has focused more on attracting investment in mineral deposits as well as in offshore oil and gas. The government has accordingly sought to create a business and regulatory environment amenable to new investments in these sectors, including by passing a revised Mining Code in 2016. Although the state has a pivotal role in securing foreign access to subsurface resources, the positions of individual state actors in negotiations have been varied. Sometimes officials have facilitated relations of trust between private companies and local populations, whereas at other times they have supported communities in their efforts to withstand the seizure of their land (Fent 2019). The involvement of state actors in opposing projects has occurred both prior to the commencement of mining operations and in response to adverse effects. One example of this was in 2010, when various local associations, municipal councillors, and administrative authorities considered the problems affecting the phosphate-producing areas of the Thiès region and developed a plan for the Senegalese mining company to increase its social commitments (Diallo 2017). In other cases, state actors and elected local officials have tacitly supported illegal or corrupt mining activities. For instance, numerous officials were arrested in 2019 for facilitating an illegal Chinese-run mine in eastern Senegal, including a local mayor, a regional director of the Ministry of Mines in Kédougou, and the state-appointed director of the Niokolo-Koba National Park (Diebakhate 2019).

In sum, the Senegalese state has not been equally interested in supporting all agricultural, biofuel, or mining projects. Instead, its interventions reflect electoral considerations as well as the personal interests, idiosyncratic behaviour, and normative positions of state officials.

Poor Investor Capabilities

The roles of social resistance and inconsistent state support in delaying or blocking projects are frequently compounded by poor investor capabilities. Many companies, in Senegal as elsewhere, have neglected "to implement an investment strategy based on a robust economic analysis" as they rushed to acquire land (de Schutter 2011, 253). Indeed, several investors lack sufficient capital, technology, or experience to carry out industrial agriculture (Cotula 2012; Schönweger and Messerli 2015).

Not only have several land deals in Senegal never been implemented, but even operational companies perform relatively poorly. It is estimated that of 58,000 ha allocated to 20 companies in the Senegal River Valley in the 2000s, only 2000 ha (3.5%) were brought under cultivation within five years (d'Aquino et al. 2013, 276). These figures indicate that investors have either acquired more land than necessary or have taken on more land than what they can actually farm (d'Aquino et al. 2013). Although there are a number of success stories of Senegalese "rural capitalists" who have made their fortune in agriculture (Oya 2007), several domestic land investors have been unable to amass the necessary start-up capital to realize their goals. Smaller land acquisitions by Senegalese nationals have often stalled for this reason (d'Aquino et al. 2013).

In her qualitative study of JTF and Senhuile, Gagné found that both companies suffered from shortcomings that impaired their business performance. Even though the two investors were similarly inexperienced in agriculture, they aimed to cultivate no less than 50,000 and 20,000 ha, respectively. Managerial difficulties contributed to the demise of JTF, even though other factors were also at play (most notably, a lack of state support). For its part, Senhuile is still technically operating, although it has not farmed since at least 2018.

There is a learning curve for all new ventures, especially in an unstructured value chain like biofuels. For JTF, however, the curve seems to have been rather steep. Several members of the management team did not have the necessary experience or agronomic knowledge to conduct a project of this magnitude. The project was also characterized by a lack of clear orientation. As remarked by a company insider, no feasibility study, business plan, or social and environmental impact assessment was conducted prior to the project's inception, except for a memorandum of understanding signed between the Senegalese Ministry of Biofuels and the investor.[10] Insufficient planning meant day-to-day improvisation and mismanagement. For instance, the company never reimbursed salary arrears to local workers after it left the community. Apart from one community liaison officer, the company managers were also handling the project from Dakar and came to supervise the plantation only periodically. For his part, the CEO of the Italian parent company reportedly visited the plantation in Senegal only twice or thrice. As a result, the investor did not ensure an adequate scheduling or monitoring of agricultural activities on the ground. Several villagers consequently "cut corners" by not properly tending the jatropha trees.

The incompetence of Senhuile is even more blatant. To acquire land, the company made ambitious promises to the Senegalese government and local populations, most of which it did not fulfil. Senhuile also has a poor track record in terms of productivity. The investor's modest agricultural prowess is largely explained by managerial ineptitude, ambitions of personal enrichment, and nepotism by its executive staff, although other factors like the poor soil quality of its concession and social opposition from neighbouring communities in the Special Avifauna Reserve of Ndiaël also negatively impacted the project. The high turnover of CEOs (four since 2012) has also created instability. In addition, some of Senhuile's employees seemingly syphoned money from the company. Alleged misappropriation of funds by Senhuile's first CEO likely delayed the pace of project realization and narrowed the company's rate of profits.[11] Even the next CEO hired by Tampieri Financial Group (the Italian shareholders of the company) to restructure Senhuile was based in a lavish office

[10] Interview by Marie Gagné, 28 August 2014.

[11] This CEO was prosecuted for misappropriating CFA f 186 million (US$388,641) of corporate assets (Ndoye 2014).

in Dakar, 450 kilometres away from the plantation. Tampieri Financial Group eventually dismissed him for his extravagant expenses, as revealed by a former executive of Senhuile.[12] One Senegalese investor in Senhuile also created subsidiary companies to which the parent company subcontracted the leasing of agricultural machinery or the hiring of security guards. He furthermore recruited unqualified friends and family members as agronomists and for other key positions, remunerating them with salaries above Senegalese standards. To illustrate the lack of rigour, a former executive explained that, when he was hired, there was not even a numbering system to inventory agricultural machines nor a bookkeeping system to monitor fuel consumption, leading workers to steal from the company with impunity.[13] Senhuile has also been unable to retain its few competent staff members. In brief, amateurish management contributed to the demise of both JTF and Senhuile.

Conclusion: The Future of Extractive Capitalism and Land Deals in Senegal

The Senegalese government has attempted to facilitate land acquisitions since the 2000s, resulting in an apparent "free-for-all" wherein investors have recklessly captured land. There was an initial surge in the number of agro-industrial and mining-related land deals in Senegal as a result of these domestic incentives as well as global economic transformations. However, many of these deals encountered severe setbacks or did not come to fruition. In consequence, the land rush has slowed down considerably in Senegal.

As accusations of illegitimate "land grabbing" have multiplied and opponents have developed more sophisticated strategies to counteract investments, it has become increasingly difficult to secure land in Senegal. Local people and organizations have targeted contentious land deals at various stages, from the approval phase to the operational phase. Many projects were revised or abandoned as a result of concerted civil society resistance.

Issues with project implementation can also be attributed to governmental and investor dynamics. The Senegalese government has been

[12] Interview by Marie Gagné, 30 July 2018.

[13] Interview by Marie Gagné, 13 July 2018.

unable to provide a stable policy environment, particularly in the biofuel sector. In addition, some state officials have rallied behind land defenders and erected obstacles to hinder proposed projects. Furthermore, the deficiencies of investors have played a role in stalling projects. Some companies did not secure funding, did not possess the know-how to run large-scale projects effectively, or made grandiose promises that they could not fulfil.

In sum, the widely touted land rush by corporations in Senegal has not materialised to the expected level, and these investments might not be as profitable an outlet for capitalist accumulation as originally envisioned. Nevertheless, the critical role of land and rents in providing a "spatio-temporal fix" to the ongoing problem of falling rates of return in capitalism suggests that land investments and broader transformations of rural economies and societies will continue for many years to come, albeit in different ways (Anseeuw et al. 2012; Knuth 2015). Global capitalists and financiers will likely continue to invest in agriculture and mining, particularly given the Sall administration's enthusiastic support for private sector involvement in the economy. Additionally, existing companies that have experienced success often gradually enlarge the surface area of their concessions, suggesting that land grabs may continue in a more insidious and less spectacular way. Whereas the wave of sensationalized land-based investments of the early 2000s seems to have waned, it is critical to consider the multiple means through which the expansion of extractive capitalism will continue to transform the socio-ecological systems that sustain rural livelihoods in Senegal.

Works Cited

Africa Intelligence. 2020. Miferso to transform iron ore at Falémé before it starts extraction. February 25. Retrieved from https://www.africaintelligence.com/mining-sector_supply-chain/2020/02/25/miferso-to-transform-iron-ore-at-faleme-before-it-starts-extraction,108395339-art.

Agence de presse sénégalaise. 2013. Louga: douze 'paysans sans terre' condamnés à trois mois avec sursis. June 12. Retrieved from http://www.aps.sn/articles.php?id_article=114486.

Agence de presse sénégalaise. 2015a. 95% des terres échappent aux Sénégalais (Moustapha Sourang). May 29. Retrieved from http://www.aps.sn/articles.php?id_article=142754.

Agence de presse sénégalaise. 2015b. Les expropriés de Diogo entre incompréhension et fatalisme. January 22. Retrieved from https://fr.allafrica.com/stories/201501230005.html.

Ahne, Aminatou. 2015. Comment la société Anoc a abusé de la naïveté et de l'ignorance des populations. *Flamme d'Afrique* 12–16 (May): 4–5.

Amanor, Kojo Sebastian. 2008. Sustainable development, corporate accumulation and community expropriation: Land and natural resources in Africa. In *Land and sustainable development in Africa*, ed. Kojo Sebastian Amanor and Sam Moyo, 127–158. London and New York: Zed Books.

Anseeuw, Ward, Liz Alden Wily, Lorenzo Cotula, and Michael Taylor. 2012. *Land rights and the rush for land: Findings of the global commercial pressures on land research project*. Rome: International Land Coalition.

APIX. 2010. African National Oil Corporation, un des pionniers dans le secteur des agro-carburants. *L'APIX Investmentnewsletter.* 2ème & 3ème trimestres (13).

Ba, Cheikh Oumar, Moustapha Ngaido, Ndèye Coumba Diouf, and Ibrahima Ka. 2013. *Rapport sur les acquisitions de terres à grande échelle (ATGE) en Afrique de l'Ouest. Étude réalisée pour le compte de Land Policy Initiative (LPI)*. Dakar: Initiative Prospective Agricole et Rurale (IPAR).

Baglioni, Elena. 2015. Straddling contract and estate farming: Accumulation strategies of Senegalese horticultural exporters. *Journal of Agrarian Change* 15 (1): 17–42.

Baglioni, Elena, and Peter Gibbon. 2013. Land grabbing, large- and small-scale farming: What can evidence and policy from 20th century Africa contribute to the debate? *Third World Quarterly* 34 (9): 1558–1581.

Bureau of Mines. 1967. *Minerals yearbook 1965 Vol. IV (Area reports: International)*. Washington, DC: United States Department of the Interior.

Bush, Ray. 2011. Coalitions for dispossession and networks of resistance? Land, politics and agrarian reform in Egypt. *Journal of Middle Eastern Studies* 38 (3): 391–405.

Ciss, Malick. 2012. Louis Seck, ministre des énergies renouvelable. *Le Soleil*, January 4. Retrieved from https://fr.allafrica.com/stories/201201040901.html.

Cotula, Lorenzo. 2012. The international political economy of the global land rush: A critical appraisal of trends, scale, geography and drivers. *The Journal of Peasant Studies* 39 (3–4): 649–680.

Cotula, Lorenzo, Carlos Oya, Emmanuel A. Codjoe, Abdurehman Eid, Mark Kakraba-Ampeh, James Keeley, Admasu Lokaley Kidewa, Melissa Makwarimba, Wondwosen Michago Seide, et al. 2014. Testing claims about large land deals in Africa: Findings from a multi-country study. *The Journal of Development Studies* 50 (7): 903–925.

CRAFS, GRAIN, & Re:Common. 2013. *Qui est derrière Senhuile-Senethanol?* Retrieved from www.grain.org/fr/article/entries/4814-qui-est-derriere-senhuile-senethanol.

d'Aquino, Patrick, Sidy Mohamed Seck, Seydou Camara, Djibril Diop, and Seydou Badji. 2013. *Projet de Développement Inclusif et Durable de l'Agribusiness au Sénégal (PDIDAS). Développement de méthodes d'allocation de terrains par les communautés rurales et identification de leurs besoins en assistance technique. Zones de Gandon et du Lac de Guiers. Rapport définitif finalisé.* PDIDAS/CIRAD.

d'Avignon, Robyn. 2018. Shelf projects: The political life of exploration geology in Senegal. *Engaging Science, Technology, and Society* 4: 111–130.

Dafrallah, Touria, and Emmanuel Kofi Ackom. 2016. Analysis of national Jatropha biodiesel programme in Senegal. *AIMS Energy* 4 (4): 589–605.

Dakaractu. 2013. Diogo: 3 producteurs condamnés à un mois ferme, 13 autres à 3 mois avec sursis. July 19. Retrieved from https://www.dakaractu.com/Diogo-3-producteurs-condamnes-a-un-mois-ferme-13-autres-a-3-mois-avec-sursis_a48490.html.

Dakaractu. 2015. Annulation des concessions minières octroyées à la Sdi: Macky casse le décret de Wade. December 3. Retrieved from https://www.dakaractu.com/Annulation-des-concessions-minieres-octroyees-a-la-Sdi-Macky-casse-le-decret-de-Wade_a101979.html.

Deininger, Klaus. 2011. Challenges posed by the new wave of farmland investment. *Journal of Peasant Studies* 38 (2): 217–247.

De Schutter, Olivier. 2011. How not to think of land-grabbing: Three critiques of large-scale investments in farmland. *Journal of Peasant Studies* 38 (2): 249–279.

Dia, Djiby, Cheickh Sadibou Fall, Aminata Ndour, and Maam Suwadu Sakho-Jimbira. 2009. *Le Sénégal face à la crise énergétique mondiale: Enjeux de l'émergence de la filière des biocarburants.* Dakar: ISRA-BAME.

Diallo, Mouhamadou Lamine. 2009. Mine d'or et développement durable: Quelques réflexions sur le site de Sabodala (Sénégal oriental). *EchoGéo* 8. Retrieved from https://journals.openedition.org/echogeo/11103.

Diallo, Mouhamadou Lamine. 2017. L'industrie du phosphate de Taïba au Sénégal: front minier et tensions locales. *VertigO* 28: np.

Diebakhate, Ibrahima. 2019. Exploitation illégale de l'or dans le Parc national Niokolo Koba: 21 personnes en prison pour association de malfaiteurs. *Le Quotidien*, June 8. Retrieved from https://www.lequotidien.sn/kedougou-exploitation-illegale-de-lor-dans-le-parc-national-niokolo-koba-21-personnes-en-prison-pour-association-de-malfaiteurs/.

Dieng, Rama Salla. 2017. 'Land grabbing' and the politics of evidence: The case of Senegal. *Africa Insight* 46 (4): 25–40.

Diop, Momar Coumba, and Mamadou Diouf. 1990. *Le Sénégal sous Abdou Diouf: Etat et Société*. Paris: Editions Karthala.

Edelman, Marc. 2013. Messy hectares: Questions about the epistemology of land grabbing data. *Journal of Peasant Studies* 40 (3): 485–501.

Enda Pronat. 2017. Analyse et mise en perspective des exploitations familiales agricoles et des agro industries au Sénégal. Retrieved from www.endapronat.org/wp/wp-content/uploads/2018/07/Etude-VFOK2018-copie.pdf.

Fairbairn, Madeleine. 2013. Indirect dispossession: Domestic power imbalances and foreign access to land in Mozambique. *Development and Change* 44 (2): 335–356.

Faye, Jacques. 2008. *Land and decentralisation in Senegal*. London: International Institute for Environment and Development (IIED). Retrieved from http://pubs.iied.org/pdfs/12550IIED.pdf.

Faye, Iba Mar, Amel Benkahla, Oussouby Touré, Sidy Seck, and Cheikh Oumar Ba. 2011. *Les acquisitions de terres à grande échelle au Sénégal: description d'un nouveau phénomène*. Dakar: IPAR. Retrieved from http://www.ipar.sn/sites/default/files/Rapport%20ATGE%20version%20finale.pdf.

Fent, Ashley. 2019. Governing alongside: Lateral state spatiality and unmet expectations amid mining negotiations in Casamance, Senegal. *American Ethnologist* 46 (1): 20–33.

Foster, John Bellamy. 2002. *Ecology against capitalism*. New York: Monthly Review Press.

Gagné, Marie. 2019. Resistance against land grabs in Senegal: Factors of success and partial failure of an emergent social movement. In *The politics of land*, ed. Tim Bartley, 173–203. Bingley: Emerald Group Publishing Limited.

Gatete, Charly, and Marie-Helene Dabat. 2017. From the fuel versus food controversy to the institutional vacuum in biofuel policies: Evidence from West African countries. *Energy, Sustainability and Society* 7 (1): 12.

GRAIN. 2018. Failed farmland deals: A growing legacy of disaster and pain. Retrieved from https://www.grain.org/article/entries/5958-failed-farmland-deals-a-growing-legacy-of-disaster-and-pain.

Hall, Ruth. 2011. Land grabbing in Southern Africa: The many faces of the investor rush. *Review of African Political Economy* 38 (128): 193–214.

Hall, Ruth, Marc Edelman, Saturnino M. Borras Jr., Ian Scoones, Ben White, and Wendy Wolford. 2015. Resistance, acquiescence or incorporation? An introduction to land grabbing and political reactions 'from below'. *The Journal of Peasant Studies* 42 (3–4): 467–488.

Harvey, David. 2003. Accumulation by dispossession. In *The New imperialism*, 137–182. Oxford: Oxford University Press.

Hesseling, Gerti. 2009. Land reform in Senegal: L'Histoire se répète? In *Legalising land rights: Local Practices, state responses and tenure security in Africa*,

Asia and Latin America, ed. Janine M. Ubink, Andre J. Hoekema, and Willem J. Assies, 243–269. Leiden: Leiden University Press.

Keck, Margaret E., and Kathryn Sikkink. 1998. *Activists beyond borders: Advocacy networks in international politics*. Ithaca, NY: Cornell University Press.

Kirsch, Stuart. 2014. *Mining capitalism: The relationship between corporations and their critics*. Oakland, CA: University of California Press.

Knuth, Sarah. 2015. Global finance and the land grab: Mapping twenty-first century strategies. *Canadian Journal of Development Studies/Revue canadienne d'études du développement* 36 (2): 163–178.

Levien, Michael. 2013. The politics of dispossession: Theorizing India's 'land wars'. *Politics & Society* 41 (3): 351–394.

Ndi, Frankline A., and Simon Batterbury. 2017. Land grabbing and the axis of political conflict: Insights from Southwest Cameroon. *Africa Spectrum* 52 (1): 33–63.

Ndoye, Makhaly Ndiack. 2014. Abus de biens sociaux: L'ex-Directeur général de Senhuile, Benyamin Dummai, écroué pour 186 million FCFA. *L'Observateur*, May 17 and 18. Retrieved from http://farmlandgrab.org/post/view/2354.

Niang, Momar. 2017. 3% des terres arables du Sénégal attribués à des étrangers? Pas de preuve. *Africa Check*, March 3. Retrieved from http://fr.africacheck.org/reports/3-terres-arables-senegal-attribues-a-etrangers-de-preuve/.

Oya, Carlos. 2007. Stories of rural accumulation in Africa: Trajectories and Transitions among rural capitalists in Senegal. *Journal of Agrarian Change* 7 (4): 453–493.

Oya, Carlos. 2013. Methodological reflections on 'land grab' databases and the 'land grab' literature 'rush.' *Journal of Peasant Studies* 40 (3): 503–520.

Oya, Carlos, and Cheikh Oumar Ba. 2013. Les politiques agricoles 2000–2012: entre volontarisme et incohérence. In *Sénégal (2000–2012). Les institutions et politiques publiques à l'épreuve d'une gouvernance libérale*, ed. Momar-Coumba Diop, 149–178. Dakar and Paris: CRES.

Prause, Louisa. 2019. Success and failure of protest actors' framing strategies in conflicts over land and mining in Senegal. *Canadian Journal of Development Studies/Revue canadienne d'études du développement* 40 (3): 387–403.

République du Sénégal. 1964. *Loi n° 64-46 du 17 juin 1964 relative au Domaine national*.

République du Sénégal. 1976. *Loi n° 76-66 du 2 juillet 1976 portant Code du domaine de l'État*.

République du Sénégal. 2001. *Loi n⁰ 2001-01 du 15 janvier 2001 portant Code de l'Environnement*.

République du Sénégal. 2011. *Loi n° 2011-07 du 30 mars 2011 portant régime de la Propriété foncière*.

République du Sénégal. 2013. *Loi 2013-10 du 28 décembre 2013 portant Code général des Collectivités locales*.

République du Sénégal. 2014. *Plan Sénégal Émergent*. Retrieved from http://www.un-page.org/files/public/plan_senegal_emergent.pdf.

Reuters. 2013. Senegal wins court case against Arcelor Mittal. September 10. Retrieved from https://www.reuters.com/article/senegal-arcelormittal/senegal-wins-court-case-against-arcelor-mittal-government-idUSL5N0H64EZ20130910.

Ribot, Jesse C. 1999. Decentralisation, participation and accountability in Sahelian Forestry: Legal instruments of political-administrative control. *Africa* 69 (1): 23–65.

Sachs, Wolfgang. 2010. *The development dictionary: A guide to knowledge and power*, 2nd ed. New York: Zed Books.

Sarr, Secou, Abdou Ndour, and Aby Drame. 2010. *Cartographie agro-environnementale du potentiel de production de biocarburants au Sénégal*. Dakar: Enda tiers monde.

Schönweger, Oliver, and Peter Messerli. 2015. Land acquisition, investment, and development in the Lao coffee sector: Successes and failures. *Critical Asian Studies* 47 (1): 94–122.

Scoones, Ian, Ruth Hall, Saturnino M. Borras Jr., Ben White, and Wendy Wolford. 2013. The politics of evidence: Methodologies for understanding the global land rush. *Journal of Peasant Studies* 40 (3): 469–483.

Seck, Sidy M. 1991. Sur la dynamique de l'irrigation dans la vallée du fleuve. In *La vallée du fleuve Sénégal. Évaluations et perspectives d'une décennie d'aménagements*, ed. Bernard Crousse, Paul Mathieu, and Sidy M. Seck, (17–43). Paris: Karthala.

Shipley, Thomas. 2018. *Country profile: Senegal: Overview of corruption and anti-corruption*. U4 Anti-Corruption Resource Centre. Retrieved from https://knowledgehub.transparency.org/helpdesk/senegal-overview-of-corruption-and-anti-corruption.

Smith, Neil. 2008. *Uneven development: Nature, capital, and the production of space*. Athens, GA: The University of Georgia Press.

Staff, Matthew. (n.d.). Senegal's grande vision. *Africa Outlook*. Retrieved from https://www.africaoutlookmag.com/outlook-features/grand-cote-operation-feb2017.

Temper, Leah. 2019. From boomerangs to minefields and catapults: Dynamics of trans-local resistance to land-grabs. *Journal of Peasant Studies* 46 (1): 188–216.

Touré, Oussouby. 1984. Le refus du travail forcé au Sénégal oriental. *Cahiers d'études africaines* 24 (93): 25–38.

Tsing, Anna Lowenhaupt. 2005. *Friction: An ethnography of global connection*. Princeton, NJ: Princeton University Press.

Veltmeyer, Henry. 2013. The political economy of natural resource extraction: A new model or extractive imperialism? *Canadian Journal of Development Studies/Revue canadienne d'études du développement* 34 (1): 79–95.

Zoomers, Annelies. 2010. Globalisation and the foreignisation of space: Seven processes driving the current global land grab. *The Journal of Peasant Studies* 37 (2): 429–447.

CHAPTER 4

Epilogue of a Short-Lived Land Rush: Private, Rural, and Urban Land Tenure in South Sudan

Patrick Wight

Introduction

The case of South Sudan is used in this chapter to analyze the outcomes of the global land rush, a topic that dominated policy literature in the late 2000s. This chapter provides an overview of three different forms of land tenure in South Sudan: (1) leasehold by private investors, (2) customary law in rural areas, and (3) freehold in urban areas. Much like the trajectories of Senegal and Cameroon, the influx of large-scale land investment in South Sudan never fully materialized (Gagné and Fent 2020; Hamann and Sneyd 2020). Nevertheless, the few existing land deals offer a cautionary tale. The promotion of an investor, market-oriented strategy in the context of a weak central state has produced adverse consequences. During the 2007–2010 period, a series of opaque land deals were signed between wartime elites and private investors that did not involve or cater to the interests of affected communities. South Sudan's civil war, which

The original version of this chapter was revised: The author name "Marie Gangé" has been changed to "Marie Gagné". The correction to this chapter is available at https://doi.org/10.1007/978-3-030-60789-0_12

P. Wight (✉)
Montreal, QC, Canada
e-mail: pwight@uoguelph.ca

L. Cochrane and N. Andrews (eds.), *The Transnational Land Rush in Africa*, International Political Economy Series,
https://doi.org/10.1007/978-3-030-60789-0_4

broke out in 2013, has since caused most investors to withdraw from the country and prevented others from developing their proposed projects (Fig. 4.1).

The story of land in South Sudan revolves around state efforts to formally incorporate the customary system of rural areas into national regimes, along with the commercialization and privatization of land in urban settings. These processes have each been associated with conflict and elite capture of resources. The scholarly debate hinges on whether these conflicts reflect pre-existing ethnic tensions between communities or if they relate to more recent events as per a political economy framework. Although conflicts in South Sudan's rural areas commonly manifest along ethnic lines, they are in fact a response to the increasing formalization of ethnic boundaries/territories, legal ambiguities over which authorities control land governance, and state encroachment on communal land. In urban areas, the commodification of land and processes of urban expansion (g., wartime displacement), drive land-based conflicts.

Fig. 4.1 Map of South Sudan (*Source* United Nations)

While foreign investments in South Sudan have since dried up due to the civil war, the state continues to pursue a strategy of land titling in urban areas and formalizing the customary system in rural areas, despite an overall lack of institutional capacity. In the absence of a strong central state, the problems associated these two systems of land tenure are similar: they heighten conflict and inequality, lead to elite capture, and compromise livelihoods. Theoretically, there are approaches to commodifying land in urban areas and formalizing customary law in rural that can reduce, rather than exacerbate, intergroup conflict over land and other resources. Given the current context in South Sudan, it is imperative to work within and amend existing systems while enhancing traditional conflict resolution mechanisms.

The research informing this study draws on the author's PhD fieldwork conducted during the South Sudan peace process in Ethiopia and Kenya for a period of 18 months between 2014 and 2018. During this time, over 50 key informant interviews were conducted with researchers, organizational representatives, diplomats, policy-makers, South Sudanese ex-pats, and delegates within the peace process, including Sudan People's Liberation Movement (SPLM)-in-Government, SPLM-in-Opposition, civil society, and faith-based groups. Two further interviews were conducted in 2019 with leading experts on the topic of land in South Sudan in 2019. The analysis of private land investments provided herein also relies on data collected from the Land Matrix. Finally, this study draws upon a review of the secondary literature on land issues in South Sudan.

Theoretical Overview of Private, Rural, and Urban Land Tenure Systems

The first system of land tenure discussed involves the promotion of large-scale private land investments in South Sudan by the World Bank and the United Nations Food and Agriculture Organization (FAO), among other international organizations. These organizations assert that foreign investment will produce a mutually beneficial situation for private investors and host communities if African states enact stringent regulatory reforms (Deng 2011a, 8). Foreign land deals are presented as a way to modernize agriculture and to develop a country's industries through commercial farming (Zambakari 2017, 198–199). According to Olivier de Schutter (2016, 12–13), "these commentators tend to underestimate the risks involved in land investments and often adopt an idealized view of the framework under which such investments are regulated." Critics point to commercial agriculture's encroachment on communal land and the marginalization of smallholders by foreign investors. From this perspective, large-scale land deals undermine tenure security, are responsible for the loss of smallholder farmland, and accentuate competition over land.

Second, the central government in South Sudan is attempting to formalize the communal systems of land tenure in rural areas so as to incorporate them into the state. Local communities generally consider customary land tenure systems to be more responsive, affordable, geographically accessible, socially accountable, and culturally appropriate (Mennen 2012, 7–9). When communal forms of property undergo formalization, however, "exclusivity of rights tends to be strengthened," benefitting the primary right holder at the expense of others (IIED 2006, 2). Communal land tenure systems can equally be problematized by pointing to the elite capture of resources at every level of administration and on the grounds that they often violate international human rights standards, particularly pertaining to women's land rights (McMichael and Massleberg 2010, 1–13). Formalizing communal land is prone to conflict given that tenure rules may recognize multiple and overlapping rights to the same land. The formal recognition of customary laws and accompanying identity-based systems of authority can produce local-level conflicts in multi-ethnic societies (Hessbruegge 2012, 300).

Third, growing population pressure, developing market economies, and the return of Internally Displaced Persons (IDPs) and refugees have produced significant changes in urban land tenure in South Sudan. These pressures have increased the demand for and monetary value of land, in many ways undermining its socio-cultural meaning and significance. Urban expansion, coupled with the commercialization of land, has imposed pressures on informal settlements and other land uses by low-income residents in urban and peri-urban areas. Land is increasingly concentrated in the hands of a few through greater privatization and commodification. Processes of urbanization have led to land insecurity for low-income city dwellers, smallholder farmers, pastoralists, women, and other marginalized groups in South Sudan. In some cases, returning refugees and IDPs who are aligned with state officials have come to represent the new elite (IIED 2006, 10–11).

South Sudan's Legal Framework

The Sudanese state's interference in the land rights of rural communities in the south led to a protracted civil war from 1983 to 2005, resulting in the formal secession of South Sudan in 2011 (De Waal 2015). Khartoum was never able to enforce its statist version of land legislation in the south and customary land ownership remained the norm in practice (Shanmugaratnam 2008, 1). The Sudan People's Liberation Movement/Army's (SPLM/A) has held the slogan the "land belongs to the people" since its formation in 1983. The SPLM/A successfully pushed for the recognition of customary rights in the Comprehensive Peace Agreement (CPA). The legal framework of South Sudan from 2005 to 2011 consisted of the Interim Constitution of Southern Sudan (ICSS), the Interim National Constitution, and the CPA. The CPA and ICSS were vague on the particularities of land administration in Southern Sudan; ensuing issues were delegated to the Southern Sudan Land Commission (SSLC) until its dissolution in 2009 (Rolandsen 2009, 20–21).

The Land Act, drafted by the SSLC and passed in 2009, lists three forms of land tenure: freehold, leasehold, and communal. In addition, there is public land that is owned collectively by the citizenry and held in trust by the appropriate level of government (Deng 2016, 3). Public land comprises land for which no customary ownership is established (e.g., roads, government facilities, and national parks) (IOM/DFID 2017, 16). Private land in South Sudan is owned by individuals and registered under freehold (permanent ownership) or leasehold (for a specified duration of time). Freehold is a form of private ownership held individually, in perpetuity, and includes the right to transfer property. Freehold ownership is most common in urban areas. Foreign investors are not permitted to own land in South Sudan under the Land Act but may lease it for a period of up to 99 years (Rolandsen 2009, 20–21).

The Land Act reinforces the government's recognition of customary land tenure and sets broad parameters for defining, demarcating, registering, and managing community land. Under the Act, community lands held under customary law possess the same legal standing as private holdings that are registered by the state. A community is defined on the basis of ethnicity, residence, or interest. Land administration is decentralized to the local level, namely, to county, payam (district), and boma (hamlet) land councils. Customary chiefs work with elected government officials with regard to matters of land allocation, registration, and dispute resolution (IOM/DFID 2017, 16). Although the ownership of rural lands rests with communities as per the Land Act, the legislation does not specify who is to represent said communities' interests vis-à-vis the government and foreign investors (De Simone 2013, 47).

In 2009, Southern Sudan's legislative assembly passed the Investment Promotion Act and the Local Government Act. The Investment Promotion Act lays out the procedures for certifying and licensing foreign investors seeking to operate in South Sudan. The Local Government Act identifies the boma level as the main domain of traditional community authority, with customary institutions also operating at the payam and county levels. Whereas the Land Act vests authority of land administration in rural areas to communities, the Local Government Act acknowledges chiefs as government officials and traditional leaders (Justin and Van Dijk 2017, 9). In practice, a pro-government interpretation is employed whereby communities are identified through county authorities (Hessbruegge 2012, 304). In the Transitional Constitution of South Sudan (TCSS) of 2011, it was proclaimed that all land is "owned by the people… and its usage shall be regulated by the government," a declaration that strengthened the influence of the state (Hirblinger 2015, 710).

The shortcomings of the SSLC, in addition to poor coordination between the three levels of government and between the formal/customary systems, undermined the implementation of the Land Act (Deng 2016, 3). A Land Policy was drafted in 2011 to clarify the policy objectives and provisions of the Land Act, by articulating the broader goals of land administration in South Sudan. The draft policy was developed through a consultative process in each of South Sudan's ten states, headed by the SSLC and its international partners (Pritchard 2013, 9). In February 2011, the Land Policy was handed over to the Ministry of Legal Affairs and approved by the Council of Ministers in February 2013. Thereafter, the Land Policy stalled in parliament and remains a draft. Further political discussion on enacting the Land Policy was disrupted by the outbreak of civil war in December 2013 and ongoing instability (Mennen 2012, 15).

Strengthening the SSLC has been the focus of land reform efforts and so little attention has been paid to the role of sub-national institutions. As of 2017, only Jonglei and the three Equatorian states instituted state land commissions, with none of these commissions devolving their administrative duties to the county, payam, and boma authorities, as per the requirements of the Land Act (Justin and Van Dijk 2017, 9). The 2015 Agreement on the Resolution of the Conflict in South Sudan (ARCSS) and the 2018 "revitalized" peace deal (R-ARCSS) mandate the transitional government to initiate a national debate to review the current land policy, including the Land Act; to establish land registries; to empower land commissions at all levels of government; and to assist in the mediation of conflict arising from land disputes (Deng 2016, 11).

Large-Scale Private Investments in South Sudan

This section unpacks the history of foreign and domestic large-scale land investments in South Sudan and details: (1) the past and present state of land deals in the country; (2) their effects within the context of a weak regulatory environment; and (3) their impacts on livelihoods and ecologies. South Sudan's land rush lasted from approximately 2007 to the onset of the civil war at the end of 2013. Since then, there has been a marked retraction in foreign land investments due to the high risks and costs involved. Meanwhile, there is evidence of an increase in domestic investments. The capacity to monitor and enforce existing laws pertaining to land governance has thus far been weak, creating challenges for large-scale land investments and market-based, export-oriented approaches more generally.

In 2008, the Government of Southern Sudan (GoSS) embarked on a campaign to promote agricultural investment with a consortium of development partners, including the International Finance Corporation (IFC) and the United States Agency for International Development (USAID), and through a subcontracted company known as Tetratec ARD. This campaign entailed granting foreign investors an assortment of privileges, such as tax holidays, reduced limits on capital repatriation, and streamlined land acquisition procedures. The 2009 Land Act and the 2011 Investment Promotion Act then mandated that the government place ceilings on land acquisitions; limit the lease period for foreign investments in agriculture and forestry to renewable terms of 30 and 60 years; oversee social and environmental risk assessments; secure informed consent from the affected communities; and prohibit interference with pastoralist grazing rights (Deng 2011a, 1–19).

Large areas of land were subsequently leased out in negotiated deals between investors, community leaders, and state officials, usually without meaningful public consultation. Consequently, many of these deals were violently contested by local communities, such as in Lainya County, Yei (Hirblinger 2015, 708–709). David Deng estimated that foreign interests sought or acquired a total of 2.64 million hectares (ha) of land in the agriculture, forestry, and biofuel sectors between 2007 and 2010. This figure rises to 5.74 million ha when domestic investments are added, the equivalent to nine percent of Southern Sudan's total land area (Deng 2011b). Many of these investors were not serious about operationalizing proposed projects, while others were waiting to see how things would play out in the 2011 referendum before developing acquired land. Although there has been less speculative investment by foreign companies since 2013, there has been an increase in domestic acquisitions (Interview 1 2019).

As of November 2019, 26 deals are listed on the Land Matrix for South Sudan. Only nine of these deals are in operation, covering a land area of 598,634 ha. Two projects were abandoned and negotiations failed in two other cases. The remaining 13 deals are non-operational (i.e., the land deal is still being negotiated or has been concluded, but there is no development actually occurring). Three of the land deals currently in operation (294,000 ha in Renk, 147,000 ha in Manyo, and 29,400 ha in Melut) involve mechanized food projects in the Upper Nile State that began in the 1970s and are listed as having "unknown" owners. There is also very little information available on three further land deals currently in operation: the Gogrial East Farmers' Union (840 ha in Gogrial East), Toch Chol Crop Production (2730 ha in Gogrial West), and Tonj East Agricultural Cooperatives (1260 ha in Tonj) (Land Matrix 2020).

There are three active land investments for which information is available. First, the Egyptian-based agricultural company Qalaa Holdings controls 105,000 ha of land in Pariang and Guit, Unity State through a 25-year agreement with the state-level government at an annual leasing fee of US$125,000. Agricultural production began in 2009 but the civil war negatively affected planting. There was no environmental or social assessment for the project and local communities were not consulted. The company promised benefits for local communities such as education and infrastructure (e.g., irrigation, tractors, machinery, and roads) but so far only a health clinic has been built (Land Matrix 2020).

Second, the Canadian Economic Development Assistance for South Sudan (CEDASS) signed a 404 ha land deal in Jebel Lado, Central Equatoria to produce food crops in 2007. There is no lease as the project is a charitable endeavor. A portion of the crops are provided to the local community and the remaining supply is sold to the World Food

Program (WFP) at market prices for distribution in South Sudan. Some community members complained that they have not been given a share of the harvested crops (Land Matrix 2020). In addition, there are few benefits to the project in terms of employment creation since CEDASS employs mechanized forms of production. The company claims that the farm has 50 fulltime employees and employs about 100 seasonal workers (CEDASS 2020). Around 100 people were displaced by the project, however, community members stated they were able to re-establish their farms outside of the plantation areas with relative ease (Deng 2011b, 34).

Third, the Equatoria Teak Company (ETC), a unit of London-based Maris Capital, operates five separate forest reserve blocks in Western Equatoria. The concession is over 18,000 ha, with a total planted area of 1700 ha (ETC 2020). The affected communities are meant to receive a lump sum of US$200,000 into a social fund (US$70,000 has been dispersed thus far) in addition to royalty payments of US$5 per cubic meter of exported sawn teak board (Land Matrix 2020). Some state-level officials complained that these terms are not competitive since ETC earns upwards of US$1000 on international markets. ETC's concession appears to have been non-competitively awarded by the central government (Verjee 2013). Some states responded by taking back land from the plantations (Toby 2019). In addition, a lack of consultation has reportedly provoked uprisings by local communities, who have not received promised roads and other assistance as part of timber extraction deals (The National 2013).

The Land Matrix lists two deals as abandoned. First, Saudi investor Prince Budr Bin Sultan signed a 25-year contract in 2010 to produce food crops, at a leasing fee US$125,000 per year to the state government. Second, in 2008, the Texas-based company Nile Trading and Development (NTD) negotiated a deal with the Mukaya Payam Cooperative in Central Equatoria for 600,000 ha in Lanya, with the possibility of obtaining 400,000 ha more). NTD never activated the lease, applied for a government license, or established any visible presence on the ground. As it turns out, the Mukaya Payam Cooperative was a fictitious entity; influential locals leased out the land without the knowledge or consent of the community (Land Matrix 2020). They leased the land at the low price of US$25,000, which works out to only US$16 a hectare. The company agreed to provide the local community with a portion of the profits from the investment, increasing from 40 to 50% of net profits over the life of the lease (Rhode 2011).

Negotiations failed in two other cases. First, in 2010, Joint Aid Management (JAM) and African Commercial Development (ACD) were negotiating a 32-year lease deal for 243,000 ha to produce food crops in Yambio, Western Equatoria. Second, in 2009, Jarch Capital, owned by American Phil Heilberg, acquired a 70% interest in LEAC in a deal to produce food crops on 400,000 ha of land in Mayom for a period of 30–40 years (Land Matrix 2020). This agreement, negotiated with local warlord Paulino Matiep, did not possess government approval nor the consent of affected communities. The local county commissioner of the new government had never even heard of Jarch Capital or the land deal. The deal between Jarch Capital and Matiep fell through in 2011.

A further seven land deals are listed on the Land Matrix as being "under negotiation": (1) a plan by the Egyptian government to produce food crops and an irrigation scheme on 16,800 ha of land along the Jur River in Western Bahr el-Ghazal; (2) negotiations by Yen Thumb Group for 3000 ha in Jonglei; (3) plans by the Eastern Equatoria State (EES) Ministry of Wildlife to purchase 280,000 ha of land in Kapoeta, Eastern Equatoria for a wildlife park; (4) the EES Ministry of Wildlife's negotiations for 13,200 ha of land in Ikotos and Magwi for conservation and tourism at Imatong National Park; (5) a Memorandum of Understanding (MoU) signed by Madhvani Group in 2007 to produce food crops; (6) interest expressed in 2008 by M.A.J. Foundation to develop the forestry industry in Wau and; (7) negotiations by Eyat Oilfield Services to produce food crops in Ezo and Tambura, Western Equatoria, based on an MoU signed in 2010 that stipulates a one-time lease payment of US$250,000 to the state government (Land Matrix 2020).

Finally, the Land Matrix lists five deals still in the "start up" phase: (1) a 6300 ha deal signed in 2010 by the Ministry of Agriculture of the Northern Bahr-el-Ghazal State to produce food crops in Aweil, wherein the local community is to receive 60% of the crop and the rest of the supply sold in South Sudan; (2) M.A.J. Foundation signed a 32-year deal for 8020 ha to produce teak in Nzara (affected communities are promised US$200,000 via a social fund and royalty payments of US$100 per cubic meter of exported sawn teak board); (3) Blue Lakes Limited signed a 30-year contract for 560 ha in 2008 to produce teak in Yambio, Western Equatoria (includes US$200,000 payment into a social fund for communities, plus US$110 in royalties per cubic meter of exported teak); (4)

in 2010, Green Resources entered into the final stages of negotiation to obtain a 99-year lease for 179,999 ha of land for a timber plantation, conservation, and carbon sequestration (the Tindilo community is to receive US$12,500 per year in rent and community support, amounting to US$0.07 per ha each year) and; (5) Al Ain National Wildlife, an Emirati company, signed a 30-year deal with the southern government in 2008 for 1,680,000 ha of land designated for tourism/conservation in Pibor, Jonglei and Kapoeta, Eastern Equatoria (Land Matrix 2020).

The Land Matrix data therefore shows a marked retrenchment in foreign investments and corporate activity on the ground. This likely fails to capture the full picture, as data availability in South Sudan is a problem and it is unclear how frequently the Land Matrix is updated. The few deals that *have* been signed are transfers arranged between the South Sudanese politico-military elite and foreign investors that often result in the dispossession of customary land (Oyono and Galuak 2015, 5–8). The SPLM/A-led government has gradually moved away from a community, rights-based model to a private sector approach to agriculture. This is grounded in a belief that relying on the communal systems will undermine the investment climate, inhibit economic growth, and reduce the state's control over development activities (Hirblinger 2015, 710). Investments are managed almost entirely at the state level, a fact that contributes to an overall lack of transparency since there is no central monitoring body responsible for keeping track of who is investing in what and where. Investors are free to negotiate land leases with power brokers at the state level without proper regulatory oversight from the central government (Deng 2011b, 18–19).

It is common for public and private actors alike to only inform community members of proposed projects after the details of an arrangement have been finalized and as a matter of formality (Deng 2011b, 32). Some agreements are entered into without any involvement from affected communities. In other cases, a government official held discussions with a local chief and a few leaders without involving the rest of the community (Deng 2011c, 16). Most land deals are signed unofficially. In addition, extremely low leasehold rates suggest that most of the money paid by investors never makes it into official accounts (De Waal 2014, 359). Companies rarely conduct environmental and social impact assessments. There are often delays in project development and/or a failure to fulfill promised social benefits such as education, health care, and infrastructure (Deng 2011a, 2–10). Instead, local populations can experience displacement from residential, agricultural, pasture, or forage land. Rural communities have, at times violently, resisted informal or forced land acquisitions given the linkage between land and ethnic belonging (Hirblinger 2015, 711–717).

The SPLM/A believes that large-scale development projects are the quickest way to improve food security and stimulate the economy. Proponents of this model assert that, by amassing large areas of "unused" land and turning that into large-scale mechanized farms, South Sudan can produce enough food to feed its population and export food to international markets (Deng 2011c, 1–2). From this perspective, customary land tenure inhibits individuals from using the land to produce for the market or to create personal wealth and so it must be subsumed by freehold or leasehold forms of tenure (Shanmugaratnam 2008, 7–11). Although 90% of South Sudan's soil is suited for agriculture and forestry, only 4% of the land is being used for crop production and the country is almost entirely dependent on food imports (SOMO 2016, 5–11). These figures suggest that South Sudan has significantly more agricultural potential than what it currently produces.

Agro-industrial investment projects, however, are more likely to undermine food security by dispossessing people from land and resources, especially considering that 70% of the population in South Sudan relies on subsistent livelihoods (McMichael and Massleberg 2010, 7). Transferring large areas of land to private interests undercuts communal systems of ownership by concentrating land in the hands of foreign and domestic companies. The lack of a functioning regulatory framework, the nascent state of government, a society reeling from decades of war, and the legal ambiguity of the post-conflict transition are all risk factors that exacerbate the likelihood that such investments will undermine livelihoods (Deng 2011a, 2). Strong frameworks are needed to govern the administration of land investments and enforce legal regulations. Insecurity provides fertile ground for high risk, high reward investors to exploit the lack of clear land acquisition procedures (Deng 2011b, 18–19).

There is a place for investment in both smallholder farmers and commercial agribusiness. The counterargument against the simultaneous use of both models or strategies is that there are financial incentives to concentrate on private investors to the neglect of smallholder farmers, especially within the context of limited government capacity. A balanced approach could support smallholder farmers alongside some forms of agribusiness (Interview 1 2019). Domestic investments in South Sudan also generally do a better job of consulting communities prior to making decisions on land allocations. Such projects are often conceived of as community ventures, including farmers' cooperatives and smaller investments by private individuals. Foreign companies tend to leverage the political capital of their domestic allies to facilitate land acquisitions, as opposed to the social capital of communities (Deng 2011b, 34).

Rural Land in South Sudan

This section engages with a number of salient land issues in South Sudan's rural areas, including: (1) the lack of clarity in land policies and institutional multiplicity, which together encourage competing land claims; (2) evidence that an identity-based approach to the recognition and formalization of communal land tenure has heightened group conflict; (3) the reality that local systems, much like the central state, are subject to elite capture in land management decision-making processes; and (4) the gender-based concerns associated with the communal system. Land conflicts may manifest outwardly along ethnic lines, but they are rooted in the SPLM's land reform policies, the tensions between statist and customary land systems, the formalization of land rights, and the commercialization of land. None of these issues are unique to the customary system. There is no choice but to rely on traditional or hybrid authorities, in one way or another, given the weak reach of the central state. Still, there is a need to promote policies that are more unifying and that rely on and strengthen local conflict resolution mechanisms so as to ensure respect for human rights vis-à-vis the customary system.

Land in South Sudan's rural areas is governed under the principles of customary law, which is administered, interpreted, and enforced by community leaders, including chiefs, clan leaders, and village elders. Within the customary system, land is considered common property. The right to access communal land derives from membership in a given community through common ancestry. Usufruct rights are passed down in four ways: allocation, inheritance, gift, and purchase or exchange. The most common way of accessing land is through inheritance, with men inheriting land from their father and daughters acquiring land rights through their husbands (Mennen 2012, 13–15). Customary tenure divides each territory into lands designated for agricultural production, residential plots, grazing, and fishing. Members claim ownership of crop production and residential land, while pasture and other resource lands are part of a common pool that any community member can access (Tiitmamer et al. 2017, 7).

Recognition of communal ownership is based on patrilineal descent from those who first cleared and settled or conquered a particular territory. Traditionally, there has been no benefit or interest in asserting exclusive property rights over land. Secondary rights holders could access land for grazing or other purposes based on friendly relations, marital ties, or long-standing agreements. A community that is a primary rights holder must then negotiate secondary rights for non-members (e.g., pastoralists) (Leonardi and Santschi 2016, 104). Since 2005, the SPLM has made efforts to integrate the communal system into the formal state by wrestling control over land administration from traditional authorities (Deng 2014, 5). The Land Act placed land in rural areas under the control of the local chiefs at the Boma level, as well as through the Payam Land Councils (PLCs) and County Land Authorities (CLAs). In practice, politico-military elites manipulate the codification of the communal system (Pritchard 2013, 12).

As Cherry Leonardi and Martina Santschi (2016, 8–9) write, South Sudan's decentralized system of governance imagines people as living in "discrete ethnic territories organized into patrilineal descent groups and governed by their own decentralized administrations." The creation of ethnically defined states, counties, payams, and bomas has increased incidences of land disputes, many of which are articulated along identity lines given the nature of the customary system. These reforms have also encouraged competing land claims between local state administrations and traditional authorities, who are forced to compete to secure the territorial advantage of their respective ethnic groups (IOM/DFID 2017, 11–12). The political and economic ambitions of elites, along with fears of exclusion, drive the promotion of rigid boundaries in land codification. The resulting intergroup competition over land produces a context marked by the militarisation of ethnic identity (De Simone 2015, 60).

The codification of customary land tenure in South Sudan is problematic, Jan Arno Hessbruegge writes, because the law becomes "petrified and can no longer reflect changing values" (2012, 310). In practice, land governance is not divided into discrete customary and statutory laws but entails an evolving and flexible negotiation of different kinds of land claims (Leonardi and Santschi 2016, 141). Statutory law simplifies and distorts the nature of customary land rights by promoting the conversion of customary rights into more exclusive property rights (e.g., land title registration). Drawing fixed boundaries between clans and tribes is impractical because settlements are interspersed between different groups. Primary rights holders are increasingly claiming exclusive land rights as a result. Meanwhile, populations that historically possessed secondary rights (e.g., pastoralists) are trying to claim primary access rights because they are afraid of losing their secondary rights (Interview 2 2019).

Communal land tenure is based on autochthony and an idea of ethnic identity based on common ancestry. Primary and secondary land rights are therefore subject to membership of a particular community, while disputes are addressed through traditional mechanisms. The legal recognition of customary land rights entails the demarcation and formalization of communal borders. The criteria used to identify a community with a certain territory are often contested. Tenure reform has strengthened ethnic definitions of citizenship, deepened inequalities, and exacerbated violent competition over communal land rights. In practice, "communities" are identified through the territory of local administrative units or local government councils, with "aliens" being excluded from the land (De Simone 2015, 60).

New localized conflicts in Unity State are grounded in the perception that access to land and resources is granted along tribal lines. As Sara De Simone (2013, 55) argues, institutionalizing county borders has created local disputes over resources that emerge from the tensions between the traditional customary domain and the "modern" administrative local government unit. The regime of exclusive land rights is spreading to rural areas where customary land tenure formerly recognized multiple, often overlapping forms of land use, access, and control. Communities are pushed to legally secure their existing land and/or to opportunistically seize other lands given the unstable and transitory situation. Many groups are now reifying distinctions between primary and secondary rights, which are asserted on the basis of competing "genealogical arguments about patrilineal descent" (Leonardi and Santschi 2016, 97).

In the absence of clear policies on customary tenure, decentralization has favored those local chiefs who have positioned themselves as intermediaries between the government and their community. Localized customary authorities are subordinate to the chiefs in the new administrative hierarchy. Public authorities gain legitimacy and authority by tactically acknowledging claims to land and by applying the regulatory framework to resolve disputes. Such interventions nurture institutional multiplicity and competition over what regulations should apply and which governing bodies are in charge (Van Leeuwen et al. 2018, 289–302). For example, attempts during the CPA period to demarcate the Kit River area of Central Equatoria were disputed by politicians in the South Sudan Legislative Assembly (SSLA), local "big men," and communities, including the Acholi and Madi (Rolandsen 2009, 24–25).

Land governance is increasingly seen by the SPLM as the domain of state authority rather than a shared responsibility between customary and state institutions (Justin and Van Dijk 2017, 20–21). The incorporation of rural areas into the local government and the designation of chiefs as state officials authorized to oversee land administration problematizes the conception of community ownership defined in the Land Act. The introduction of ambiguously worded "community rights" through state-mandated legislation opens up new possibilities for local groups to stake claims by redefining "community." State powers have expanded their authority to exert control over communal land at the expense of localized customary authorities (Van Leeuwen et al. 2018, 305–307).

The County Land Authority (CLA) in Bor County, Jonglei State was one of the only localities wherein the administrative and governance structures were set up during the CPA period. The Bor CLA received support from the Sudan Rural Land and Governance (SRLG) Project, a USAID-funded initiative implemented by the American firm Tetra Tech. The project's main goal was to provide financial, institutional, and technical support to implement the Land Policy. In practice, there was a lack of substantive interaction between CLA members and the rural communities they are mandated to represent. Bor CLA members were appointed through a top-down process and therefore did not feel accountable to the rural communities. Community members, the customary owners of the land, were not officially involved in land administration or governance decision-making processes (Oyono and Galuak 2015, 1).

Many scholars point to the ambiguous and over-ambitious nature of South Sudan's communal land tenure system and its contribution to local identity-based conflicts. These are not, however, arguments to abandon communal tenure altogether. South Sudan is committed to a system based on customary law and thus the question is how to incorporate this system into the state in a way that is unifying and reinforces national identity. Investing in pre-existing or traditional institutions at the local level can help strengthen governance in South Sudan. The practice of supporting local or hybrid institutions lessens the burden on the formal state to deliver services (Interview 1 2019). When it comes to the formalization of communal title, the academic and policy literature calls for a shift from land rights "registration" to "recording and documenting" processes (Interview 2 2019).

South Sudan's approach to land tenure is criticized for fuelling elite capture by powerful local and national figures. Chiefs are supposed to defer to county authorities on land issues in towns, but in practice do not and commonly exploit land deals for personal gain (Mennen 2012, 23). The process of aligning administrative boundaries with community lands creates incentives to reify ethnic identities, as a political tool to amass power. Land governance is skewed in favor of wealthy and powerful members of national or local governments regardless of the laws and procedures used (formal or informal; customary or statist; private or communal). The administration of customary land tenure is therefore subject to the same inequalities that exist in South Sudan's broader political economy (Leonardi and Santschi 2016, 9–11).

Some scholars argue that the government should not interfere with community lands and landholders. From this perspective, state regulation of the customary system opens up space for individuals at the local level to manipulate laws and policies to their advantage. However, population pressure and the growth in land acquisition and development creates a need to formally recognize community structures to ensure their survival. The general trend in the literature is to acknowledge the utility of customary systems, while also recognizing their shortcomings (Interview 1 2019). Any approach to land reform is only as good as the dispute resolution mechanisms that underpin it, the most effective of which are likely to be found in the mediation practices that characterize customary land governance (Interview 2 2019).

At the same time, it is important not to romanticize customary institutions. The ideal of equality in terms of access to land is problematized by a hierarchy of rights. Access to land is circumscribed by rules of descent, gender, and ethnicity (Pantuliano 2007, 7). For instance, women's rights to land in South Sudan are entangled in conflicting customary and formal legal systems. The Transitional Constitution and the Land Act assert that women can own land, while customary law denies this right (Mennen 2012). In practice, women's land rights are largely conditional on their marital or childbearing status (Stone 2014, 7–8). Women do, however, possess usufruct rights, that is, their lack of property rights does not obviate their legal right to access land within the communal system (Leonardi and Santschi 2016, 127–142).

Despite the limitations of customary law, there is no institutional capacity to rely on other systems of tenure in South Sudan. Customary institutions enjoy a high degree of legitimacy because they are rooted in and adapted to local contexts. Current best practice in land governance is to afford equal protection of customary land rights and then upgrade associated institutions when certain issues arise, including those of gender inequality and inheritance. Cultural changes are slow and gradual, and must be encouraged in ways that are institutionally and socially sustainable. There is no use in crafting laws that will not be implemented (Interview 2 2019). It is also unfair to "measure the customary systems against the benchmark of an idealized, fully human rights-compliant central state, because this ideal is removed from post-conflict realities" (Hessbruegge 2012, 300). Instead, progress must be measured in comparison to existing state institutions, which in South Sudan have been characterized as patriarchal, unaccountable, and exploitative.

In rural areas, there is a need to shift toward recording and documenting land uses rather than registering land title. This approach would allow for a greater degree of fluidity and continual negotiation as opposed to reifying ethnic territories. Unfortunately, the SPLM-introduced legislation is mainly focused on building new institutions. In the lead up to independence in 2011—when USAID was pumping aid money into land governance in South Sudan—the SPLM managed to set up only two county land authorities in the entire country and those were flawed. It is therefore necessary to build on existing communal institutions in rural areas. Improvements to the customary system in terms of protecting the rights of women, ethnic outsiders, and other marginalized communities can be made over time (Interview 2 2019).

Urban Land in South Sudan

This section presents a survey of the complex and overlapping land issues in South Sudan's urban and peri-urban areas, including: (1) the consequences associated with the commercialization and privatization of land; (2) the effects of urban expansion and increased competition for land; (3) weak administrative capacity, institutional fragmentation, and legislative ambiguity and; (4) the difficulties brought on by the need to integrate returning IDPs and refugees. Scholarly debate focuses on the saliency of ethnic animosities versus issues of political economy in explaining conflicts of urban land governance (Hirblinger 2015, 708–709). The Juba and Yei cases demonstrate that while conflicts often manifest along ethnic lines, the deeper causes are the processes of commercialization, privatization, and urban expansion.

Since 2005, land issues in South Sudan's urban areas have been defined by the increasing commercialization and privatization of land. Access to urban land holdings is determined by an individual's capacity to purchase leaseholds and, often times, by one's privileged access to the government officials (Leonardi 2011, 2019). Individuals therefore access land in urban areas through market-based and crony or relational mechanisms, as opposed to asserting their belonging to a particular community like in the case of rural areas. In practice, however, most cities and towns operate through parallel systems of statutory and customary law that compliment and conflict with each other at varying times (Mennen 2012, 12). Some communities claim land in urban areas despite the fact that urban areas are supposed to be administered under an individual private property regime. The SPLM's efforts to formalize land tenure systems in and around urban areas are limited by ambiguous legislation and overlapping jurisdictions (De Simone 2015, 64).

Gabriella McMichael (2016, 2735) argues that ethnicity was not the primary driver of land conflict in the informal settlements around Juba. Instead, communities, government authorities, and commercial interests are forced to compete for a scarce amount of legally available and affordable land, leading to a sharp rise in the cost of buying or renting formally demarcated urban plots. The development of informal settlements creates opportunities for individuals to exercise power and accumulate capital at the expense of others. Similarly, Anne Walreat (2011, 1–35) suggests that, although local inhabitants commonly espouse ethnically based narratives, the underlying cause of land conflict in urban areas is the varying ability of individuals to access land as per their military and/or political connections. The competition for land produces processes of class formation that are veiled by discourses of ethnicity.

Rather than portraying land conflicts as being driven by ethnicity, Leonardi and Santschi (2016, 103–141) emphasize the disruptive effects caused by the commodification of land. Whereas land always possessed productive, moral, social, and spiritual values in South Sudan, the process of rapid urbanization since the 1990s has assigned a strict monetary or market value to land. The commodification of land in South Sudan is a product of overlapping factors: political struggle between various levels of government administration, the return of IDPs and growing urbanization, new patterns of population density, and new opportunities for resource extraction and commercial agriculture. Historically, conflicts over land involved grazing lands in cattle-keeping areas. Competition for land now tends to focus on cultivable land, urban and peri-urban plots, and new development sites.

As land is privatized, commodified, and concentrated in the hands of the few, the general trend in South Sudan is one of increasing land tenure insecurity for low-income city dwellers, smallholder farmers, pastoralists and other marginalized groups, including women. Titling and other formal land tenure registration systems tend to be expensive, badly tailored to local needs, and inaccessible for marginalized groups. Informal land markets still exist, but lower-income buyers and sellers are typically exploited in these systems (IIED 2006, 10–11). In this context of growing insecurity, communities seek to protect their land rights by asserting membership in patrilineal kinship groups or by finding the means to purchase and register private land titles (Leonardi and Santschi 2016, 142). Rapid urbanization has generated tensions as towns and cities expand into formerly rural areas, thus infringing on or conflicting with communal territorial rights (Mennen 2012, 5).

The incompetence or corruption of state and customary institutions and the ambiguity of South Sudan's legislative framework further undermine land governance (IOM/DFID 2017, 6–7). The trends in urban expansion involve politicians and military officials acquiring land from communities living around urban areas. This phenomenon has taken place throughout the Equatorias as well as in the cities of Malakal and Wau (Interview 1 2019). In many cases, IDPs and refugees return to the area where they hold customary land rights only to find that this land has been allocated to influential parties, resulting in conflict and displacement (Pantuliano 2007, 7–11). Disputes also arise between newcomers and communities with autochthonous claims to the land near an urban center, as has been the case in Juba and Yei. As Matthew Pritchard writes, overlapping land claims are "rooted in decades of conflict and competition between recently politicized and militarized groups of pastoralists and agriculturalists" (2013, 9).

The ambiguities of South Sudan's legislative framework and the state's weak capacity in urban and rural land governance creates a situation wherein most South Sudanese depend on customary systems to access land (Deng 2014, 1). In the few urban areas where land administration structures are functional, "statutory and customary land administration systems co-exist in an uneasy relationship, generating disputes as the national, state and community level compete with each other over land access and control" (IOM/DFID 2017, 5). Another locus of contestation over land rights in urban settings lies between country commissioners and town mayors (Rolandsen 2009, 21–22). Conflicts have also frequently erupted between customary chiefs because the existing legislation does not clearly distinguish between communal and individual rights over land in urban and peri-urban areas (McMichael and Massleberg 2010, 27).

In the case of Juba, conflicts over land are often depicted as being driven by ethnic tensions between "Equatorians" and "Dinka." Many inhabitants of the fertile agricultural land of the Central Equatoria region fled during the war and, on their return, found their former plots occupied by soldiers, government officials, and displaced people who are commonly, but not always accurately, labeled as Dinka (Rolandsen 2009, 19). As a result, the widespread perception among communities in the Equatorias is that the SPLM/A has been actively seizing land in Juba and other towns for the benefit of Dinka newcomers rather than protecting the land rights of indigenous communities. Naseem Badley (2013, 56–60) suggests that the main conflict lies between newcomers (who are not exclusively Dinka) and the previous owners of communal land around the capital, most notably the Bari. Both newcomers and poorer long-term inhabitants, however, are increasingly disadvantaged in the competition for access to urban land, regardless of their ethnicity. McMichael (2016, 2724) argues that powerful elites seek to reify ethnic categories through informal land transactions and formal demarcation processes to further their parochial interests. Relevant power brokers included the settlement leaders, public officials within the southern and the Central Equatoria State (CES) governments, military actors in the SPLA, and Bari chiefs. Displaced persons who have resettled in the Equatorias are often better connected to military and government powers than the patrilineal clan authorities and local land governance structures (Leonardi and Santschi 2016). As a result, conflicts and resulting agreements often cut across ethnic lines.

In Juba, the land claims made by each set of actors were informed by their respective state-building agendas. SPLM leaders used the language of development to justify their claims to land in the capital, carve out political jurisdictions, and increase the power of the state government within the decentralized system. Bari leaders invoked customary rights to land in and around Juba as a means to preserve their ethnic privilege, while non-Bari Equatorian leaders of the CES government promoted Bari land rights in an attempt to resist state encroachment. These communities were not only asserting antecedent land rights against other groups but also resisting the penetration of the SPLM/A's military and political culture into rural areas (Leonardi 2011, 225). Returning refugees, IDPs, and ex-combatants articulated claims to land by emphasizing citizenship rights, ethnic privilege, elite status, and/or contributions to the liberation struggle (Badley 2013, 60). The central debate therefore hinges on whether land rights should be based on wartime effort, nationality, ethnicity, autochthony, or use and occupancy.

In Yei, many returnees found that soldiers, migrants, and IDPs occupied their land. Some of these land-based conflicts possessed an ethnic dimension in that many of the soldiers occupying land were Dinka and those returning were mainly ethnic Kakwa. To complicate matters further, the pre-war inhabitants of the area and the "newcomers" possess their own respective local leaders and authorities who voice their claims to land and settlement rights. SPLA soldiers often assumed that, as the liberators of the south, they held the right to land and land governance; migrants and displaced people often agree with this arrangement. In contrast, the Kakwa consider the rural Bomas to be the domain of their own people. The Kakwa complained that the administration of Yei Town was filled with newcomers and government officials who represented the interests of the state (Van Leeuwen et al. 2018, 286–306).

As Peter Hakim Justin (2016, 419) details, local public authorities leverage decentralization policies to vie for legitimacy among returning SPLA soldiers, refugees, and IDPs arriving in the wake of the civil war. Transformations in land governance, ambiguously worded national policies, and shifts in population demographics are capitalized upon by chiefs and state powers at the expense of more localized customary authorities. The politics of land control and identity turn land disputes between displaced people and returnees into a major source of instability. The historical grievances in Yei between the Dinka and Equatorian communities mean that displaced people are often portrayed as agents of the Dinka-led state, sent to occupy territory in the Equatorias. Chiefs in Yei are accused of allocating land belonging to local communities to displaced people from the Dinka tribe, resulting in conflicts (Justin and Van Dijk 2017, 18–20).

Various public authorities, including chiefs, local government officials, and state representatives, vie for influence in land governance in and around Yei. State attempts at land tenure reform and ambiguously worded decentralization policies have fed into contestations by legitimizing certain local authorities over others. These processes effectively increase the state's authority in local land governance despite its limited institutional presence in Yei. State officials selected many of the chiefs in Yei on the basis of SPLA membership, replacing the existing chiefs of local communities. Although state legislation acknowledges the power of customary authorities to govern communal land, the state maintains discretionary powers in recognizing and formalizing customary authorities (Van Leeuwen et al. 2018, 286–297).

Land-based conflicts in South Sudan's urban areas are therefore explained by: the privatization and commodification of land; processes of urban expansion; the return or resettlement of IDPs and refugees; land grabbing by politico-military elites; the insecure land rights of women and other marginalized groups within market-driven and customary systems and; low institutional capacity at all levels of government (McMichael and Massleberg 2010, 13). The return of refugees and IDPs, along with the influx of international investors and humanitarian aid workers, caused the economic value of available plots to skyrocket. Meanwhile, poor governance hindered the formation of effective institutions in the development and management of urban land. Most new urban inhabitants were unable to access land legally and were forced to reside in informal settlements, leading to increased competition for land (Van Leeuwen et al. 2018, 286–297). From a political economy perspective, these conflicts are symptomatic of a shift from a subsistence system to one which commodifies land, as opposed to being produced by ethnic tensions (McMichael 2016, 2721–2737).

Conclusion

In conclusion, the brief land rush experienced in South Sudan between the signing of the CPA in 2005 to the onset of the country's civil war in 2013 offers a cautionary tale. Large-scale, particularly foreign land investments are a risky strategy in South Sudan given the ambiguous legal framework and weak regulatory institutions. At the same time, government, military, and local elites favor uncertainty since it opens up opportunities for personal enrichment, often at the expense of marginalized groups. The customary system of land tenure prevails in rural areas, however, the SPLM/A seeks to formalize borders and define territories on the basis of ethnic belonging, in turn heightening inter- and intra-group conflict. Local systems, much like those of the central state, are subject to elite capture in land management decision-making processes and can undermine respect for human rights. These limitations do not mean that customary systems should be abandoned altogether; rather, a hybrid approach is needed to de-escalate and resolve land conflicts. While conflicts are typically framed as being driven by ethnic tensions, political economy factors related to the commodification and privatization of land are more salient in urban areas.

Bibliography

Badley, Naseem. 2013. The strategic instrumentalization of land tenure in 'state-building': The case of Juba, South Sudan. *Africa* 83: 57–77.

CEDASS. 2020. The Jebel Ladu Farming Project. https://cedass.squarespace.com/farm.

Deng, David. 2011a. Understanding land investment deals in Africa. Oakland Institute: 1–54.

Deng, David. 2011b. The new frontier: A baseline survey of large-scale land-based investment in Southern Sudan. Norwegian People's Aid: 1–48.

Deng, David. 2011c. Land belongs to the community: Demystifying the 'global land grab' in Southern Sudan. Land Deal Politics Initiative Working Paper: 1–29.

Deng, David. 2014. South Sudan synthesis report: Findings of the Land Governance Assessment Framework (LGAF). South Sudan Land Policy: 1–7.

Deng, David. 2016. Between a rock and a hard place: Land rights and displacement in Juba, South Sudan. South Sudan Law Society: 1–21.

De Schutter, Olivier. 2016. Tainted lands: Corruption in large-scale land deals. International Corporate Accountability Roundtable and Global Witness: 1–112.

De Simone, Sara. 2013. Post-conflict decentralization: Dynamics of land and power in Unity State, South Sudan. UNISCI Discussion Papers: 35–56.

De Simone, Sara. 2015. Building a fragmented state: Land governance and conflict in South Sudan. *Journal of Peacebuilding and Development* 10: 60–73.

De Waal, Alex. 2014. When kleptocracy becomes insolvent: Brute causes of the civil war in South Sudan. *African Affairs* 113: 347–369.

De Waal, Alex. 2015. *The real politics of the horn of Africa: Money, war and the business of power*. Cambridge: Polity.

ETC. 2020. Equatoria Teak Company. http://equatoriateak.com/.

Friis, Cecilie, and Anette Reenber. 2010. Land grab in Africa: Emerging land system drivers in a teleconnected world. Global Land Project: 1–46.

Gagné, Marie and Ashley Fent. 2020. The faltering land rush and the limits to extractive capitalism in Senegal. In *The transnational land rush in Africa*, ed. Logan Cochrane and Nathan Andrews. Cham: Springer.

Hamann, Steffi and Adam Sneyd. 2020. Agribusiness development in Cameroon: Colonial legacies and recent tensions. In *The transnational land rush in Africa*, ed. Logan Cochrane and Nathan Andrews. Cham: Springer.

Hessbruegge, Jan Arno. 2012. Customary law and authority in a state under construction: The case of South Sudan. *African Journal of Legal Studies* 5: 295–311.

Hirblinger, Andreas. 2015. Land, political subjectivity and conflict in Post-CPA Southern Sudan. *Journal of Eastern African Studies* 9: 704–722.

IIED. 2006. Innovation in securing land rights in Africa: Lessons from experience. International Institute for Environment and Development (IIED): 1–12.

IOM/DFID. 2017. Key Housing, Land and Property (HLP) issues in urban areas of South Sudan: Context, actors and legislation, a background brief for shelter actors. International Organization for Migration (IOM) and the UK's Department for International Development (DFID): 1–20.

Justin, Peter Hakim. 2016. The politics of displacement-related land conflict in Yei River County, South Sudan. *The Journal of Modern African Studies* 54: 419–442.

Justin, Peter Hakim, and Han Van Dijk. 2017. Land reform and conflict in South Sudan: Evidence from Yei River County. *Africa Spectrum* 52: 3–28.

Land Matrix. 2020. South Sudan. https://landmatrix.org/data/by-target-country/south-sudan/.

Leonardi, Cherry. 2011. Paying 'buckets of blood' for the land: Moral debates over economy, war and state in Southern Sudan. *Journal of Modern African Studies* 49: 215–240.

Leonardi, Cherry, and Martina Santschi. 2016. Dividing communities in South Sudan and Northern Uganda. Rift Valley Institute: 1–161.

McMichael, Gabriella. 2016. Land conflict and informal settlements in Juba, South Sudan. Urban Studies: 2721–2737.

McMichael, Gabriella, and Asa Massleberg. 2010. Landmines and land rights in Southern Sudan. Geneva Centre for Humanitarian Demining: 1–31.

Mennen, Tiernan. 2012. Customary law and land rights in South Sudan. Norwegian Refugee Council: 1–40.

Oyono, Phil René, and Deng-Athoi Galuak. 2015. Land governance, local authorities and unrepresentative representation in rural South Sudan: A preliminary exploration. RFGI Working Paper: 1–58.

Pantuliano, Sara. 2007. The land question: Sudan's peace nemesis. Overseas Development Institute (ODI): 1–14.

Pritchard, Matthew. 2013. Land tenure reforms and food security in South Sudan. Institute for the Study of International Development (ISID): 1–19.

Rhode, Michaela. 2011. Is South Sudan's largest land deal a land grab? *Think Africa Press*.

Rolandsen, Øystein. 2009. Land, security and peace building in the Southern Sudan. PRIO Paper: 1–33.

Shanmugaratnam, Nadaraja. 2008. Post-war development and the land question in South Sudan. International Symposium on Resources Under Stress organized by the *Afrasian Centre for Peace and Development*, Ryukoku University, Japan, 23–24 February.

Sindayigaya, Willy. 2011. Foreign investments in agriculture—'Land grabbing.' *GLS*: 1–19.

SOMO. 2016. *Country profile, South Sudan: Main economic sectors and multinational companies*. Amsterdam: SOMO Centre for Research on Multinational Corporations: 1–14.

Stone, Anna. 2014. Nowhere to go: Displaced and returnee women seeking housing, land and property rights in South Sudan. Norwegian Refugee Council: 1–78.

The National. 2013. Hardwood to Help South Sudan Wean Itself from Oil Dependence. https://www.thenationalnews.com/business/hardwood-to-help-south-sudanwean-itself-from-oil-dependence-1.290462?videoId=5754807360001.

Tiitmamer, Nhial, Augustino Ting Mayai, and Nyathon Hoth Mai. 2017. Land tenure in South Sudan: Does it promote climate change resilience? Sudd Institute: 1–16.

Toby, Hellen. 2019. Amid upheaval in South Sudan, the country's teak forests fall. Reuters.

United Nations. n.d. Map of South Sudan.

Van Leeuwen, Mathijs, et al. 2018. Transforming land governance and strengthening the state in South Sudan. *African Affairs* 117: 289–302.

Verjee, Aly. 2013. Is all well in the teak forests of South Sudan? African Arguments.

Walreat, Anne. 2011. Displacement in post-war Southern Sudan: Survival and accumulation within urban perimeters. MICRON Research Working Paper No. 57: 1–35.

Zambakari, Christopher. 2017. Land grab and institutional legacy of colonialism: The case of Sudan. *Consilience: The Journal of Sustainable Development* 18: 193–204.

CHAPTER 5

Behind Accumulation and Dispossession: State and Large-Scale Agricultural Land Investments in Nigeria

Noah Echa Attah

Introduction

The debate on large-scale land investments since the 2007/2008 commodity price spike remains alive and well, particularly in Africa as a target destination for investors. The massive "rush" for land produced reports of dispossession and attendant consequences (Cotula et al. 2009). The convergence of global crises in finance, food, and fuel – "the triple-F crisis" – drove powerful transnational and national economic actors to re-evaluate the value of land and to invest in the production of fuel and food crops. The ongoing land grab involves a complex set of actors, including governments, foreign firms, multilateral institutions, and community-based leaders (Nhamo and Chekwoti 2014).

N. E. Attah (✉)
Department of History and Diplomatic Studies, Federal University of Kashere, Kashere, Nigeria

L. Cochrane and N. Andrews (eds.), *The Transnational Land Rush in Africa*, International Political Economy Series,
https://doi.org/10.1007/978-3-030-60789-0_5

The Land Matrix lists 15 million ha in Africa, 6.8 million ha in Asia, 14.5 million ha in Eastern Europe, and 9.2 million ha in Latin America. Sub-Saharan Africa accounts for about 1/3 of concluded deals and thus is the primary destination for land grabbing. Based on the 2019 Land Matrix database, 84 deals involving 1,097,003 hectares (ha) total were concluded in Nigeria. Nigeria, Africa's most populous country, ranks among the top 20 most targeted countries for large-scale land investments globally and among the top ten in Africa (Osabuohien 2014; GRAIN 2013). Studies estimate that Nigeria has between 79 to 84 million ha of arable land, in addition to an agriculture-friendly climate, coastal marine resources of over 960 km of shorelines, and 120,000 square kilometres of rivers and lakes. These factors provide favourable conditions for the cultivation of a wide range of food crops (Akanbi 2011; Nwajiuba 2001).

Despite its vast land resources and enormous agricultural potential, Nigeria ranks 93rd out of 117 in the Global Hunger Index (GHI 2019). The Nigerian government is committed to reviving its agriculture sector through large-scale investments in land, as part of its strategy of economic growth and development. The need for alternatives to fossil fuels also drove investments in agriculture for the production of biofuel. Together, these factors drove major investments in Nigeria's agricultural land beginning in the 2000s. The steadfast support of the Nigerian state to foreign investors made the country a prime destination for land deals.

The involvement of the Nigerian state in large-scale land deals is reflected in its attraction of more than US$30 billion of Foreign Direct Investment (FDI) in the agricultural sector, which it views as indispensable to the development of rural areas (Yusuff and Ajiboye 2015). Proponents of large-scale agricultural projects, the state, and multilateral institutions included, claim that food security in host communities can be increased through such investments (Yusuff and Ajiboye 2015). Agencies like the World Bank embarked on a wholesale transformation of rural areas through investments in agricultural projects, dams, and irrigation systems (GRAIN 2010). This strategic focus on commercial farming is mirrored in Nigeria's national policy on agriculture. Nigeria imports US$1,417.5 million worth of livestock, US$400 million of dairy products, US$987 million of fisheries, US$267 million of rice, US$640 million of sugar cane, US$102 million of wheat, and US$50 million of tomatoes on an annual basis (Mustapha 2011). The government's priority is to attract FDI in large-scale agricultural land deals, as exemplified by the establishment of Shonga Farms owned by white Zimbabwean farmers in Kwara State, among other foreign farms in Nigeria.

The perception that land is abundant in Africa should be treated cautiously. In Nigeria, there are many cases where land is already under cultivation by rural smallholders, however, their rights are not recognized or excluded from formal ownership regimes. Land ownership can sometimes be complex and contentious, especially in rural communities where there are no means of title registration under the existing Land Use Act. Reports suggest that, in some cases, the government failed to undertake formal consultations with the communities whose lands had been acquired (Abdullahi 2008). The rights of individuals and groups, especially pertaining to communal livelihoods, are often overlooked. Land deals are commonly carried out without the involvement of the communities in Nigeria. Certain leaders are sometimes consulted on land acquisitions and may agree to land deals in exchange for promises of job opportunities, improved facilities, and compensation (Amanor 2012).

There are gaps between the stated policy commitments, company promises, and the actual benefits for communities in the context of large-scale land acquisitions. In other words, there are no clearly observable developmental gains at the local level. In sub-Saharan Africa, the land grabbing processes driven by transnational elites and African states disposses "powerless" people of their land (Ariyo and Mortimore 2015; Liversage 2010; Gouverneur 2009). This chapter critically examines the trajectories of large-scale agricultural deals in Nigeria against the background of the global land grab, using three case studies: Shonga Farms, Wilmar International, and Dominion Farms. The Nigerian state was instrumental to the development and conclusion of these land deals. The chapter evaluates the impacts of these projects on the land rights and livelihoods of rural people. Furthermore, it identifies the political and economic forces responsible for reconfiguring land use patterns and ownership rights in Nigeria, in a continuing processes of primitive accumulation through large-scale investments in land.

Overview and Trends in Large-Scale Land Deals

The concept of "land grabbing" is distinct from the processes of encroachment in Nigeria's urban areas, known as "*omo'nile*". Omo'nile involves the multiple sales of a single piece of land, a phenomenon which has led to conflict in South West Nigeria. Similarly, land grabbing is not be misconstrued with local conflicts over land in communities such as the Tiv-Jukun, Aguleri-Umuleri, and Ife-Modakeke, nor the perennial Fulani herdsmen crisis concerning grazing land in the Middle Belt of Nigeria. Land grabbing is better understood as transnational process involving large-scale land acquisitions by national, international, and multi-national corporate actors for the production of export crops, agrofuels, minerals, and oil and gas (Cochrane 2016).

"Land grab" is a catch-all phrase employed by the media and critical scholars to describe the recent growth in large-scale (trans)national land acquisitions. Land appropriation is not a new phenomenon, however, as the history of colonialism demonstrates. The contemporary land grab is distinguishable from previous ones in its dimensions and purpose, namely the global and growing need for food, fuel, and financing. The lack of transparency and public consultation in state-driven land deals is familiar, however, as countries seek to transition from predominantly agricultural economies to industrial, modernized ones. In this process, land use patterns switch from subsistence into other forms of utilization such as urban and infrastructure development.

There are three distinctive periods in the history of land grabbing in Africa: pre-colonial, colonial, and contemporary. This chapter concerns the contemporary epoch, focusing particularly on the risks associated with modern land grabs such as the loss of land, water, and other natural resources; marginalization and inequality; environmental degradation and reduced ecosystem services; food insecurity; and political instability (Nhamo and Chekwoti 2014). The impacts of large-scale agricultural projects lead to profound and long-standing changes in rural societies and local livelihoods. In Nigeria, powerful foreign governments and firms seek to produce commodity crops, primarily for export. The World Bank and the multi-national companies it supports often claim that they are investing in land for the purpose of sustainable development. However, the levels of rural development in host communities have not improved with the growth in large-scale land investments. In fact, empirical evidence suggests that agro-industrial investments are exacerbating food crises, environmental degradation, and rights violations in affected communities.

The land transfers involved in processes of industrialization are often accompanied by coercion and authoritarian actions. Local residents are displaced from their land for the sake of "development" and their rights usurped. Land is consequently declared as state-owned and there compensation is either minimal or non-existent. Samir Amin (2011) characterizes this phenomenon as "primitive accumulation by dispossession" and Harvey (2003) as "possession by dispossession". The growth of corporate investments in land concentrates ownership of the means of production in the hands of a few, engendering greater inequality. Ironically, economic "development" multiplies the number of near- and absolute-landless peasants who become excluded from agricultural activity and dependent upon wage labour. In Nigeria, there is a long history of land grabbing in the name of development. The state has forced peasant farmers from their land and reallocated it to multi-national corporations, as exemplified by the Bakolori Dam project (Yahaya 2002). The Land Use Act of 1978 vests the administration (but not the ownership) of land to state governments, setting the stage for the large-scale take-over of communal lands for the economic growth and "development" of Nigeria.

Contemporary debates on the current wave of large-scale agricultural land acquisitions revolve around the concept of "land grabbing". Some argue that large-scale land acquisitions are concentrated in the Global South, that is, in Africa, Central America, and South and East Asia (Cotula et al. 2009; Wilkinson et al. 2012). However, there is evidence that land grabbing extends to the former Union of Soviet Socialist Republic (USSR), Eastern Europe, the Middle East, Melanesia, Australia, and New Zealand (Visser and Spoor 2011; Anseeuw et al. 2012). Amanor (2012) observes that the debate on the acquisition of land "extends beyond the phenomenon of global land grabbing to the consolidation of power over the trans-regional value chain in particular and a component of the global 'mission' to control food and bio-fuel supply chains". Amanor's argument highlights the power and hegemonic role of foreign capital in land grabbing, as exemplified by the Kwara State government's unconditional support for the white Zimbabwean farmers under the administration of Bukola Saraki. Harvey (2003) similarly pointed out that transnational land acquisitions are rooted in the global capitalist development framework and attempts to address the triple "F" crisis – that is, the need for food, fuel, and finance (Hall 2011; White et al. 2012). Land grabbing is the combined outcome of globalisation, foreign direct investment, and the liberalisation of "land markets" (Zoomers 2010).

Crucial to land grabbing is the element of "control", which allows investors to reap the financial benefits of resource extraction and development (Peluso and Lund 2011; Borras, Franco et al. 2012). Importantly, the seizure of large tracts of viable agricultural land is often accompanied by the seizure of water (re)sources. In some cases, investors seek to acquire elements of the natural environment like forests and wildlife in order to "save it"—what is known as green grabbing (Ganho and Woodhouse 2011; Fairhead et al. 2012; Kay and Franco 2012). Conceptualizing the full scope of land grabbing permits a comprehensive and inclusive understanding of the costs and benefits involved in land deals. There is a propensity to characterize all transnational land acquisitions as land grabbing without nuance and appreciation for their particular contexts. The most common definition of land grabbing, although contested, is the large-scale acquisition of farmland for agricultural production by foreign investors (GRAIN 2008; Cotula et al. 2009; Mitta et al. 2009). Borras and Franco (2010) view commercial land transactions involving both domestic and transnational deals as land grabbing, irrespective of their size and intended markets. In contrast, Graham et al. (2011) view land grabbing as the appropriation of land for commercial agricultural production that is incongruous with the needs of local or small-scale landholders.

Studies by the Food and Agriculture Organisation (FAO) on land grabs in Latin America and the Caribbean stipulate three conditions for a deal to be qualified as a "grab": the project must be more than 1000 ha of land, involve the direct participation of a foreign government and/or company, Oxfam Internationaland possess a negative impact on the food security of the host community and/or country (Borras, Kay et al. 2012). This definition of land grabbing centres crises in food and farmland. The size of the land acquired and project scale are also distinct features of contemporary transnational acquisitions, though this framing is contested since it excludes those deals less than 1000 ha which negatively impact rural livelihoods (Oxfam International 2011; Anseeuw et al. 2012). Borras, Franco et al. (2012) conceptualise land grabbing as deals involving two broadly interlinked, but distinct, dimensions, namely the size of the land transaction and the amount of capital required.

The Tirana Declaration, agreed to by governments, international organizations, and civil society groups following a major conference on land rights organised by the International Land Coalition in May 2011 defines land grabs as involving one or more of the following:

> Violation of human rights, particularly the equal rights of women;
> Not based on free, prior and informed consent of the affected land-users;
> Not based on a thorough assessment, or are in disregard of social, economic and environmental impacts, including the way they are gendered;

> Not based on transparent contracts that specify clear and binding commitments about activities, employment and benefits sharing, and;
> Not based on effective democratic planning, independent oversight and meaningful participation. (ILC 2011)

A land grab is thus uniquely characterized by the neglect or violation of recognized human rights standards. The Land Matrix further describes land acquisitions as involving a transfer of rights to use, control, or own land not less than 200 ha through sale, lease, or concession. The Land Matrix implies land "grabbing" to be the conversion of land from smallholder production or important ecosystem service provision to commercial use.

The International Law Commission (ILC) identifies the wave of large-scale land acquisitions as a phenomenon driven by both foreign and national governments and multi-national firms. The ILC points out that popular conceptions of "land grabbing" are misleading in that they imply the illegitimate or illegal acquisition of land by investors when it is the domestic policies that (1) permit foreign investments projects, and (2) fail to recognize customary use rights. In contrast to the position of ILC, this chapter considers land grabbing to occur so long as the interests of the local owners/users are disrespected. Whereas some view land grabbing as a major threat to the lives and livelihoods of the rural people, particularly agrarian peasants, others see it as an economic opportunity for impoverished communities despite the possibility of negative economic, environmental, and social consequences. Borras and Franco (2010), for one, regard the most important issue in land grabbing as the rights of the dispossessed in relation to the issues of consent and appropriate compensation.

To expand on the issue of scale and the extent of dispossession in the debate about large-scale land investments, one must examine the role of international processes and actors. Ironically, land deals are posited as the universal solution to crisis-ridden global financial markets where increased agricultural production for food and agrofuels is needed to address the energy problems of rich countries. The accumulation of international capital, however, comes at a cost: African peoples are often dispossessed of their land, livelihoods, and resources. The new class relations produced agricultural modernization are not without tension or inequality. The World Bank narrowly views the role of international capital in Africa from the perspective of the potential benefits that may accrue from sales, leases, and new cropping patterns. However, foreign investment in African farmlands creates false expectations and leads to unfulfilled promises as the enclosure of common rural resources dispossesses peasants from their farmlands and livelihoods. The capitalist imperatives of large-scale agricultural investments coerce the dispossessed to become wage labourers or proletarians. The case of the white Zimbabwean-owned Shonga Farms, examined later in this chapter, illustrates the processes by which peasants are forced to became agricultural workers for foreign investors.

While private companies are behind most land deals, with the support and approval of the national governments, lands are also acquired by state-owned companies. Investments take a number of forms, depending on the local situation and the relevant legal regime. Although some lands are purchased, they are leased more often than not – in some cases for up to 99 years. In Nigeria, land laws bestow state governments as custodians of land on behalf of communities. Traditional and local institutions, however, are seldom consulted or considered in large-scale land deals in Nigeria, thereby generating conflict (Amanor 2012). The federal and state governments spearhead acquisitions of land on behalf of foreign capital while promising job creation and economic development to rural populations.

The 1978 Land Use Act and Large-Scale Land Acquisition

The Land Use Decree (No. 6) of 1978, which officially became an Act in the 1979 Constitution, marked a watershed in the history of land use in Nigeria (Ako 2009). One of the goals of the Land Use Act (hereinafter "the Act") is to ensure that land is available for the sustenance of all Nigerians and their families. As stated in the Act's preamble: "it is in the public interest that all the rights of all Nigerians to use and enjoy land in Nigeria and the natural fruits thereof in sufficient quantity to enable them to provide for the sustenance of themselves and their families should be assured, protected and preserved". The right of all Nigerians to access to land, especially for agricultural purposes, must be protected if the Act's stated goal is to be achieved (Oshio 1986). Cases of land grabbing in Nigeria, however, contradict the tenets and principles of the Act on account of the displacement experienced by peasants from their farmlands.

The Act, in its (mis)application/(mis)interpretation, serves to undermine rural people's rights to land. Paradoxically, the Act shifted the balance of rights against autochthonous owners by terminating usufructuary rights to ancestral lands and vesting them in the state, which can exercise its right of eminent domain (Attah 2013a; Akpan 2005). There is an erroneous and commonly held perception in Nigeria that the government "owns" the land on account of these post-colonial land reforms; however, the provisions of the Land Use Act are grossly misunderstood and often misapplied (Odoemene 2015). Land is only *vested* in the state, which holds it in trust for the people, a position supported by Section 14(2)(a) of Chapter 2 of the Constitution. The Act stipulates that in the event of the state's acquisition of community farmlands, alternative farmlands and/or appropriate compensation must be given to the affected populations. Government officials often misapply the provisions of the Land Use Act and instead collude with foreign capital to dispossess communities of their lands (Odoemene 2015). Some government officials have taken advantage of the Act to acquire lands for their own forms of primitive accumulation (Nwaka 2005). Such corrupt practices related to land governance are common in rural communities where local populations possess limited capacity to resist due to their material poverty and lack of formal rights.

Section 29 of the Act addresses compensation for land compulsorily acquired by the government for public purposes. Compensation is calculated using the estimated market value of the land at the time of its acquisition. When acquired land is developed with residential buildings, the government may provide monetary compensation or offer a resettlement plan by providing reasonable alternative accommodation where circumstances permit. Where the land acquired is undeveloped, available compensations is limited and assessed based on the unexhausted improvements on the land. In all cases, an officer employed by the state government performs the assessment of compensation for land, which often leads to the under-evaluations. When land is compulsory acquired for public purposes, the state Governor is expected to provide compensations to the owners. In some cases, however, the Governor either fails to pay the required compensation or provides an inadequate amount.

Another provision of the Act germane to this discourse is Section 28, which confers state governors the powers to revoke rights of occupancy where such land is required by government for public purposes. To guard against the use and abuse of this power by the Governor, the Act details strict procedures that must be followed by the Governor, otherwise the revocation will be declared null and void:

> The notice of the state government's intention to compulsorily acquire the land mentioned therein must be published to the whole world with specific deadline for the raising of objections by interested parties. The revocation of the right of occupancy shall be made under the hand of a public officer duly authorized in that behalf, by the Governor and the notice thereof shall be given to the holder.

There is a lack of compliance with the above stated guidelines, as the cases discussed in this chapter illustrate. In each land grab surveyed, there was no public notice of the government's intention to compulsorily acquire land, that is, to exercise the rights of eminent domain. Such violations can be explained in part by the misapplication/misinterpretation of the post-colonial land law, wherein public officials view land as belonging to the state. The Nigerian courts developed two tests to determine the validity of the acquisition of land for "public purposes", as defined in Section 28(3) of the Act: Does the reason advanced for the revocation fall within the statutorily defined public purpose? Has the government followed the required procedures for the revocation of rights of occupancy? The person whose right of occupancy is to be revoked has the right to be informed by the government. The notice of revocation must clearly state that the land is intended for public purposes only.

In sum, the provisions of the Land Use Act are often disregarded by public officials in their management of large-scale land deals. In the case of the Shonga land deal discussed later in this chapter, the government initially claimed the acquisition was for public purposes but ended transferring leasehold rights to private actors, specifically white Zimbabwean farmers. The government failed to comply with the conditions set out in Section 28(3) of the Act in the process of the Shonga land acquisition. On the issue of what constitutes public purposes, the courts have consistently held that it does not include the revocation of rights of occupancy of an individual/company and the re-allocating of these same rights to another individual/company, as this would amount to "robbing Peter to pay Paul". The actions of Nigerian government officials in large-scale land deals are usually fraught with illegality and corruption, as demonstrated by the stories of Shonga Farms, Wilmar International, and Dominion Farms (Fig. 5.1).

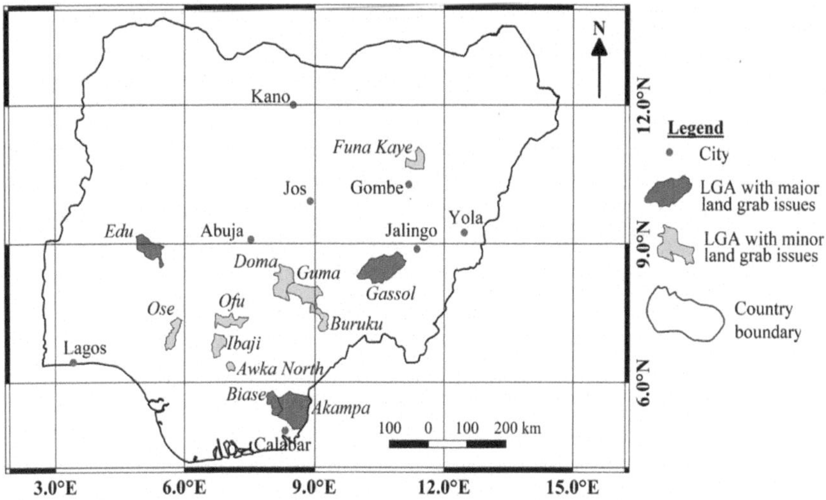

Fig. 5.1 Map showing Land Grabbing in Nigeria

White Zimbabwean Commercial Farmers and Large-Scale Land Acquisition

In an effort to modernize agriculture in Kwara State, former Governor Bukola Saraki invited displaced white farmers to invest in commercial agriculture under the 2002 Zimbabwe fast-track land reform programme (Mkodzongi and Lawrence 2019). A total of 13,000 ha of farmlands in the Shonga District were initially appropriated from local farmers for the white Zimbabwean commercial farmers by the Kwara State in 2005. The land was acquired on the basis of a renewable 25-year lease, at no cost to the white Zimbabwean farmers. An additional 4656 ha was appropriated for collateral uses arising from the unforeseen consequences of large-scale commercial farming in the area. Shonga is located at about 110 kilometres (68 miles) north of Ilorin, the Kwara State capital. The area lies in the Guinea Savannah along the bank of the River Niger. The mean annual rainfall is about 1,500 mm and the rainy season runs between the months of March and October (Ariyo and Mortimore 2015). The vast arable land, favourable climate, and presence of the River Niger are pull factors for large-scale commercial farming. The land acquisition for the Zimbabwean farmers led to the eviction of some 400 families and 1289 local farmers in 28 communities from their ancestral lands (Hofstter 2004; Mustapha 2010). The appropriation of such a large expanse of land restricted the area available for rotational bush fallowing and pastoral nomads to graze their livestock.

The state government approved some financial compensation to the displaced, however, sums were either inadequate or non-existent. Ariyo and Mortimore (2015) found that a total of US$58,000 was paid to 1990 out of the 2771 displaced in the Shonga District, representing about US$30 per person. In addition, about 781 people were not paid at all on the basis that their claims were questionable, as opined by officials in the State Ministry of Agriculture and Natural Resources. A monetized agricultural incentive package amounting to US$73 per ha for land preparation was paid to the affected people (Ariyo and Mortimore 2015). The totality of actual compensation does not adequately cover the losses arising from the land dispossession. Crop trees such as shea butter and locust beans were destroyed, affecting the livelihoods of local women who depended upon these resources for their incomes. Although the Kwara State government claimed that the lands allocated to the white Zimbabwean farmers were not under cultivation at the time of the acquisition, the resultant displacement and dispossession proved otherwise and led to violent conflict (Mustapha 2011; Odoemene 2012).

The federal and state governments cast the Zimbabwean farmers as foreign investors with enormous capital, capable of successfully financing an agrarian revolution (Mustapha 2011). The initial Memorandum of Understanding (MoU) between the government and the Zimbabwean farmers stipulated that the latter would operate as an independent company. However, the farmers did not come with any capital to invest in the farms. Instead, the Kwara State government provided the Zimbabwean farmers with interest-free loans in the region of US$3 million in 2005 to enable start-up operations (Ariyo and Mortimore 2015). In addition, the Zimbabwean farmers formed a consortium known as the "New Nigerian Farms" in partnership with the state government and used this platform to access a loan of US$5 million from the federally owned Nigeria Agricultural, Cooperative and Rural Development Bank (NACRDB) in 2006 (Odoemene 2012; Ariyo and Mortimore 2015; Mustapha 2011). The loan was backed by an Irrevocable Standing Payment Order (ISPO) from the Federal Ministry of Finance and authorized deductions from the Kwara state government's monthly statutory financial allocation in the event of default. Only 19% of the loan was repaid (Mustapha 2011), with both the white farmers and the state government defaulting on their loan obligations to the NACRDB. The Central Bank and the Federal Ministry of Finance thereby commenced deductions from the Kwara State.

Beside the loan from the NACRDB, the Kwara state government, through a consortium of five commercial banks, further guaranteed an investment of US$6.6 million as equity in the farming enterprises and another credit advance of US$6.6 million to the white farmers (Ariyo and Mortimore 2015). The "spectacular support" of the Kwara state government to white Zimbabwean farmers and the failed agricultural revolution led to accusations of money laundering by then-Governor Bukola Saraki (Mustapha 2011). The near collapse of Shonga Farms is reflected in the project's reduction from thirteen to three farms, specifically for poultry, cattle, and soya bean farms, each with limited acreage (Attah 2016).

In addition the massive financial support provided to white commercial farmers, support which indigenous farmers in Nigeria did not receive, the state government provided the Zimbabwean nationals with a host of infrastructural facilities, including a network of roads, housing estates, boreholes for water supply, electricity, and irrigation facilities. Mustapha (2011) summarizes the government's commitment to Shonga Farms as such:

> The government invested over N400 million (US$2.6 million) on roads, housing, and electricity; each farmer received a bungalow of up to 2500 square feet, complete with a generator, storage sheds, and fencing. N870 million (US$5.8 million) was spent on irrigation by the federal government while N1 billion (US$6.6 million) was provided for electrification.

Wilmar International and Land Grab

Wilmar International is a Singaporean firm and one of the world's largest oil palm plantation owners, traders, and processing companies. Wilmar international controls about 45% of the global oil palm trade (ALIMENTERRE 2014; Colchester 2011). The firm is valued at $US17.9 billion and holds a "land bank" of over 600,000 ha worldwide through its subsidiaries (Ojo et al. 2019). The company is expanding its frontiers in Africa, particularly in the Cross River State of Nigeria, amidst the current global wave of land grabbing (Odoemene 2015). Wilmar

International is mainly financed by investors from Europe and the United States through bank loans and bond issuances.

There is a joint venture between PZ Cussons and Wilmar for agrofuel production in Nigeria. The joint venture, PZ-Wilmar Ltd, has built a state-of-the-art oil palm refinery for the processing of agrofuels in Lagos State. In 2014, PZ-Wilmar announced an aggressive expansion of its oil palm production through a planned 240,000 ha of plantations within five to six years; the expansion would employ over 250,000 individuals within the same period. Although these plans are in harmony with the Nigerian government's active promotion of private sector investment in the agricultural sector and its commitment to the G8 New Alliance for Food Security and Nutrition, the consequences of these plans are not always considered or adequately mitigated.

Wilmar's land deals in Cross River State fall into two categories, namely a northern and western triad involving the Biase, Ibiae, and Calaro plantations, and a southern and eastern flank consisting of the Obasanjo plantation in Ekong-Anaku. The Biase, Ibiae, and Calaro plantations cover about 19,173 ha and were earmarked for oil palm development in 1963 by the defunct Eastern Nigerian Development Corporation (ENDC), when communities entered into a 99-year lease agreement with the government (Friends of the Earth/Environmental Rights Action 2015). However, the ENDC abandoned its plans to establish an oil palm plantation, making it possible for the local farmers to return to the land and crop cultivation given the usurpation.

In 2011, Wilmar bought the Biase, Ibiae and Calaro plantation lands from the Cross River State government, even though about one-third of the land was already under use by small-hold farmers who depended on it for their livelihoods and, therefore, assumed the rights over the land in perpetuity. The controversy resulting from Wilmar's acquisition of land brought to light the ambiguity of land rights in Nigeria. In Nigeria, it is individuals and families, not communities, who can claim legal ownership of land title as per the Land Use Act (Friends of the Earth/Environmental Rights Action 2015). Most rural communities are characterized by fragmented social dynamics and as such no agreement signed with a community representative is considered binding on the entire population.

The Cross River State government owned the Investment Promotions Bureau and administered it via the state's Privatization Council, which sought the consent of the Councils of Chiefs and Elders on behalf

Wilmar. The chiefs were apprehensive of the proposal, however, the government assured them that Wilmar would bring development to the communities through the construction of schools, hospitals, clean water, and electricity, and other infrastructure. However, it was reported that Wilmar began developing the lands before the process of consultation was concluded, a situation which aggravated communities (Friends of the Earth/Environmental Rights Action 2015). The lack of consent from members of the affected communities and the attendant loss of farmlands, water sources, and non-timber forest products collections resulted in demands for the return of the land (Schonevelde 2013).

The case of Ekong-Anaku, the southern axis land acquisition by Wilmar, was equally controversial. The land was originally ceded to the Cross River State government by the indigenes in 1992 under an agreement that allowed for the conservation of 10,000 ha of traditional forestlands – Ekinta forest – into a reserve (Odoemene 2015). The agreement was based on the promise of agroforestry programmes, credit facilities for small farmers, and development for the people (Odoemene 2015). Unfortunately, but unsurprisingly, the promises were not redeemed in the manner characteristic of governments in Nigeria. By 2002, the then-Governor of Cross River State, Donald Duke, gifted the same 10,0000 ha of land to then-President Olusegun Obasanjo when he made an official visit to the state (Friends of the Earth/Environmental Rights Action 2015; Odoemene 2015). The deception of state officials and lack of regard for local people represented a gross abuse of office and caused the community to protest this unlawful act.

Then-Governor of Cross River State Donald Duke later transferred – at no cost – the controversial Ekong-Anaku forestland to the Obasanjo Farms Company, a private company owned by former President Olusegun Obasanjo, for the establishment of a large-scale oil palm plantation. Obasanjo eventually invited Wilmar International in 2012 to buy the land for an undisclosed amount of money, in the range of millions of dollars (Friends of the Earth/Environmental Rights Action 2015). These types of fraudulent land acquisition are common in Nigeria and typical of land grabbing processes in Africa. The people of Ekong-Anaku, upon realising the irregular manner in which their land was sold to Wilmar by Obasanjo, protested violently and received international attention for their resistance.

Despite this popular resistance, Wilmar went ahead with the oil palm plantations on the premise that it had acquired the land legitimately from the relevant authorities (Friends of the Earth/Environmental Rights Action 2015). Evidence shows, however, that Wilmar acquired the land without proper consultation. According to Orok (cited in Odoemene 2015), "[t]he land was never Obasanjo's to sell, if you buy something stolen, then you cannot say it is yours". The manner by which Wilmar acquired the land reproduces the corrupt legacy of the state and political elite in Nigeria. The irregularities involved in the Wilmar land deal led to litigation and struggles by the indigenous owners/users to repossess the land. The Rainforest Resources Development Centre (RRDC) also brought a case to the Roundtable on Sustainable Palm Oil (RSPO) in November 2012 (Odoemene 2015).

Dominion Farms and Large-Scale Land Acquisition

Dominion Farms is an Oklahoma-based agribusiness in the United States that acquired 30,000 ha of land in Gassol in Taraba State for rice production in 2012. The firm invested an initial US$40 million for rice production, monies not provided by the state like in the case of the white Zimbabwe commercial farmers in Kwara State. The land deal was a tripartite arrangement involving the federal government, the Taraba State government, and Dominion Farms (Odoemene 2015). The fertile land is located at the edge of the Rivers Benue and Taraba, which was originally under cultivation and grazing by peasant farmers and herders who possess autochthonous rights to the land.

The State government transferred the land to Dominion Farms without the free, prior, and informed consent of the indigenous cultivators and the traditional authorities of the area. Further, no compensation was paid despite initial promises and after protest by the rightful landowners. Furthermore, young men who were recruited to work on the Dominion Farms were not paid promised allowances after attending training in Kenya. Dominion Farms then refused to employ them after their return, as the company struggled to initiate its project.

The failure of the company's project denies the host community the anticipated economic and agricultural benefits promised to them. The expectation of such benefits hinged on the community's previous experience with the defunct Upper Benue River Basin Development Authority (UBRBDA) land deal. Under the supervision of the UBRBDA, peasant farmers were allocated pieces of land, which they managed based on modern farming methods. Dominion Farms was expected to be provide an improvement on the existing system, however, the project was ultimately abandoned due to disagreement among the relevant stakeholders and the violent resistance of some community members.

Other Large-Scale Land Deals and Dispossessions

Another notable land deal involved Ollam International, which invested US$49.2 million into its first rice farming and milling facility in the Middle Belt zone of Nigeria. The firm acquired 6000 ha of farmland in Rukubi of the Doma Local Government Area of the Nasarawa State, one of Nigeria's main rice growing areas. Aside from Ollam International, numerous hectares of land have been appropriated from vulnerable rural people for agrofuel production across the country. Some land under food crop production has also been converted for the production of jatropha through the provision of government incentives such as hybrid seeds and guaranteed markets. Recognizing the opportunity of agrofuel production, the Nigerian state, through the Nigeria National Petroleum Corporation (NNPC), is attracting both foreign and domestic investment in large-scale land deals for the production of agrofuel feedstock. Such programmes can involve negative consequences for the livelihoods of original landowners/users.

In some cases, land for agrofuel projects is secured through local and state authorities and detailed feasibility studies involving both international experts and public institutions. For example, Germany's Renewable Energy and Energy Efficiency Partnership supported feasibility studies for lands targeted for agrofuel production with a grant of €70 000 in 2007 (NNPC 2007). The NNPC acquired land for sugar cane plantations in Kupto of the Funa Kaye Local Government Area (Gombe State), in Buruku and Agasha of the Guma Local Government Area (Benue state), and in Kwali (the Federal Capital Territory); production, however, has yet to start. Cultivations are planned for areas greater than 15,000–20,000 ha and are expected to produce 1.8 million tons of sugar cane to yield 75 million litres of ethanol per year (NNPC n.d.). In the case of Kupto, many rice and maize farmers were forced from their land without due compensation, a situation involving once again the abuse of eminent domain (Abdullahi 2008). Lands have not been returned to their original owners/users, despite the fact that production has not yet started almost a decade after these acquisitions.

The federal government and its corporate partners also acquired 15,000 ha of land for integrated cassava plantations and ethanol production in the Ebenebe and Ugbenu communities of the Awka North Local Government Area in Anambra State, at a cost of over $300 million for the production of about 200,000 litres of ethanol fuel annually (Odogwu 2012). The land was acquired from the two communities on promises of job creation and development. Following the general pattern of land grabbing in Nigeria, the dispossessed were neither compensated for the land nor resettled. In another case, the Ondo State government, in conjunction with the NNPC, signed an agreement with an agribusiness to establish a cassava ethanol project on a 15,000 ha of land, which was originally a forest reserve in Okeluse of the Ose Local Government Area.

In Kogi State, under the administration of former Governor Ibrahim Idris, a Memorandum of Understanding (MoU) was signed with CSECC International of China for the establishment of an agrofuel refinery on 450 ha of land in Itobe (Maritz 2008). Similarly, 31,000 ha of land was acquired in Odogwu, Kogi State for the construction of an ultra-modern sugar factory. The sugar factory, worth US$510 million, is a partnership deal between the Kogi State government and US-owned International Trans Oil Corporation and is expected to produce about 87million litres of ethanol annually (Aruwa 2011). The agreement did not provide compensation or a resettlement plan for the peasant farmers that were dispossessed of their land. The Kogi State government promised that the project would generate about 400 jobs, a promise yet to be fulfilled (Aruwa 2011). The expropriation of arable land from vulnerable farmers for the purpose of agrofuel production compounds issues of food insecurity, which are already exacerbated by the adverse effects of climate change and ongoing attacks of herders on farms/farmers.

Conclusion

The emergent commercial farming complex in Nigeria and the large-scale land acquisitions that accompany it offer the possibility of profitable investments for foreign capital, but leaves Nigerians more food secure and vulnerable to environmental crisis and conflicts. The state's support for agribusiness in Nigeria has attracted enthusiastic and ambitious investors. Resulting processes of dispossession, however, raise concerns about the impact of such land deals on the so-called development of rural Nigeria.

Large-scale agro-industrial projects have not produced concrete benefits for the local populations, but instead served to further the financial and economic interests of foreign and national investors and encouraged the primitive accumulation of their government partners. The case of the white Zimbabwean farmers in Shonga, Kwara State showcases this type of state-corporate collusion, where the state mortgaged its monthly financial allocations to the central government in order to provide bank loans to the white farmers (Attah 2016). Most of the peasant farmers affected by Shonga Farms became landless and, if paid compensation at all, received meagre restitution. Unable to invest in new farmlands, peasants were coerced by their economic disadvantage to become impoverished farm labourers.

The manner in which most of these land deals were conducted – without the consultation of the original owners and users – has provoked violent protests in some cases (Attah 2013b). The irregularities involved in Wilmar International's acquisition of land led to a formal complaint by the RRDC against the company at the RSPO in November 2012 (Odoemene 2015). Conflicts over land rights and access to land are predictable given the ongoing displacement and dispossession of peasants. Land grabbers are cognizant of the geopolitical and socioeconomic conditions of Nigeria, but instead leverage attendant issues to their advantage. The majority of rural people whose lands have been taken for corporate profit do not see the developmental benefits promised to them and are continually excluded from the policy- and decision-making processes involved in land deals. Notably, most of the forcibly acquired lands have not yet been put to productive use after almost a decade since acquisition, except in a few cases such as the white Zimbabwean farmers and Wilmar International. Impacted rural people not been adequately resettled or duly compensated, nor has land been returned to its original owners/users.

Acknowledgements I wish to acknowledge the permission granted by *The Public Sphere Journal* to republish part of my paper "White Zimbabwean Farmers and Land Grabbing in Shonga of Central Nigeria: Development or Dispossession?" exclusively in *The Transnational Land Rush in Africa: A Decade After the Spike*.

References

Abdullahi, Salihu. 2008. NNPC's Ethanol project and the fate of Gombe communities. *Daily Independent*, May 20. http://www.punchontheweb.com/Articl.aspx?theartic=Art200805151433562.

Akanbi, Festus. 2011, 6 November. Agriculture Policy Review Draws Applause. http://www.thisdaylive.com/articles/agriculture-policy-review-draws-applause/102137/, accessed 23 September 2017.

Ako, Rhuks T. 2009. Nigeria's land use act: An anti-thesis to environmental justice. *Journal of African Law* 53 (2): 290–321.

Akpan, Wilson. 2005. Putting oil first? Some ethnographic aspects of petroleum-related land use controversies in Nigeria. *African Sociological Review/Revue Africaine de Sociologie* 9 (2): 134–152.

ALIMENTERRE. 2014. Palm oil giant Wilmar Ranked the worst company in the world. Accessed September 13, 2014. http://www.alimenterre.org/en/breve/palm-oil-giant-wilmar-ranked-the-worst-company-in-the-world.

Amanor, Kojo Sebastian. 2012. "Global resource grabs, agribusiness concentration and the smallholder: Two West African case studies." *Journal of Peasant Studies* 39 (3–4): 731–749.

Amin, Samir. 2011. *Ending the crisis of capitalism or ending capitalism?* Translated byVictoria Bawtree. Cape Town: Pambazuka Press.

Anseeuw, Ward, Mathieu Boche, Thomas Breu, Markus Giger, Jann Lay, Peter Messerli, and Kerstin Nolte. 2012. Transnational land deals for agriculture in the global South analytical report based on the land matrix database. Bern/Montpellier/Hamburg: CDE/CIRAD/GIGA. Available at: http://www.landcoalition.org/sites/default/files/publication/1254/.

Ariyo, Joseph A., and Michael Mortimore. 2015. State, land & agricultural commercialisation in Kwara state, Nigeria. In *Africa's land rush: Rural livelihoods and Agrarian change*, edited by Ruth Hall, Ian Scoones, and Dzodzi Tsikata, 30–45. Woodbridge, Suffolk: James Currey.

Aruwa, Aduku. 2011. Kogi state governor Launches Bio-fuels Refinery in Itobe. *Graphic Newspaper*, Nigeria: 18.

Attah, Noah Echa. 2013a. Possession by dispossession: Interrogating the new wave of land Grabbing in Nigeria. *Journal of Land and Rural Studies* 1 (2): 213–228.

Attah, Noah Echa. 2013b. Land Grabbing in Nigeria and responses: Protest or acquiescence? *African Notes: Journal of the Institute of African Studies, University of Ibadan, Nigeria* 37 (1–2): 185–214.

Attah, Noah Echa. 2016. White Zimbabwe farmers and land grabbing in Shonga of Central Nigeria: Development or dispossession? *The Public Sphere LSE Africa Summit Edition 2016*: 37–60.

Borras, Saturnino M., and Jennifer C. Franco. 2010. Towards a broader view of the politics of global land grab: Rethinking land issues, reframing resistance. Working paper 1, The Hague: International Institute of Social Studies (ISS).

Borras, Saturnino M., Cristóbal Kay, Sergio Gómez, and John Wilkinson. 2012. Land grabbing and global capitalist accumulation: Key features in Latin America. *Canadian Journal of Development Studies/Revue canadienne d'études du développement* 33 (4): 402–416.

Borras, Saturnino M., Jennifer C. Franco, Sergio Gómez, Cristóbal Kay, and Max Spoor. 2012. Land Grabbing in Latin America and the Caribbean. *Journal of Peasant Studies* 39 (3–4): 845–872.

Cochrane, Logan. 2016. Land grabbing. In *Encyclopedia of food and agricultural ethics*, P.B. Thompson and D. Kaplan (Eds.), 2nd Edition, Springer Press. https://doi.org/10.1007/978-94-007.

Colchester, Marcus. 2011. *Palm oil and indigenous peoples in South East Asia*. Rome: ILC.

Cotula, Lorenzo, Nat Dyer, and Sonja J. Vermeulen. 2009. *Fuelling exclusion? The agro-fuels boom and poor people's access to land*. London: IIED/FAO.

Fairhead, James, Melissa Leach, and Ian Scoones. 2012. Green grabbing: A new appropriation of nature? *Journal of Peasant Studies* 39 (2): 237–261.

Friends of the Earth US/Environmental Rights Action, Nigeria. 2015. *Exploitation and empty promises: Wilmar's Nigerian land grab*. Washington DC: Friends of the Earth US.

Ganho, A.S., and P. Woodhouse. 2011. Is water the hidden agenda of agricultural land acquisition in Sub-Saharan Africa? Land Deal Politics Initiative (LDPI) in collaboration with the *Journal of Peasant Studies* and hosted by the Future Agricultures Consortium at the Institute of Development Studies, University of Sussex.

Global Hunger Index. 2019. Nigeria.

Gouverneur, Cédric. 2009. The Palm Oil Land Grab. *Le Monde diplomatique*, December 5.

Graham, Alison, Sylvain Aubry, and Rolf Künnemann. 2011. *The role of the EU in land grabbing in Africa—CSO Monitoring 2009–2010 "Advancing African Agriculture" (AAA): The impact of Europe's policies and practices on African agriculture and food security*. Global Land Grabbing. Paper presented at the International Conference on Global Land Grabbing.

GRAIN. 2008. *Seized. The 2008 land grab for food and financial security*. GRAIN briefing. www.grain.org.

GRAIN. 2010. *World Bank report on land grabbing: Beyond the smoke and mirrors*. http://www.grain.org/articles/?id=70.

GRAIN. 2013. Stolen land: Nigerian villagers want their land back from wilmar. *Grain, December 7*. http://www.grain.org/article/entries/4844-stolen-land-nigerian-villagers-wanttheir-land-back-from-wilmar.

Hall, Ruth. 2011. Land grabbing in Southern Africa: The many faces of the investor rush. *Review of African Political Economy* 38 (128): 193–214.

Harvey, David. 2003. *The new imperialism*. Oxford: Oxford University Press.

Hofstter, Stephan. 2004. Zimbabwean farmers get 200,000 land hectares in Kwara state. *This Day*, Lagos, May 5.

International Land Coalition (ILC). 2011. *Tirana declaration: Securing land access for the poor in times of intensified natural resources competition*. Rome: International Land Coalition available at www.landcoalition.org/about-us/aom2011/tirana-declaration.

Kay, Sylvia, and Jennifer Franco. 2012. *The global water grab: A primer*. http://www.tni.org/sites/www.tni.org/files/download/watergrabbingprimer-alt cover.

Liversage, Harold. 2010. *Land access for rural development and poverty alleviation: An IFAD perspective*. Presentation at the Global Donor Platform for Rural Development Meeting, Rome, 24 January. www.donorplatform.org/content/view/332/210.

Maritz, J. 2008. Can bio-fuels kick-start Nigeria's Agric-economy? *Nigeria Business Times*, March 17.

Mitta, Anuradha, and Daniel Shepard. 2009. *The great land grab: Rush for world's farmland threatens food security for the poor*. Oakland: The Oakland Institute.

Mkodzongi, Grasian, and Lawrence Peter. 2019. The fast-track land reform and Agrarian changes in Zimbabwe. *Review of African Political Economy* 46 (159): 1–13.

Mustapha, A. Rauf. 2010. Zimbabwean farmers and Nigerian agriculture. *West African Insight*. Centre for Democracy and Development, December. www.independentngonline.com.

Mustapha, Abdul Raufu. 2011. Zimbabwean farmers in Nigeria: Exceptional farmers or spectacular support? *African Affairs* 110 (441): 536–561.

Nhamo, Godwell, and Caiphas Chekwoti. 2014. *Land grabs in a green African economy: Implications for trade, investment and development policies*. Pretoria: Africa Institute of South Africa.

Nigerian National Petroleum Corporation (NNPC). 2007. Nigeria's NNPC launches four major bio-fuel projects. http://biopact.com/2007/01on12.

Nwajiuba, Chinedum. 2001. Nigeria's agriculture and food security challenges. Federal Ministry of Health, Mission Report on field visits to Sokoto, Kano, Borno and Gombe States; Abuja: Federal Republic of Nigeria/FEWS NET.

Nwaka, Geoffrey I. 2005, May. The Urban Informal Sector in Nigeria. *Global Urban Development Magazine* 1 (1).

Odoemene, Akachi. 2012. White Zimbabwe farmers in Nigeria: Issues in 'new Nigerian' land deals and the implication for food and human security. *African Identities* 10 (1): 63–76.

Odoemene, Akachi. 2015. Socio-political economy and dynamics of government-driven land grabbing in Nigeria since 2000. Working paper 2015/103, *Global Economic Governance*, University of Oxford.

Odogwu, Emeka. 2012. Federal government establishes $300 m Ethanol Project. *The Nation*, Nigeria, July 29.

Ojo, G.U., A. Uwagie-Ero, and N. Tokunbor. 2019. Bottom-up accountability initiatives to claim tenure rights in Sub-Saharan Africa: Securing community tenure rights to land in Betem, Akpet, Idoma and Akampa in Cross River State, Nigeria. International Development Research Centre (IDRC)-Canada. Available at: https://www.tni.org>files>bottom-upaccountabilityinitiatives.

Osabuohien, Evans S. 2014. Large-scale agricultural land investments and local institutions in Africa: The Nigerian case. *Land Use Policy* 39: 155–165.

Oshio, P.E. 1986. Agricultural policy and the Nigerian land use decree: The conflict. *Journal of African Law* 30 (20): 130–142.

Oxfam International. 2011. *Land and power: The growing scandal surrounding the new wave of Investments in Land*. Oxfam Briefing Paper 151. Oxford: Oxfam International.

Peluso, Nancy Lee, and Christian Lund. 2011. New frontiers of land control: Introduction. *Journal of Peasant Studies* 38 (4): 667–681.

Schonevelde, George Christoffel. 2013. The politics of the forest frontier: Negotiating between conservation, development, and indigenous rights in cross river state, Nigeria. *Land Use Policy* November.

Visser, Oane, and Max Spoor. 2011. Land Grabbing in the former Soviet Union. *Journal of Peasant Studies* 38 (2): 299–323.

White, Ben, Saturnino M. Borras Jr., Ruth Hall, Ian Scoones, and Wendy Wolford. 2012. The new enclosures: Critical perspectives on corporate land deals. *Journal of Peasant Studies* 39 (3–4): 619–647.

Wilkinson, John, Bastiaan Reydon, and Alberto Di Sabbato. 2012. Concentration and foreign ownership of land in Brazil in the context of global Land Grabbing. *Canadian Journal of Development Studies/Revue canadienne d'études du développement* 33 (4): 417–438.

Yahaya, Mohammed Kuta. 2002. Development and challenges of Bakolori irrigation project in sokoto state, Nigeria. *Nordic Journal of African Studies* 11 (3): 411–430.

Yusuff, Olabisi, and Ajiboye, Olarewaju. 2015. Foreign land acquisition: Food security and food chains—The Nigerian experience, available at: https://www.

researchgate.net/publication/281651436, https://doi.org/10.4018/978-1-4666-7405-9.ch008.

Zoomers, Annelies. 2010. Globalisation and the foreignisation of space: Seven processes driving the current global land grab. *Journal of Peasant Studies* 37 (2): 429–447.

PART II

Informality and 'New' Customary Land Tenure Landscapes

CHAPTER 6

Under the Disguise of Participation: Community Forestry as a New Form of Land Rush in Liberia

Ricarda Roesch

Introduction

Following the end of Liberia's civil war in 2003, a variety of actors, including donors, international organizations, the government, and civil society, launched a comprehensive peacekeeping and peacebuilding effort. The attraction of Foreign Direct Investment (FDI) was a core component of the liberal peacebuilding strategy (Paffenholz 2015, 861; Pugh 2005; Radelet 2007, 1; Waldorf 2018, 445). President Ellen Johnson Sirleaf became a strong ally in this respect, making "rapid, inclusive and sustainable economic growth" a core priority of the Liberian Poverty Reduction Strategy in the post-conflict period (Republic of Liberia 2008, 35). The World Bank and the International Monetary Fund viewed Liberia as a success story during Johnson Sirleaf's first term (International Monetary

R. Roesch (✉)
Friedrich-Alexander-University of Erlangen-Nuremberg, Erlangen, Germany
e-mail: ricarda.roesch@fau.de

L. Cochrane and N. Andrews (eds.), *The Transnational Land Rush in Africa*, International Political Economy Series,
https://doi.org/10.1007/978-3-030-60789-0_6

Fund 2010, 1; Paczynska 2016, 1). By 2014, the government granted approximately 45.8% of the Liberian landmass to investors (The Rights and Resources Group 2013, 1); of that, mining accounted for 56% of the identified area, timber products for 21%, and agricultural products for 19%.

In the meantime, the Liberian government revisited its agricultural concession policy on account of (1) the conflicts between companies and communities in the context of governmental-sponsored oil palm and rubber concessions, (2) the pending Land Rights Act, which was finally passed in 2018 and recognizes customary land ownership, and (3) the United Nations Collaborative Program on Reducing Emissions from Deforestation and Forest Degradation (REDD +). The Liberian government committed to granting no more agricultural concessions, although existing concessions remained in place. The Norwegian government even provided Libera with a US$100 million grant on the condition that the state halt agricultural concessions (Atyi 2018, 52).

Consequently, the logging sector gained in importance, with new forest governance approaches emerging. Most notably, the government passed the Community Rights Law with Respect to Forest Lands (CRL) in 2009, which grants communities ownership over forest resources and the right to manage their customary forest land. Despite the introduction of community forestry, a growing area of land is under commercial logging licenses (Halton 2013, 13). Forestry could therefore become one of Liberia's most prominent economic sectors.

This chapter (1) provides a brief overview of the post-war legal reforms in Liberia, (2) illuminates the legal framework for community forestry, and (3) describes the implementation of community forestry in two community forests: Beyan Poye and Sehzueplay. It draws from ethnographic data obtained in Liberia to critically explore the land tenure dimension of community-based forest governance.

Methodology

I collected data in different parts of Liberia between October 2017 and January 2018 and February to March 2018. I was hosted by the Kofi Annan Institute for Conflict Transformations during my first research visit. During the second visit, I collaborated with the United States (US)-based economic development organization Agricultural Cooperative Development International–Volunteers in Overseas Cooperative Assistance (ACDI-VOCA). In Liberia, ACDI-VOCA is implementing a USAID-funded community forest project known as "Forest Incomes for Environmental Sustainability." I visited two authorized community forests that entered into commercial use contracts with companies. It is likely that the majority of Liberian community forests will enter into such agreements (Senior Forestry Expert 2018, para 151; Global Witness 2018, 41).

The actors involved in the implementation of community forestry were the variable distinguishing the two cases: one community forest, Sehzueplay, receives ongoing financial and technical support from successive USAID-funded projects. Sehzueplay is classified as neither the most successful, nor the most unsuccessful of the four USAID-supported community forests in Southern Nimba in terms of sustainable forest governance, making it a typical case (Liberia Strategic Analysis 2018, 3). The other community forest, Beyan Poye, has not seen any ongoing external support, with only the Liberian Forestry Development Authority (FDA) facilitating its registration process. I conducted semi-structured interviews with members of the forest management bodies, local politicians, and other community leaders to understand how the community forest registration process was implemented in practice.[1] Additionally, I tried to visit as many villages—or towns as they are generally called in Liberia—as possible within the two community forests.[2] I conducted two focus group discussions within the different towns.[3] Research assistants facilitated these discussions.

My research faced several limitations. Firstly, a large number of community forests are still undergoing the authorization process. It is possible that new patterns will emerge in these community forests and so the cases examined herein might not be representative. Secondly, my positionality led to certain difficulties. In the community forest that did not receive USAID support, I depended on the goodwill of the forest management body whose members walked me to the different towns and

[1] 45 interviews with elders, women leaders, youth leaders, local USAID-funded project staff, members of the Community Assembly, Community Forest Management Body and Executive Committee.

[2] In the first community forest, I walked to 6 different villages in a radius of 3 hours walking distance. In the second one, I managed to cover all villages (8 plus 4 smaller settlements).

[3] 15 general focus groups with 6–10 participants and 12 women's focus groups (6–8 participants).

acted as interpreters. While this helped to render some of the tensions between ordinary community members and the managers of the community forest visible, it also impaired the willingness of people to share their concerns. Moreover, the FDA instructed my hosts to make sure that I was safe. They took this very literally and their undoubtedly good intentions strongly interfered with my free choice of interview partners. After a few days, the logging company convinced the management body to not support me in my study, which brought my field research to an end. In the second community forest, I was supported by a field facilitator of the USAID-funded project. This, too, impacted the way I was perceived as a researcher. Generally, my presence as a young white foreigner raised certain expectations in many places, which influenced the way people interacted with me.[4] I did not always manage to explain the purpose of my research sufficiently.

Thirdly, my positionality, together with the technical nature of the community forestry, made it very difficult to reconstruct specific steps of the authorization processes. I regularly received contradictory claims about what happened (or not) at which point in time. One woman had to remind me that "we don't remember things [exact dates]. We are not Kwi [educated, civilized]" (Women's FGD 2017c, para 35). While I tried my best to triangulate all information, the absence of documentation, the politicization of community forestry, and my positionality made it difficult to reconstruct events at times. At the same time, these ambiguities highlighted the multiplicity of experiences and challenges in the implementation of the highly technical community forest program.

Liberia's Post-war Logging Sector

Post-war Reform of the Logging Sector: The Four Cs

In 2003, the UN Security Council recognized the impact of the timber industry on the war in Liberia and imposed timber sanctions for the first time in its history (United Nations Security Council 2003). Despite the UN's negative perspective of the logging industry, and the forestry sector more generally, many peacebuilders shared the assumption that bringing Liberian forestry "back on track" would lead to economic development and prevent further conflict (Beevers 2015, 31). Hence, a coalition of

[4] Other researchers in Liberia describe very similar experiences (Utas 2003, 54).

different actors endeavored to rebuild the sector and its legal framework from scratch to fill the "governance vacuum" (Beevers 2015, 28).

The first step in Liberian forest sector reform was the adoption of the 2006 National Forestry Policy (Forestry Development Authority 2006). It formalized the so-called "3 Cs"—commercial, conservation, and community—that still govern the Liberian forestry regime. The underlying idea is that Liberian forests should be zoned by designating areas for commercial, conservation, and community use (Halton 2013, 8–9). In 2006, the National Forestry Reform Law (NFRL) was adopted (United Nations Security Council 2005, 32ff). The NFRL only regulates commercial forestry and conservation, as no consensus on the community-C could be found at the time (Russell et al. 2011, 39). Based on the NFRL, the Liberian government began granting logging concessions in 2009, including seven Forest Management Contracts (FMCs) and ten Timber Sale Contracts (TSCs) (World Bank 2018, 12). At least 28% of the 6.6 million hectares (ha) of Liberian forest are now under commercial concessions (FMCs and TSCs); protected and proposed protected areas cover 18%, and 6% are under rubber and oil palm plantations (World Bank 2018, 7–8).

Massive negative publicity on the illegality of many logging licenses and the pending Land Rights Act, which was expected to enter into force much earlier than in 2018, made the government rethink its concession policy (Global Witness 2017). In 2011, Liberia stopped granting FMCs and TSCs, the most common logging concessions. Subsequently, a high number of private use permits (PUPs) were issued, a type of license that was largely unregulated under the NFRL. The PUPs covered approximately 23% of the Liberian territory and allowed for any forest use, including the clearance of the forest (Global Witness, Save My Future Foundation, and Sustainable Development Institute 2012). Non-Governmental Organizations (NGOs) played a significant role in the revelation of forged deeds and corruption in this context (President of Liberia 2013). As a consequence, the President canceled the PUPs in 2013.

More recently, a fourth C has emerged: carbon. With Liberia becoming a REDD + partner country, a variety of international actors have invested considerable resources in Liberia's forest governance to meet the REDD + goals. They hope that, in the long run, the international emission trading system will help make community forestry economically viable (ACDI/VOCA 2019b, 21).

The Emergence of Community Forestry

The community-C has been neglected in the Liberian forestry regime. The NFRL required the FDA to pass a "comprehensive law governing community rights with respect to forest lands" to ensure that the stated goals of the NFRL were fulfilled (Republic of Liberia 2006, sect. 10.1.c). However, the conceptions of community forestry varied to a large extent: while NGOs envisioned a (forest) land tenure law, the FDA sought to designate small areas for community management (Tissari et al. 2008, 36). The fact that the government granted several illegal forest concessions just a few weeks before the CRL was adopted is symptomatic of the government's prioritization of FDI over community needs (Wily et al. 2010, 4). Despite these challenges, the CRL was finally adopted in 2009. In 2011, it was complemented by a regulation governing its implementation that was amended in 2017.

With the government no longer granting FMCs, TSCs, and PUPs, community forestry is the only way of obtaining a logging license under a so-called commercial use contract (CUC) (CRL Chapter 6). By 2018, approximately 130 communities applied for community forest status. The World Bank estimates that 3 million hectares of forest land or 27% of the Liberian landmass could fall under these yet-to-be-authorized community forests (World Bank 2018, 18). The FDA approved 36 of those applications involving more than 700,000 ha as of late 2018, and at least 12 of them signed commercial use contracts with companies (World Bank 2018, 15, 18; Sustainable Development Institute 2019, 2–3). According to experts, the majority of Liberian community forests are planning to enter into these logging contracts (Senior Forestry Expert 2018, para 151; Global Witness 2018, 41).

Liberia thus underwent a paradigm change concerning its forest resources. The government has moved away from large-scale logging concessions to community-based forest governance, recognizing customary land rights to some extent. The following section explores the procedure for obtaining community forest status and the actual impact of community forestry on customary land rights.

The Legal Framework of Community Forestry

The CRL and its accompanying Regulation outline a specific procedure for registering community forests on customary land. Departing from previous legislation under which all forest resources belonged to the state, communities own all forest resources within these community forests and can decide how to use them (CRL sect. 1.3, 2.2.a). Community is defined as a self-identified and publicly or widely recognized coherent social group that shares common customs and traditions and that resides in a particular area of land over which they exercise jurisdiction (CRL sect. 1.3). While the statutory recognition of customary tenure is not a requirement for establishing a community forest, communities are restricted in the free designation of their forest land by the requirement that community forests must be between 5 001 and 49 000 ha in size (CRL sect. 2.3).[5] In theory, communities may apply for community forest status without any geographical restrictions. However, it is unlikely that the FDA would knowingly grant community forest status for land that is part of a government-granted concession or a protected area.[6]

Under the CRL and its Regulation, the protection of forest land rights is qualified by the need to register as a community forest and to go through the so-called nine (or 11)[7] steps. The steps involve four core elements: (1) community self-identification, (2) identification of customary land, (3) election of a forest governance structure and adoption of forest governance rules, and (4) the decision on how to use the forest (Fig. 6.1).

For the first element of community self-identification, community members must write a letter of application to the FDA and the FDA conducts a socio-economic resource reconnaissance (SER) survey thereafter to identify the appropriate community unit. The second element, the identification of community land, is done through the demarcation of the community forest and the cutting of its boundaries. The third element consists of the election of the governance structure, involving a Community Assembly (CA), the highest decision-making body; the Executive

[5] However, the CRL Regulation also contains provisions on smaller and bigger community forestry indicating that the FDA in practice does not stick to the size requirement of the CRL.

[6] For instance, the community forests around East Nimba Natural Reserve, one of the protected areas, only extend to the buffer zones of the park but not to the park itself (Gill 2017, 36–7).

[7] Those additional steps consist of the implementation requirements of a Community Forest Management Plan.

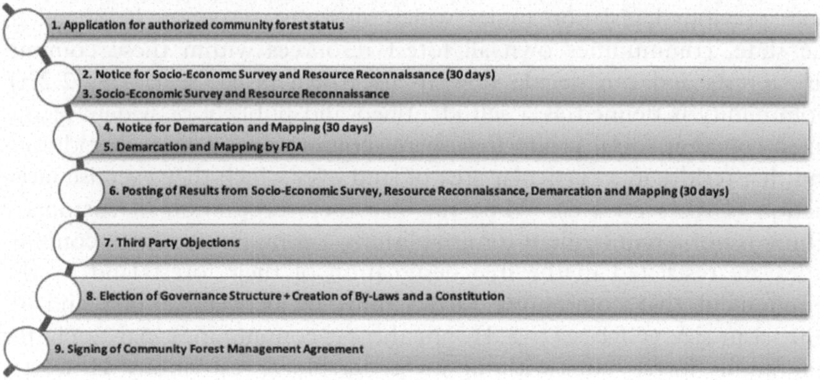

Fig. 6.1 Nine steps required by the CRL to register as a community forest (Author's figure)

Committee (EC), whose members are also members of the CA and which convenes the meetings of the CA; and the Community Forest Management Body (CFMB), which is in charge of day-to-day activities and which has to report back to the EC. Forest governance rules are then incorporated in the Constitution and by-laws of the community forest. When these conditions are met, the community and the FDA sign a Community Forest Management Agreement (CFMA). Moreover, as a fourth element, the communities are obliged to adopt (step 10) and implement (step 11) a Community Forest Management Plan (CFMP) (Forestry Development Authority 2017b, Chapter 2). In the CFMP, the community outlines how it wants to use the forest and may designate different zones for different forest uses.

The procedure not only can take years, but also comes with considerable costs. Within the process, the FDA takes a prominent role: it is in charge of conducting the SER survey, and the demarcation process, posting notices, and reporting results. The self-identification procedure and the identification of community land are thus largely taken out of the communities' hands. Still, the CRL protects the customary rights to forest land to a considerable extent and allows the communities to decide about how they want to use their land. Even though the Liberian government could, in theory, make use of its right to eminent domain to grant concessions, it has not done so in the past. The community forest framework has thus, in theory, put an end to the governmental alienation of customary land.

Community Forestry in Practice: A New Form of the Land Grab?

This section explores whether the community forest legislation lies a sound foundation for the protection of customary land rights. It does so by comparing the implementation of community forestry in the Beyan Poye and the Sehzueplay community forests. Beyan Poye was an FDA pilot community forest, while Sehzueplay has seen ongoing support by two successive USAID-funded projects.

Beyan Poye Community Forest

Background

The Beyan Poye community forest is located in Margibi county but overlaps with Bong and Grand Bassa counties. To reach Beyan Poye, one has to take a 1.5-hour drive to Kakata, the capital of Margibi county, on a paved road, and from Kakata another 1.5-hour drive on a dirt road to Worhn, the capital of Gibi district. The Beyan community was founded in the late nineteenth century by Gio and Mano migrants from Nimba (Forestry Development Authority, 5). In the early twentieth century, settlers from Grand Bassa joined them. Other ethnic groups arriving in the region in the 1950s include the Kpelle, Vai, and Lorma. In 1973, the Beyan and Poye communities merged. According to estimates, 93 towns are located within the Beyan Poye community forest (Forestry Development Authority 2007, 4; Tetra Tech/ARD 2012, 8). It takes about 12 hours to walk from Worhn to the most distant towns within the community forest (District Commissioner 2017, para 46). Dirt tracks connect most of the towns in the forest, and no cars, motorbikes, or bicycles can reach the towns beyond Poie town (Fig. 6.2).

The map illustrates the high number of towns located within the community forest area. It is therefore not surprising that the forest plays an essential role in the lives of the communities living within it. One elder explained that "the forest is the first thing in our life" (FGD 2017a, para 21). Statements like "we were thinking that the forest is for us, but it's

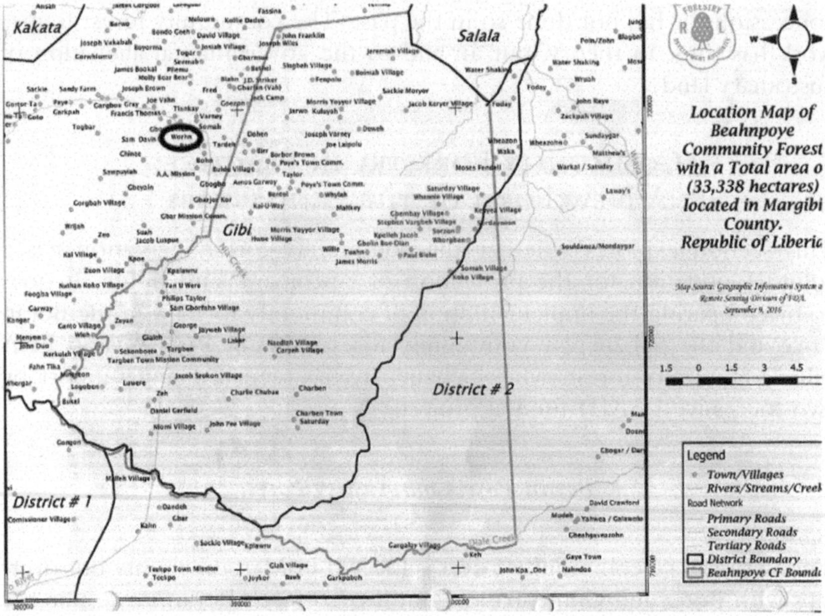

Fig. 6.2 The Beyan Poye community forest. The district capital Worhn is circled in black Photo taken at the Forestry Development Authority's office, January 2018

for the government" (Women's FGD 2017e, para 23) were ubiquitous in all of the towns visited. Communities see themselves as the owners of the forest and explained that the government has interfered with their customary governance in the past decades. During the war, the forest played a pivotal role for many community members. Many of them spent several years in the forest hiding. Forest products are used in all of the towns visited. Some communities live and farm in more remote parts of the forest. Those at the fringe of the forest collect rattan and cut wood to build furniture or houses, install traps, produce charcoal, and collect snails and wild palm nuts for the production of palm oil (Women's FGD 2017e, para 28; Women's FGD 2017c, paras 42, 47; Women's FGD 2017b, para 22).

In 2010, the District Commissioner sent an application for a PUP in the name of the "citizens of Worhn" (Boyer 2010) to the FDA.

Even though the applicants possessed an Aborigines Land Grant Deed,[8] interviews in the district suggested that most community members were not aware of the existence of such a deed (Tetra Tech/ARD 2012, 8–9). The PUP was granted to the community in 2011, and the FDA brokered a social agreement between the community and the Nigerian logging company Akewa. Akewa had already started its operations when the government canceled all PUPs (Sustainable Development Institute 2018, 3).

The Nine Steps in Practice

Following the cancelation of the PUP, it became clear that community forestry was the only option for commercial use of the forest. In 2014, one elder submitted a letter of application on behalf of the "citizens of the Beyan Poye community in Gibi District" (Beyan Poye Community 20 June 2014, 1) to the FDA. The letter stated that the community forest—just like the PUP—comprises 22,000 ha. The FDA made Beyan Poye one of their pilot community forests and funded the SER (Technical Manager 2015, 1). The survey took three days and was conducted by the FDA in the presence of the Environmental Protection Agency (EPA) and a civil society representative (Forestry Development Authority 2016a).

The demarcation of the community forest began in October 2015 when the FDA patrolled the community for three days. The map produced was inaccurate due to technical problems and time constraints. Community members complained that several towns were missing. Moreover, the size of the forest increased from 22,000 to 39,895 ha, including towns in Bong county and a considerable area of Grand Bassa county (Forestry Development Authority 2015b, 2, 6). The validation in January 2016 largely confirmed the contours of the proposed community forest. The second map is, however, even less accurate than the one produced during the first mapping exercise (Forestry Development Authority 2016b, 4). In September 2016, a final map was produced which shifted the Eastern boundary line inwards. Much of the area located in Grand Bassa was excluded from the community forest.

The results of the demarcation were posted in September 2016, and, in December 2016, the FDA confirmed that no third-party objections had been raised (Forestry Development Authority Planning Officer 2016).

[8] Deeds are a pre-condition for obtaining a Private Use Permit.

However, the results of the mapping were not reported in all towns. For instance, community members from Poie town noted that the map was only posted in other towns (FGD 2017d, para 15; Women's FGD 2017a, para 55). In Morris town, community members complained that they could not read the map and nobody explained it to them (FGD 2017c, para 15). In September 2016, the FDA informed the Beyan Poye community that, while the FDA provided funding for the first four steps of the authorization process, the community itself would have to fund the cutting of the boundary line and that it would cost approximately US$2310 USD (Office of the Managing Director 2016). A Liberian NGO suspects that, given the high costs involved in boundary cutting, Akewa likely provided the financial means since the logging company held the previous PUP for the area (Sustainable Development Institute 2018, 3).

In 2017, the CFMB signed a CUC with Akewa, granting the company the right to exploit the entire forest. Under the forest legislation, CUCs may only be signed after the adoption of the CFMP. In the records of the FDA, no indication could be found that the Beyan Poye community submitted a CFMP. It is unlikely that a forest inventory and zoning was conducted in the short period of about four weeks between the authorization and the CUC. Moreover, the forest size in the CFMA and the CUC is identical, which indicates that, at least formally, no part of the community forest has been designated for non-commercial uses.

The signing ceremony for the CUC was a more memorable event than the nine steps involved in regulating a community forest; most community members remember the ceremony vividly as the "cow business" (Women's FGD 2017f, para 94), an event where the women slaughtered a cow.[9] The CUC granted Akewa the right to use to entire community forest area for 15 years, and the contract may be renegotiated after five years. A breach of the agreement does not render the agreement "null and void" (Forestry Development Authority 2017a, para 30), and it cannot be revoked by any party (2017a, paras 28, 30, 32). Akewa began its operations in early 2018.

[9]The cow business may have been noteworthy for community members as cattle are scarce in Beyan Poye.

Outcome of the Nine Steps
The following section explores in further detail the identification of community land, the meaning of community, and the forest use decision.

A New Understanding of Community
During the authorization procedure of the PUP, the FDA identified only 11 towns and four villages whereas the SER survey found 21 towns (Resident Country Surveyor Margibi 2010). According to the FDA, two clans owned the forest. The interviewees only referred to the Beyan section and the Poye section when describing the community forest (Forestry Development Authority, 3). The two sections may correspond to the two clans, but it should be noted that the migration history of the area has contributed to considerable heterogeneity. Several languages are spoken in all of the towns (Forestry Development Authority, 6).

The size of the community forest raises issues of representation: Only a small proportion of the towns located in the forest have been officially recognized as being part of the community. There are many more settlements within the community forest than those identified in the SER survey. Moreover, the size of the towns vary greatly: the Benthol and Gaye villages have 20 inhabitants whereas Worhn, the district capital, has 5000 (Forestry Development Authority, 8). Nevertheless, In theory, the 21 towns possess the same number of votes in the community forest governance structure. In addition, not all towns have the same kind of relationship to the forest. Towns like Worhn and Poie Town are identified as forest owning communities even though they are several walking hours away from the forest. Residents of the two towns may use the forest economically or for cultural purposes, but most likely do not do so to the same extent as the residents living within the forest that directly depend on the forest for farming. Several informants shared this sentiment (Women's FGD 2017d, para 32). For instance, the general town chief of Worhn held that "the whole district [owns the community forest]. But the affected area, where the forest is, the people there have more care over it than the people on this side" (General town chief 2017, para 25).

The inclusion of Worhn as the district capital in the boundaries of community forest indicates that prominent local actors felt that community forest governance should be a district matter. Several factors support this theory: firstly, informants repeatedly stressed that the whole district endorsed the creation of the community forest and thus the whole district should benefit from the forest resources (General town chief 2017, para 23; District Commissioner 2017, para 64). Secondly, the District Commissioner was elected to be a member of the EC in violation of the CRL, according to which government officials must not be members of the governance structure.[10] Only after protest by a national NGO was he deposed (FGD 2017e, para 18). And thirdly, Worhn is the place where most of the community forest decisions taken. Statements from the CFMB like, "isn't Worhn everybody's big town?" (CFMB member 2017a, para 93) highlight the centralized nature of decision-making. One woman in Kaiuway shared this feeling and explained: "everything that happens here, the order where it comes from is there in the city [Worhn]" (Women's FGD 2017d, para 40). Moreover, most of the actors involved in the nine-step procedure reside in Worhn, and the Community Assembly's headquarter is also in Worhn (Forestry Development Authority 2015a; Republic of Liberia 2015; Beyan Poye Community Forest 2017, art V sect. 6).

The district-level understanding of community means that the Beyan Poye is not particularly close-knit. Some interviewees were under the impression that the FDA had "told the 24 [21] towns to work together" (FGD 2017e, para 10). They also believed that "the citizens together agree to become a community for the community forest. We weren't a community before" (FGD 2017e, para 8). These popular conceptions and discourses have thus contributed to the reframing of community from "those who own the forest" to "those who should benefit from it," which, in this case, is principally the district (District Commissioner 2017, para 34).

Drawing Boundaries with a Ruler—Again

The mapping of the community forest caused the eruption of an "age-old" (FDA employee 2018c, para 299) land dispute (EPA employee 2018, para 85). At the time, the conflict was exacerbated by the fact that the Land Authority bill had not yet been adopted and the other agencies took the position that as "foresters, we're not there to solve land issues, we are not the Land Authority" (EPA employee 2018, para 85). The main issue of contention was the boundary between the counties Margibi, Grand Bassa, and Bong. The Beyan Poye community claimed a

[10] According to the CRL, no government official must be elected into the EC (2009, art 4.1.b).

strip of Grand Bassa as part of the community forest. However, a community in Grand Bassa was in negotiation with a company for the same parcel of land (District Commissioner 2017, para 72). The Superintendents and the land surveyors of the two counties, upon meeting, decided to shift the Eastern boundary line inwards to avoid delays in the authorization of the community forest, ensuring that the community was able "to get the required hectares" (District Commissioner 2017, para 72). Informants explained that the FDA told them "how much hectares makes a community forest and we were even able to even go a little beyond that" (District Commissioner 2017, para 50). This revelation implies that the FDA asked the community to designate a sufficiently big area or even proposed the demarcation itself. While the Southern demarcation line follows the boundaries between District Gibi and Districts 1 and 2, the Northern, Eastern, and Western boundaries seem to have been drawn with a ruler. Community members thus had no ownership in the demarcation process, mirroring the way the boundaries were drawn during the colonial era.

Commercial Logging as a Necessity

The decision to opt for the commercial exploitation of the forest was likely taken well before the authorization of the community forest. In the view of many community members, no clear line is drawn between the PUP and the community forest, in part because the same community members spearheaded both processes and the company Akewa was continuously present in the negotiations (FGD 2017a, para 14). NGOs suspect that the community only applied for community forest status to allow the company to resume their logging activities (Sustainable Development Institute 2018, 3). When one of the USAID-funded projects approached the communities of the Beyan Poye forest, members told them that "as much as we want to preserve, we want our area now for commercial purpose, so at least that can get we few lines of streets, and roads and then at least we can get the benefits" (District Commissioner 2017, para 70).

Community members were aware of Akewa's continued interest in the forest during the nine-step procedure (District Commissioner 2017, paras 17ff). The first letter of application announced that "the proceed derived from the extraction of the forest resources will be equally shared in the communities" (Barnyou 2013, 1). When problems arose during the demarcation concerning the accuracy of the maps produced by the

FDA, community members were eager to not delay the authorization process further "as they [...] yearning for investor to come in their area" (Forestry Development Authority 2016b, 2). As a result, community members agreed to the loss of considerable areas of forest land to the neighboring counties.

While it is challenging to uncover and reconstruct how the decision to opt for commercial logging was taken, it is clear that community forestry was, from the onset, seen as a source of income for the district. Alternative forest uses were never discussed. In all of the towns visited, community members declared that "they told us [...] [the forest] should be used to benefit us, by using it only for logging [...]" (FGD 2017d, paras 13, 14; Women's FGD 2017e, para 19).

Criminalization of Local Forest Uses

The decision to opt for commercial logging went hand in hand with the criminalization of local forest uses. In all of the towns visited, community members explained that they were told not to use the forest anymore. The construction of local forest uses as unsustainable and the portrayal of "development" as a modern necessity justified the extinction of customary rights to forest land. Interviewees expressed this finding through two different narratives: (1) the narrative of ignorance and (2) the narrative of powerlessness.

Narratives of ignorance were regularly used by powerful, educated, and geographically mobile actors. Statements like "they were just damaging the forest. [...] Because we have some knowledge from school [...]. So we should not damage that tree. Because in the future, it will benefit us" (District Commissioner 2017, para 30) reflect this narrative. What follows from this logic is that local forest uses must be prohibited and community members need to be taught to embrace modern forestry practices, i.e., commercial forestry. Traditional forest uses are thus reconstructed as a form of land encroachment.

In a few cases, community members echoed the narrative of ignorance. Inhabitants from Weirlii stated that, "we didn't understand that we couldn't just use the forest" (FGD 2017d, para 20). However, this internalization of the narrative of ignorance remained the exception. Instead, narratives of disempowerment were more common, and the phrase "they told us to not use the forest anymore" (FGD 2017d, para 13) was a recurring theme in all of the towns visited. The identity of "them" varies: informants sometimes referenced "the government and the radio" (FGD

2017d, para 20), the FDA (Women's FGD 2017f, para 34), Akewa (FGD 2017b, para 11), or "people from the city" (Women's FGD 2017e, para 15). It is still evident that "they" are the decision-makers, while the ordinary community can do nothing but comply.

The narrative of ignorance and the narrative or powerlessness produce a common outcome. From the narrative of ignorance follows that local forest uses must be prohibited. The narrative of powerlessness highlights that community dwellers have no other option but to respect that prohibition. The sense of disempowerment goes so far that some community members fear repercussions if they continue to use the forest: "if we continue to use this forest, a storm will be coming" (Women's FGD 2017e, para 15). Moreover, a CA member admitted that they did not inform the company that they needed a part of the forest for farming, as they were afraid that the company might reconsider the investment (CA member 2017, para 56).

The community forest framework thus contributed to land conflicts, both within the Beyan Poye community and with neighboring communities. It impaired the livelihood opportunities of many residents, particularly those living within the forest. The strong development discourse accompanying the formalization of the community forest contributed to silencing and criminalizing those negatively affected. In this respect, the CFMB is in an extraordinary position of power since it determines how the forest may be used, while also depending on the company's goodwill. It is in charge of investigating and sanctioning violations of the no-forest-use policy. Community members' continued use of the forest for non-commercial uses, however, indicates that they have retained space for counter-practices or acts of resistance despite the framing of local livelihood practices as unsustainable (CA member 2017, para 53; CFMB member 2017b, para 126).

Sehzueplay Community Forest

Background

Sehzueplay is located in Southern Nimba. From Monrovia, it takes about four hours on a paved road to reach Ganta. Ganta and Sehzueplay are connected by a dirt road that is only accessible during the dry season and which takes two hours to drive. Seven towns belong to the Sehzueplay forest: Graie town, Zuolay, Volay, Sehyee village, Kenpea, Zeonghn, and Korlay. A dirt road connects them and, unlike in Beyan Poye, they are all located outside of the authorized community forest. Sehzueplay has approximately 25,000 inhabitants, with the major ethnic groups being Gio, Mano, Kpelleh, and Lorma (Sehzueplay Community Forest 2017, sect. 3.1) (Fig. 6.3).

Sehzueplay is one of the forests supported by two successive USAID-funded projects. The Peoples, Rules, and Organizations Supporting the Protection of Ecosystem Resources (PROSPER) project was active in Sehzueplay from 2012 to 2017, followed by the Forest Incomes for Environmental Sustainability (FIFES) project which runs from 2015 to 2020. Both projects received significant financial support from the USAID under its biodiversity earmark and, consequently, could not support any activities contributing to deforestation.

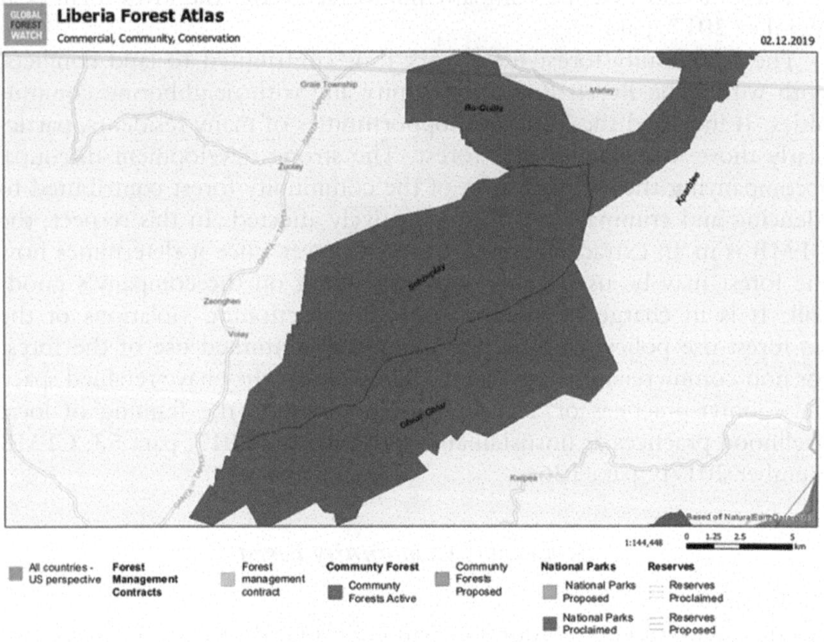

Fig. 6.3 Map of Sehzueplay. Retrieved from Forest Atlas, https://gis.forest-atlas.org/server/rest/directories/arcgisoutput/print/ExportWebMap_GPServer/_ags_9483c1a5ba9b4d0a995dfceaf3822619.pdf (last accessed 2 December 2019)

Before its recognition as a community forest, the Sehzueplay forest was part of the 58,000 ha-large Gio National Forest which stretched across three districts, namely Doe, Boe-Quilla, and Kparblee, and which was created in 1952. The government of President William Tubman introduced national forests in the 1950s "to serve the industrial development in Liberia" (United States Operations Mission to Liberia 1961, 19, 22). National forests were declared uninhabited and constantly controlled by forest guards "to keep the artificial boundaries clear, to keep out farmers and to control hunters" (Sachtler 1968, 1). According to community members, a logging company operated in the forest during the war (CFMB member 2018a, para 264). After the war, the government classified it as an unallocated forest concession (Vogt 2012).

In 2011, the FDA granted a 25-year long PUP to the Doe Chiefdom for a tract of land covering 79,263 ha (Forestry Development Authority 2011, sect. 1 art 5). The PUP was canceled in 2013 and the Land Commission found that the deed had been forged (Tetra Tech/ARD 2014, 11). In the same year, the communities surrounding the Gio National Forest, including Sehzueplay, Boe-Quilla, Gbear-Gblor, and Kparblee, decided to opt for separate community forest status. Today, the Sehzueplay community forest comprises 6890 ha (Tetra Tech/ARD 2016b).

Historically, community members in Sehzueplay did not use the forest as much as the Beyan Poye community. One woman explained that "during before, the forest, it was not in the hand of the community, so the good thing [about community forestry] is, that the forest to rest in the hand of the community, to manage their own forest" (FGD 2018e, para 24). The FDA most likely never managed to fully prevent community members from entering the forest entirely, even though forest rangers burned the farms of so-called perpetrators and brought them to court (CA member 2018b, para 60; former FDA employee 2018, para 30). During the war, the FDA no longer possessed the capacity to patrol the forest (Tetra Tech/ARD 2013, 18). Community members and those from neighboring places went into hiding in the forest and began using it for farming. Population growth increased the pressures on the Gio National Forest and drove some community members farther into the forest in search of farmland. The continuing presence of families in the forest causes conflicts within the community of Sehzueplay.

The Nine Steps in Practice

In April 2013, six towns of the Sehzueplay community submitted their letter of application to the FDA (Sehzueplay clan 2013). During these first steps, the community had no formal governance structure in place and so PROSPER established Community Forest Organizing Committees (CFOCs) to lead them through the process (Tetra Tech/ARD 2013, 13). PROSPER also had one staff member living and working in the community as a mobilizer (Social Impact's Liberia Strategic Analysis 2016, 29). Moreover, PROSPER introduced Community Awareness Teams (CATs) to spread information about biodiversity conservation.

The FDA, together with the EPA and PROSPER, posted the SER survey notices in April 2015 (Tetra Tech/ARD 2015, 19). PROSPER sought to enable the self-determined identification of the community forest's external boundaries and provided GPS training to community members toward this goal (Tetra Tech/ARD 2016a, 27). However, the demarcation just confirmed the 1952 boundary line of the national forest and, after the demarcation, community members complained that their farmland was now behind the demarcation line and asked the FDA to move the boundary line 600 m inwards (Sehzeplay Clan 2016). The FDA was apparently reluctant to comply and argued that if the proposed area was smaller than 9000 ha, they would not receive authorization (Clan chief 2018, para 90). As a compromise, the FDA agreed to move the 1952 boundary line 200 m inwards, thereby decreasing the size of the community forest (Clan chief 2018, para 92; Zone chief 2018, para 44). Given ongoing complaints by community members about their loss of farmland, FIFES, came to the conclusion that PROSPER had not sufficiently ground-truthed the demarcation coordinates (ACDI/VOCA 2019a, 18). Beyond the demarcation process, PROSPER supported the community in drafting its Constitution and by-laws wherein it was agreed that each town would have three representatives in the CA.

After the signing of the Community Forest Management Agreement in February 2017, it became evident that the CFMB did not possess sufficient funds for maintaining the community forest (ACDI/VOCA 2018, 18). For instance, most community forest boundaries became overgrown and needed to be cleared again. Generating funding for the zoning of the forest and the forest inventory also exceeded the CFMB's capacities. While FIFES envisioned to support the CFMB in the writing of the CFMP, the process took much longer than expected and community members became impatient.

In autumn 2017, the Chief Officer of the CFMB secretly signed a memorandum of understanding (MoU) with the US logging company Opulence. The Chief Officer was subsequently dismissed, but the other CFMB members still felt bound by the MoU and, in December 2017, signed a CUC with Opulence. The 14-year contract covers the whole community forest (Republic of Liberia 2017, sects. 1, 2). The CUC's land rental and stumpage fees are relatively low and the social obligations of Opulence are vague in the contract terms. In addition, the community commits to support Opulence in the maintenance of roads and to provide building materials free of charge (Republic of Liberia 2017, sects. 3, 5, 7.5). On top of that, community members remain in charge of the costly boundary cleaning, which must be done twice a year to ensure that the boundaries do not overgrow (Sehzueplay Community Forest 2017, 18).

The CFMP was adopted after the CUC with Opulence was signed, thereby violating the CRL and its Regulation (Republic of Liberia 2017, sect. 4). Opulence drafted the CFMP in Monrovia and the CA subsequently adopted it. One of the main objectives of the CFMP is to engage in logging activities (Sehzueplay Community Forest 2017, 1), however, it otherwise remains vague and does not zone the forest to allow for different forest uses.

The Outcome of the Nine Steps

The Forest as a no-Go-Zone

The local FDA and PROSPER staff felt that the forest should not be used during the nine steps, a position which departed from the official stances of the FDA and PROSPER (PROSPER employee 2018, paras 82, 84; FDA staff member 2018b, para 40). According to community members, the FDA told them not to enter the forest anymore (FGD 2018c, para 10). Others remember that PROSPER taught them that the forest was a "no-go zone" (FGD 2018e, para 6) and that they should stop hunting and fishing there.

The CFMP echoes the no-use-forest policy and states that community members do not have the right to farm in the forest (Sehzueplay Community Forest 2017, 18). However, the CFMP simultaneously speaks of determining quotas for the use of forest resources by community members upon the granting of a license, without providing details (Sehzueplay Community Forest 2017, 20ff). It is the CFMB's duty to ensure that nobody illegally enters the forest and to designate forest guards to enforce the no-forest-use policy (Sehzueplay Community Forest 2017, 21).

The District Commissioner and the paramount chief have also become involved in the conflict with community members living in the forest the District Commissioner ordered community members to burn down rice farms in the forest and to report hunters, and the paramount chief apparently offered money to community members to make them leave the forest (FIFES employee 2018a, para 166; FGD 2018d, para 8; Women's FGD 2018d, para 2).

Even though some community members possessed farmland within the forest before the demarcation, most community members have adopted the rhetoric of forest protection and supported—at least publicly—the outlawing of local forest uses. For instance, one woman explained that the community forest is the "forest that is being protected from the things of the community" (Women's FGD 2018a, para 23). The exercise of governmental authority over the forest has thus extinguished customary use rights to a large extent (Sehzueplay Community Forest 2017, 18). If community members complained about the FDA and its management of the forest, these complaints mainly targeted the lack of benefits generated from the commercial exploitation of the forest but not the alienation of the forest itself (CA member 2018c, para 8; Women's FGD 2018b, para 25; Women's FGD 2018d, para 2).

The Odd Case of the Buffer Zone

While most community members agree that the community forest should not be used by locals (CA member 2018f, para 97), the situation is different for the so-called tribal reserves located in the buffer zone, i.e., the area located between the towns and the former national forest.

Under pre-war land legislation, tribal or native reserves were land to be used for essential farming activities (Stevens 2014, 255). In Sehzueplay, the government granted some of these reserves as compensation to the communities affected by the 1952 boundary line (FGD 2018d, para 4; Former town chief 2018, para 24; Former FDA employee 2018, para 44). According to community members, some of the reserves are even older than the Gio National Forest (Community member 2018b, para 4). One old man explained: "the village in which I was born on this side, that the village we're talking about, you see my gray hair, where I was born, today they say I should leave it, which is very impossible" (Community members 2018, para 34). The tribal reserves had been used for planting eddoes, rubber trees, cocoa, plantains, and oil palm (Women's FGD 2018d, para 224; FGD 2018d, para 4).

Buffer zones, in contrast, represent "best management practices" (International Forestry Experts 2018, para 33) in forestry and function to delimit the forest zones used for different purposes. The Liberian forest legislation does not mandate the creation of buffer zones for community forests. However, the FDA suggested creating a 3 m buffer strip around the forest. At the time, PROSPER expressed caution about the idea and there is no indication that it was introduced in Sehzueplay (PROSPER employee 2019).

The FIFES project, in contrast, makes explicit reference to buffer zones. One of FIFES' stated objectives is to improve the management of the "community forest (CF) and buffer zone natural resources" (ACDI/VOCA 2017a, 4). FIFES reported that the Sehzueplay CFMB "agreed to set aside areas along CF boundaries that will be managed as protective zones to the CFs" (ACDI/VOCA 2017a, 26). It is likely that FIFES pushed community members to introduce a buffer zone (International Forestry Experts 2018, para 33). According to community members, one leading staff member of FIFES gave them training on buffer zones (FGD 2018a, para 10; FGD 2018g, para 12).

Community members were unsure at what point in time the buffer zone was introduced. Several informants took the position that it was demarcated after the nine steps (International Forestry Experts 2018, para 31; FIFES employee 2018a, para 181; FDA staff member 2018b, para 32). It was probably the CFMB that decided to establish a 3 km buffer zone[11] surrounding the Sehzueplay community forest (EC member 2018c, para 176), although some members of the governance structure argued that it was the FDA who proposed the size of the buffer zone (CA member 2018a, para 86; EC member 2018d, para 60).

The local FDA officer took the position that, although the buffer zone could be used for farming by community members, it should not be so as to ensure the integrity of the community forest as a biodiversity habitat (FDA employee 2018a, 253). Local FIFES staff members argued that the CFMB could not allow farming in the buffer zone because then community members would encroach upon the community forest (FIFES

[11] Community members were unsure about the width of the buffer zone, with some of them suggesting that it was 3 miles, 3 kilometres or 300 metres. FIFES staff members and other the key people in the governance structure took the position that it is 3 kilometres.

employee 2018b, para 198). In their understanding, buffer zones are necessary to protect watersheds and biodiversity (FIFES employee 2018b, para 216). The Commissioner, the CA, and the CFMB began informing the people about the prohibition on the use of the buffer zone, and many community people moved from their farmlands in the buffer zone back to their home towns (EC member 2018b, para 138). Members of the CF governance structure, forest guards, and other community members patrol the buffer zone (ACDI/VOCA 2017b, 12).

Conflicts between the FDA and community members arose during the demarcation of the buffer zone (CA member 2018a, para 86). Five of the seven towns reported that some or most of their community members were negatively affected. People repeatedly stressed that they lost their "old area" (Women's FGD 2018d, para 2) and that "no big tree here, that only [in the] Doe [community forest], but they take everything from us" (Women's FGD 2018c, para 71). A FIFES staff member admitted that he did not know about the number of people affected by the loss of native reserves since nobody collected data on the number of farms in the buffer zone either before or during the buffer zone demarcation process (FIFES employee 2018b, para 208).

Community members, including members of the CA, informed the CFMB about the issue of buffer zone demarcation to no avail. They also brought the issue to FIFES' attention (FGD 2018d, para 4). In the eyes of many community members, they were "appealing to FDA that they should at least, the other area, that they are already occupied with old, old farming area, that they should give it back to them, so that they will be able to eat from there"(CA member 2018a, para 80). This sentiment corresponds to the findings of FIFES' midterm evaluation: the restrictive forest rules contributed to degraded livelihoods and alternative livelihood activities were less productive than the swidden cultivation that occurred within the CF and its buffer zone prior to the demarcation (Liberia Strategic Analysis 2018, 8). Yet, the FDA officer in charge of the community forest argued that they were not aware of any problems (FDA employee 2018a, para 299). The fact that even CA members appealed to the FDA about the width and function of the buffer zone strongly indicates that the CA was not involved in decision-making processes.

The conservation discourse propagated by PROSPER and FIFES legitimized the no-forest-use policy in both the buffer zone and the community forest. It also motivated the addition of roughly 6000 ha to the existing 6890 ha of land to the community forest, a considerable extension in jurisdiction and a major alienation of farm land which occurred without any indication of community consent.

Fragmentation of Community and Authority
The introduction of community forestry in Sehzueplay led to frictions within the community.

Firstly, conflicts exist between the towns affected by the buffer zone and those outside of the community forest. The towns affected by the buffer zone portray outside community members as violators and perpetrators, alleging that they as still farming or hunting in the buffer zone or the community forest (CFMB member 2018a, para 278). Often times, they did not distinguish between those members who had lost their native reserves and those who had moved into the forest during the war (former District Commissioner 2018, para 8). Those affected by the demarcation, however, distinguished more clearly between those living within the community forest and those living within native reserves in the buffer zone (former town chief 2018, paras 28, 36). Many assigned responsibility to PROSPER and the FDA for their loss of farmland, not knowing that it was likely the CFMB who decided to introduce the buffer zone.

Secondly, ordinary community members contest the new governance system. Women from Volay complained that, "during PROSPER time, that only the big people, the chiefs, not us, the town chiefs, they used to go for the meeting, but when they come, the only thing that they can tell is say we not go in the forest, we not go in the forest. That only thing" (Women's FGD 2018d, para 56). This statement corresponds to the findings of PROSPER's evaluation: knowledge about the community forest was concentrated among individuals more closely connected to the governance structure or belonging to PROSPER (Social Impact's Liberia Strategic Analysis 2016, 25). Other community members argued that, "they can't tell us. [As long as they get] their sitting fee [for attending meetings] over there, when they come they go in their various houses then [without giving us information]" (Women's FGD 2018a, para 93). Particularly people from those communities that lost farmland who complained about the lack of information received from their CA representatives (FGD 2018d, para 11; Community members, para 10; Women's FGD 2018a, para 86).

Thirdly, conflicts persist within the governance structure, particularly between the CA and the CFMB. Several CA members complained that they received insufficient information from the CFMB during the nine step process (CA member 2018a, para 40; CA member 2018e, para 42). One CA member even posed that they "don't know whether the CA is the big man for CFMB or the CFMB is the big man for CA" (CA member 2018i, para 56).

Finally, the relationship between outside actors, particularly the FDA, and community members remains unclear. Community members possess a limited or restricted sense of forest ownership. One member of the EC, for example, explained that the FDA entrusted them with the management of the forest but that they needed the FDA's approval for any forest use decision (EC member 2018c, para 140). The fact that CA members complained to the FDA about the buffer zone instead of taking the matter in their own hands equally highlights the FDA's power.

These examples indicate a wide gap between the procedures stipulated in Liberia's forest legislation and community forestry in practice. The fragmentation of authority and communities enhances the risk of land grabbing, like in the case of Sehzueplay's buffer zone, to the disadvantage of the most vulnerable community members.

Commercial Logging as a Form of Forest Conservation

Strikingly, the strong conservation discourse legitimizes the redefinition of commercial logging as a form of forest conservation. Both PROSPER and FIFES possessed a clear conservation focus and hoped that communities would dedicate their forests for this purpose. Most community dwellers agreed that PROSPER taught them how to preserve and manage the forest in a sustainable way (CFMB member 2018a, para 182; CFMB member 2018b, para 50; FGD 2018c, para 10; FGD 2018f, para 7).

However, members of the governance structure also strongly felt that PROSPER and FIFES could no longer participate in decision-making processes once the community forest received authorized status. According to the CFMB Chair, "PROSPER had nothing to do whether to agree or not [to the commercial use of the forest]. Because they have turned [the forest] over to us, and then the FDA was the only authority that we were meeting with so long" (CFMB member 2018a, para 142). In the view of the CFMB, it was the FDA who informed them of the commercial use option (CFMB member 2018a, para 182; FGD 2018c, para 10; FGD 2018h, para 8). Influential community stakeholders like the District Commissioner and the lawyer representing the community also supported and facilitated the negotiation of a commercial use contract

(FIFES employee 2018a, para 116). Apparently, a secret meeting with Opulence took place at the District Commissioner's residence with a few selected members of the governance structure and prominent community members (CFMB member 2018a, paras 176–8, 237).

The weak sense of forest ownership expressed by interviewees reveals that community members do not see community forestry as a way of securing their rights to forest lands, but rather as a mechanism for benefitting financially from the forest. The no-forest-use policy and the buffer zone contributed to reduced household incomes and coerced members into believing that a logging contract was the only viable economic option (Liberia Strategic Analysis 2018, 15). In that sense, community members understood that "as a CFMB Chief Officer, your responsibility is to go and lobby for [a] company" (Zone chief 2018, para 210). However, the CA never gave the CFMB the mandate to "go and lobby for a company" (CFMB member 2018d, para 40). It is likely that the governance structure's motivation to sign the CUC was enhanced by Opulence's offer of a "signing fee" worth approximately US$4000 (EC member 2018c, para 112). This claim, though speculative, reflects how different actors influenced the decision to opt for commercial forestry.

My findings suggest that community members have internalized the conservation discourse in a way that redefines commercial logging as a form of forest conservation. Local forest uses are constructed as (a) not benefitting the whole community and (b) being harmful to the forest. Meanwhile, commercial operations are not seen as interfering with biodiversity (CAT member 2018, para 28; CFMB member 2018a, para 186; CFMB member 2018c, para 164). One CA member explained that, "our forest is most important. If there is no forest, there is no good life, because there we have drinking water from, cold breeze, and we use the forest [...] to make for out of it to generate money. We live on it" (EC member 2018b, para 6). Given the persuasiveness of development discourse, this redefinition of conservation makes it very difficult for community members to question the commercial exploitation of the forest, as they would be seen as prioritizing their individual interests over the interests of both the community and the environment.

Conclusion: From Commercial to Community Back to Commercial

There are several differences between Beyan Poye and Sehzueplay with regard to their respective community forests: first of all, and quite obviously, Beyan Poye is nearly four times the size of Sehzueplay. In general, the community forests without external support are much larger than those that have been supported by USAID (Global Witness 2018, 18–9). Larger forests are more attractive for investors and many communities apply for authorization with the explicit intention of entering into a CUC. Consequently, the Beyan Poye community is less close-knit than Sehzueplay as reflected in the hierarchical and non-participatory decision-making practice. Secondly, PROSPER and FIFES invested considerable time and human resources in Sehzueplay's self-identification and land mapping processes. Moreover, they provided extensive training to support the governance structure. Conflicts about forest governance were more evident in Sehzueplay than in Beyan Poye, very likely because community members possessed a more comprehensive understanding of forest governance. Community members in Sehzueplay felt empowered to bring their complaints to the relevant management bodies. Thirdly, the relationship between the community and the forest differs in the two places. In Sehzueplay, the creation of the Gio National Forest resulted in the usurpation of customary land rights, whereas in Beyan Poye, the community possesses a close relationship to the forest and its resources.

However, Beyan Poye and Sehzueplay also share some characteristics. In both cases, the participation of the CA and the broader community is inadequate or insufficient. Instead, the CFMB is in an extraordinary position of power and can negotiate single-handedly with a company with little to no CA oversight. Moreover, In both cases, the nine step process led to the criminalization of local forest uses. The narrative that local agricultural practices destroy the forest is prevalent in both cases, though it is stronger in Sehzueplay with its strong conservation discourse. In Beyan Poye, community members more frequently employ a customary ownership discourse to counteract the no-forest-use policy. A common feature to both community forests is the de facto extinction of customary land rights. It is difficult to estimate how many community members are negatively affected by community forestry in Beyan Poye. In Sehzueplay, five of the seven towns reported a considerable loss of a farmland and the deterioration of livelihood opportunities.[12] This dispossession made the community more susceptible to the offers of a logging company. Community members in both Beyan Poye and Sehzueplay expressed narratives of disempowerment centered around their exclusion from governance structures, their lack influence with regard to the implementation of community forestry, their limited access to information, and their weak sense of ownership. The purpose of community forestry is to protect customary land rights and empower communities, however, interviewees often characterized it as another government or donor program in which communities have little say.

Liberia's forest legislation has been hailed for its progressiveness, particularly for recognizing customary rights to forest land and allowing for community-based forest governance. The promise of participation, however, has not translated into practice and community forests can indeed be seen as a new form of land grabbing (Global Witness 2018). In a context where the state fails to provide the most basic infrastructure like roads, schools and health facilities, different actors compete in pursuit of various agendas. USAID projects and some elements within the FDA seek to promote conservation, while other elements within the FDA alongside companies and powerful government agents pursue their commercial interests, Communities risk getting caught in the crossfire in all instances. The cases of Zimbabwe, Ethiopia, and Nigeria (see Chapters 5, 8 and 9 of this volume), like Liberia, illustrate how strong conservation and development discourses are deployed to silence "disagreeable" community members.

Moving from a process-oriented to a rights-based approach to community forestry may help actualize the legislative goal of enhanced participation in Liberia. If not, the land rush in Liberia could reach new highs. It is estimated that up to 27% of the Liberian landmass could be converted to community forests and put to commercial use (World Bank 2018, 18). There is a substantial risk that more rural Liberians will lose access to their customary land under the disguise of participatory forest management.

[12] With the exception of Sehyee village and Zeonghn.

References

ACDI/VOCA. 2017a. Forest Incomes for Environmental Sustainability (FIFES), Annual Report: November 6, 2016 to November 5, 2017. Washington D.C.: USAID.

ACDI/VOCA. 2017b. Forest Incomes for Environmental Sustainability, FY2018 First Quarterly Report: October–December 2017. Washington D.C.: USAID.

ACDI/VOCA. 2018. Forest Incomes for Environmental Sustainability, FY2018 Quarterly Report: January–March 2018. Washington D.C.: USAID.

ACDI/VOCA. 2019a. Forest Incomes for Environmental Sustainability, FY2019 Quarterly Report: October–December 2018. Washington D.C.: USAID.

ACDI/VOCA. 2019b. FY10 Fourth quarter & annual report: October 1, 2018–September 30, 2019. USAID.

Atyi, Richard Eba'a. 2018. *Assessing Progress in Forest Law Enforcement and Governance in Africa*. African Development Bank Group.

Barnyou, Sam. 2013. *Letter of Application Beyan Poye Community*. Monrovia.

Beevers, Michael D. 2015. Peace resources? Governing Liberia's forests in the aftermath of conflict. *International Peacekeeping* 22 (1): 26–42. https://doi.org/10.1080/13533312.2014.992568.

Beyan Poye Community. 20 June 2014. *Letter of Application Beyan-Poye Community*. Monrovia.

Beyan Poye Community Forest. 2017. *Constitution*.

Boyer, Amos. 2010. *Letter Requesting a PUP*. Monrovia.

Focus Group Discussions (5) with Community Members in different towns in Beyan Poye. 2017a–e. Interviewer: Marthaline Borma.

Focus Group Discussions with Women (7) in different towns in Beyan Poye. 2017a–f. Interviewer: Marthaline Borma.

Focus Group Discussions (8) with Community Members in Sehzueplay. 2018a–h. Interviewer: Gbangaryisi Johnson.

Focus Group Discussions (4) with Women in Sehzueplay, 2018a–d. Interviewer: Gbangaryisi Johnson.

Forestry Development Authority, Republic of Liberia. 2006. *National forestry policy and implementation strategy*. Monrovia.

Forestry Development Authority. Social, Economic and Reconnaissance Survey to Establish Authorized Forest Community: Field Information Easy Notes, Beyan Poye.

Forestry Development Authority. 2007. Forest data.

Forestry Development Authority. 2011. Private use permit contract between the Forestry Development Authority & The People of Doe's Chiefdom.

Forestry Development Authority. 2015a. Letter Receipts Log. For Signing Affidavit of Consent.

Forestry Development Authority. 2015b. *Report covering the validation and mapping of Beyan Poye community forest*, Gibi District, Margibi County.

Forestry Development Authority. 2016a. *Authorization page socio-economic and reconnaissance survey*. Beyan Poye.

Forestry Development Authority. 2016b. *Validation exercise report on the Beahn Poye's community forest*.

Forestry Development Authority. 2017a. *Community forest management agreement between the Beyan Poye community forest management body and Akewa group of companies Liberia Inc*. Gibi District, Margibi County.

Forestry Development Authority. 2017b. Regulation to the community rights law of 2009 with respect to forest lands, as Amended, edited by Republic-of-Liberia. Monrovia.

Gill, Ghislaine Z.D. 2017. *Managing Liberia's forests: Community forestry for social justice*, Master's diss., Wageningen University.

Global Witness. 2017. *Holding the line*.

Global Witness. 2018. *Power to the people? How companies are exploiting community forestry in Liberia*.

Global Witness, Save My Future Foundation, and Sustainable Development Institute. 2012. *Spoiled: Liberia's private use permits*. Monrovia.

Halton, Anna. 2013. *Background: A snapshot of forest governance assessment for REDD+In Liberia*. FCFP World Bank.

International Monetary Fund. 2010. *Staff report for the 2010 article IV consultation and fifth review under the three-year Arrangement under the Extended Credit Facility*.

Interview with a CA member in Beyan Poye. 2017. Interviewer: Ricarda Roesch.

Interview with the Clan Chief of Sehzueplay. 2018. Interviewer: Ricarda Roesch.

Interview with a Member of the Community Awareness Team (CAT) in Sehzueplay. 2018. Interviewer: Ricarda Roesch.

Interviews with Members (2) of the CFMB in Beyan Poye. 2017a–b. Interviewer: Ricarda Roesch.

Interview with General Town Chief from Beyan Poye. 2017. Interviewer: Ricarda Roesch.

Interview with the District Commissioner of District Gibi. 2017. Interviewer: Ricarda Roesch.

Interview with CA Members (10) in Sehzueplay. 2018a–j. Interviewer: Ricarda Roesch.

Interviews with EC Members (4) in Sehzueplay. 2018a–d. Interviewer: Ricarda Roesch.

Interview with CFMB Members (4) in Sehzueplay. 2018a–d. Interviewer: Ricarda Roesch.

Interviews with Community Members in Sehzueplay. 2018. Interviewer: Ricarda Roesch.

Interview with Staff Member of the Environmental Protection Agency (EPA). 2018. Interviewer: Ricarda Roesch.

Interviews with FDA employees (3). 2018a–c. Interviewer: Ricarda Roesch.

Interviews with FIFES Staff Members (2). 2018a–b. Interviewer: Ricarda Roesch.

Interview with former District Commissioner. 2018. Interviewer: Ricarda Roesch.

Interview with former FDA Employee. 2018. Interviewer: Ricarda Roesch.

Interview with former Town Chief in Sehzueplay. 2018. Interviewer: Ricarda Roesch.

Interview (Skype) with International Forestry Experts. 2018. Interviewer: Ricarda Roesch.

Interview with Senior Forestry Expert. 2018. Interviewer: Ricarda Roesch.

Interview with a Zone Chief from Sehzueplay. 2018. Interviewer: Ricarda Roesch.

Interview and Email Communication with PROSPER employee. 2018/2019. Interviewer: Ricarda Roesch.

Liberia Strategic Analysis. 2018. *Forest incomes for environmental sustainability midterm performance evaluation*. Monrovia: USAID.

Office of the Managing Director, Forestry Development Autority. 2016. Confirmation Steps 1 to 4. Monrovia.

Paczynska, Agnieszka. 2016. Liberia rising? Foreign direct investment, persistent inequalities and political tensions. *Peacebuilding*, 1–20.

Paffenholz, Thania. 2015. Unpacking the Local Turn in Peacebuilding: A Critical Assessment Towards an Agenda for Future. *Third World Quarterly* 36 (5): 857–874.

Planning Officer, Forestry Development Authority. 2016. *Memorandum: No third party objection to SER Survey and preliminary demarcations results*. Monrovia.

President of Liberia. 2013. *Executive order No. 44: Protecting Liberian forests by a temporary moratorium on private use permits*.

Pugh, Michael. 2005. The political economy of peacebuilding: A critical theory perspective. *International Journal of Peace Studies* 10 (2): 23–42.

Radelet, Steven. 2007. *Reviving economic growth in Liberia*. In Working Paper Number 133, Center for Global Development.

Republic of Liberia. 2006. An act adopting the national forestry reform law of 2006 (Amending the National Forestry Law of 2000, As Amended; And Amending An Act Creating the Forestry Development Authority, as Amended).

Republic of Liberia. 2008. *Liberia: Poverty reduction strategy paper*. International-Monetary-Fund.

Republic of Liberia. 2015. Beahn-Poye community affidavit.

Republic of Liberia. 2017. Third party forest management Agreement between Sehzueplay community forest management body and opulence logging company.

Resident Country Surveyor Margibi. 2010. Verification & Reconnaissance Survey of 65,445,00 acres of land in Whorhn Gibi District, Margibi County. 22 November 2010.

Russell, Diane, Andrew Tobiason, Kenneth Hasson, David M. Miller, and Paul de Wit. 2011. *Final evaluation of the land rights and community forestry programme (LRCFP)*. USAID Liberia.

Sachtler, M. 1968. *General report on national forest inventory in Liberia German forestry mission to Liberia in cooperation with the Bureau of forest and wildlife conservation*, Department of Agriculture, Republic of Liberia.

Sehzueplay Clan. 2013. *Letter of application for authorized forest community status.*

Sehzueplay Clan. 2016. *MoU.*

Sehzueplay Community Forest. 2017. *Sehzueplay community forest management plan.* Monrovia.

Social Impact's Liberia Strategic Analysis. 2016. Performance evaluation of people, rules, and organizations supporting the protection of ecosystem resources ("PROSPER"). USAID.

Stevens, Caleb J. 2014. The legal history of public land in Liberia. *Journal of African Law* 58 (2): 250–265.

Sustainable Development Institute. 2018. *What do communities want? A rapid assessment of local preferences for community-owned forest enterprises.* Duazon.

Sustainable Development Institute. 2019. *Practical potential conflict and implementation challenges for the CRL and the LRL.* Monrovia.

Technical Manager, Community Forestry Department. 2015. *Submission of socio-economic cost estimated for the revised Beyan Poye community forest.* Monrovia.

Tetra Tech/ARD. 2012. *Preliminary site assessment report.* Burlington: USAID.

Tetra Tech/ARD. 2013. People, rules, and organizations supporting the protection of ecosystem resources, Annual report, FY2013. Burlington: USAID.

Tetra Tech/ARD. 2014. People, Rules, and Organizations Supporting the Protection of Ecosystem Resources (PROSPER), Seventh quarterly report, 1 January–31 March 2014. Burlington: USAID.

Tetra Tech/ARD. 2015. People, Rules, and Organizations Supporting the Protection of Ecosystem Resources (PROSPER), 12th Quarterly report, 1 April–30 June 2015. Burlington: USAID.

Tetra Tech/ARD. 2016a. *Annual Report, FY2016.* Burlington: USAID.

Tetra Tech/ARD. 2016b. Peoples, Rules, and Organizations Supporting the Protection of Ecosystem Resources (PROSPER), Quarterly report, FY16 Q1, 1 October–31 December 2015. Burlington: USAID.

The Rights and Resources Group. 2013. *Investments into the agribusiness, extractive, and infrastructure sectors of Liberia*.
Tissari, Jukka, Anthony Taplah, and Edward S. Kamara. 2008. Draft Report: World Bank Diagnostic Trade Integration Study: Wood Industry Component.
United Nations Security Council. 2003. Resolution 1521 (2003) Adopted by the security council at its 4890th Meeting, On 22 December 2003. New York.
United Nations-Security Council. 2005. Letter Dated 13 June 2005 from the chairman of the security council committee established pursuant to resolution 1521 (2003) Concerning Liberia addressed to the president of the security council.
United States Operations Mission to Liberia. 1961. Third report on forestry progress. Washington D.C.
Utas, Mats. 2003. Sweet battlefields: Youth and the Liberian civil war. *Cultural Anthropology*, PhD diss., Uppsala University.
Vogt, Martina. 2012. *Biodiversity assessment report*. USAID.
Waldorf, Lars. 2018. Legal empowerment and horizontal inequalities after conflict. *The Journal of Development Studies* 55 (3): 437–455.
Wily, Liz Alden, David Rhodes, Madhu Sarin, Mina Setra, and Phil Shearman. 2010. *The end of the hinterland: Forest, conflict and climate change*. Washington D.C.: Rice and Resource Initiative.
World Bank. 2018. Liberia forest cover note. Washington, DC.

CHAPTER 7

Agro-Industrial Mega-Land Deals in Sierra Leone: Beyond the Rhetoric of Beneficiation, Employment and Economic Development

Solomon Peter Gbanie and Alec Thornton

Introduction

Global demands on agricultural land are increasing due to population growth, dietary changes, and the use of biofuels (Mann and Bonanomi 2017; Phoenix et al. 2019; The Oakland Institute 2012). The global surge in food prices in 2007/08 heightened the investor interest in large-scale land acquisitions (LSLAs) for the purpose of biofuel crops

S. P. Gbanie (✉)
Geography Department, Faculty of Pure and Applied Sciences, Fourah Bay College, University of Sierra Leone, Freetown, Sierra Leone

A. Thornton
School of Science, University of New South Wales, UNSW Canberra, Kensington, Australia

School of Humanities and School of Tourism, University of Johannesburg, Johannesburg, South Africa

L. Cochrane and N. Andrews (eds.), *The Transnational Land Rush in Africa*, International Political Economy Series,
https://doi.org/10.1007/978-3-030-60789-0_7

cultivation, including sugar cane and oil palm. According to the land matrix database (https://landmatrix.org/global/-December, 2020), 1949 deals accounting for 79,238,508 hectares (ha) of transnational land deals have been completed globally. At the same time, another 165 land deals covering 12,682,154 ha are being negotiated and 162 land deals covering 16,372,949 ha were considered failed.

The increase in LSLAs across sub-Saharan Africa over the last decade has generated serious academic and policy discussions around three important concepts: beneficiation, job creation, and economic development. The main thrust of the debate has been the question of whether such large-scale agricultural investments will transform rural economies and map new development pathways or entrench poverty in their operational areas (Baxter and Schaefter 2013; Hansen et al. 2016; Phoenix et al. 2019; Yengoh and Armah 2016).

Commonly referred to as "land grabs," global agribusiness and governments of developing countries promote LSLAs in search of agricultural transformation, job creation, and economic development. Many argue that large-scale investments in agriculture will produce new opportunities for income generation by stimulating rural economies (Deininger and Byerlee 2011). While there is renewed investor interest in LSLAs across developing countries, inquiries into their impacts on national development indicators and contributions to local economies demonstrate a mismatch between the promises of agribusiness and actual outcomes (Baxter and Schaefter 2013; Phoenix et al. 2019; Yengoh and Armah 2016). This discrepancy leads authors like Cotula (2013) and Li (2011) to characterize such promises as propaganda, pointing out that LSLAs often lead to a loss in the rights of local people to access and own land. In their view, LSLAs produces new forms of vulnerabilities and heighten livelihood insecurity.

The re-emergence of the "land grabbing" concept following the 2007/2008 food and fuel price hike has been accompanied by various scholarly attempts to define the buzzword. Kay and Franco (2012) interpret land grabbing as the purchase or lease of land by foreign investors for the purpose of agricultural production. An expanded definition is provided by Cotula (2013) and Yengoh and Armoh (2016) who consider land grabbing as transactions involving acquisitions of large-scale (trans)national commercial land. The latter definition is broader in that it does not exclude domestic investors and includes land acquisitions for both agricultural and non-agricultural purposes. The latest installment of this debate centres around the emerging process of "green grabbing," whereby land and its associated resources are appropriated for environmental ends (Fairhead et al. 2012; Maconachie 2019). We adopt the earlier definition of LSLAs which defines grabbing as those acquisitions for agro-industrial production.

The practice of land grabbing possesses a long history dating back to the colonial era when land was violently enclosed by European empires for the purpose of global capitalist expansion. Its contemporary re-emergence following the 2007/2008 commodity price hike involves new entrants, including Saudi Arabia in Ethiopia and South Korea in Madagascar (Deininger and Byerlee 2011; Kay and Franco 2012; The Oakland Institute 2012). The recent land grabbing episode is different from that of the colonial era in that it is occurring at a faster rate and most LSLAs are for food and bioenergy crop production. Furthermore, LSLAs are primarily characterized by long-term leases ranging from 30 to 50 years—and even up to 90 years in some cases (Kay and Franco 2012). Although Africa is the hotspot for the new land rush, the phenomenon is widespread across the globe (Saturnino and Franco 2011; Schoenberger et al. 2017).

The land rush for capitalist agro-industrial farming in the Global South is underpinned by the intractable problem of underdevelopment and the elusive search for a solution (Ayelazuno 2019). Growing concerns around the impact of climate change granted agro-industrial investors leverage to access more land. Investors posit a "win-win" solution, arguing that their interventions will lead to reductions in greenhouse emissions without compromising consumption and growth levels (Maconachie 2019). In the following sections, we explore LSLAs in the Sierra Leone context to assess the beneficiation, job creation, and economic development rhetoric of agro-industrial investors. Specifically, we evaluate whether these investments are truly transformative as promised or if they represent a threat to rural livelihoods.

Sierra Leone in Context

Sierra Leone is a West African country that gained independence from Britain in 1961. It has a monsoon climate, a rainy season from May to October, and a dry season from November–April. Although this type of climate is favourable for food crop production, the country is ranked 103 out of 117 countries on the 2019 Global Hunger Index (GHI) with a score of 30.4.[1] The United Nations Human Development Report ranked Sierra Leone 184 out of 188 countries, with a score of 0.42 (UNDP 2018a). Poverty remains widespread. Over 60% of the population lives below the US$1.25 per day poverty benchmark, life expectancy at birth is a mere 52 years, and the country has one of the highest infant mortality rates in the world (Phoenix et al. 2019).

Sierra Leone has an agrarian-based economy with more than 60% of its population dependent upon on small-scale farming for their food and other livelihood needs (UNDP 2018b). For rural households, land is both an economic and social asset. Almost half of the country's population is food insecure, meaning they have insufficient access to food in terms of quantity, quality, and diversity for a healthy life (Phoenix et al. 2019). The country is experiencing a slow recovery process from the civil war of the 1990s, which claimed an estimated 50,000 lives, displaced thousands of people, destroyed infrastructure, crippled the economy, undermined rural livelihoods, and caused untold human suffering (Gbanie et al. 2018; Maconachie 2019). Post-conflict recovery and development was further stalled by the 2014 West African Ebola outbreak and the 2017 landslide near Freetown, which claimed over 1000 lives.

The 1990s civil conflict, which ended in 2002, had a significant social and economic impact on the country. Approximately 70% of youths are underemployed in Sierra Leone (Danish Trade Council for International Development and Cooperation 2017). Successive governments identified foreign direct investment in large-scale agricultural production as a panacea to development challenges (Kay and Franco 2012). Amidst high unemployment levels and rising poverty, the agricultural sector was positioned as the key to job creation and economic growth (Maconachie and Binns 2007). Approximately 5.42 million ha of the country's land mass is cultivable but only 15% is currently under cultivation (Phoenix et al. 2019). As such, the call for foreign investment in the agricultural sector created a business environment favourable to the establishment of large-scale agro-industrial farms.

Traditional farming practices in Sierra Leone are rooted in slash-and-burn farming methods. Land parcels are cleared and crops such as cassava, rice, maize, groundnut, and sesame are cultivated for a year or two as either monoculture or mixed crop production; thereafter, the land is left

[1] Global Hunger Index 2019. https://www.globalhungerindex.org/results.html.

to fallow for five to seven years in order to regain fertility (Mann and Bonanomi 2017). This traditional farming system is dismissed by proponents of LSLAs as inefficient and unproductive; such discourses seek to justify their investment in 'idle' lands.

Land is a valuable economic, social, and cultural resource in many sub-Saharan African countries. In Sierra Leone, the bulk of LSLAs are directed towards upland, inland valley swamps, and boli-lands, which are of great importance to food crop production, especially rice. Since 2007, multinational companies have been granted access to thousands of hectares of productive land in Sierra Leone. It is uncertain whether households will see any benefits from these investments, despite the desire of the post-conflict government to create jobs in the rural areas.

Land Tenure and Lease Arrangement

Sierra Leone's dualistic land tenure system is a legacy of the British colony and protectorate administrations (Njoh and Akiwumi 2012; Renner-Thomas 2010; SLIEPA 2019; Unruh and Turray 2006). The Western Area of Sierra Leone is characterized by a freehold system, whereas the Provinces possess a communal and customary system of ownership that entrusts land administration to tribal authorities and chiefdom councils headed by Paramount Chiefs (Phoenix et al. 2019). This means that provincial Chiefs hold land in trust on behalf of the indigenous families who are the de facto owners of the land and have usufruct rights to its use (Hansen et al. 2016; Renner-Thomas 2010; Ryan 2018; The Oakland Institute 2012; Unruh and Turray 2006). In the provinces, land use rights for non-native people, including foreigners, are restricted to an initial period of 50 years. Leases can be renewed twice on a 21-year term each, as per the Province Land Act of 1961 (SLIEPA 2019; The Government of Sierra Leone 1927).

Communal and customary land ownership dictates that land is the property of extended families that can trace their lineage to indigenous ancestors. Customary land is inherited from one generation to another. Within this structure, land lease arrangements with foreign investors involve three principal actors: the landholding family, the chiefdom council headed by the Paramount Chief, and the land user (Hansen et al. 2016). Landholding families are usually represented by the head of the extended families and elders. The central government most often facilitates LSLAs, even though they are not formally involved in lease arrangements. The Cabinet of Sierra Leone announced a new policy in 2009 entitled, "Investment Policies and Incentives for Private Sector Promotion in Agriculture in Sierra Leone," which replaced the previous equal proportional payment sharing arrangement of lease rent among landowners (30%), the Chiefdom Council (30%), and the District Council (30%), in addition to the 10% allocated to the central government. Now, landowners, the Chiefdom Council, the District Council, and the central government receive 50%, 20%, 20%, and 10%, respectively (Baxter and Schaefter 2013; Ministry of Agriculture, Forestry, and Food Security 2009). Prior to the 2009 Cabinet policy, only a third of the lease rent was paid to families whose livelihoods were compromised by the leasing of fertile land to large-scale agricultural investors. The new land rent sharing agreement provides half of the lease rent to families directly affected by LSLAs. While the change in policy certainly benefits landholding families, there is still room for improvement. The allocation of 50% of the lease rent to groups not directly affected by LSLAs, namely the Chiefdom Council, the District Council, and the Government of Sierra Leone, creates room for compromise during the negotiation process.

Sierra Leone's Mega Agro-Industrial Land Deals at a Glance

Following the end of Sierra Leone's decade-long civil war, the post-conflict government sought to attract foreign direct investment to create jobs, increase exports, and thus grow its tax revenue base (Millar 2015). The country's agricultural sector is key to this post-conflict development strategy. The Sierra Leone Investment Promotion Act (2004), designed to attract foreign direct investment in the agricultural sector, prompted the establishment of the Sierra Leone Investment and Export Promotion Agency (SLIEPA) by an Act of Parliament in 2007. The SLIPEA receives support from both the World Bank and the European Union (Palliere and Cochet 2018; The Government of Sierra Leone 2007).

The SLIEPA encourages increased foreign direct investment in the agricultural sector by conveying Sierra Leone's availability of fertile lands, its cheap rents (US$12 per hectare/year), secure investment environment, a 60-month tax holiday, flexible laws, and cheap labour. The SLIEPA's call for foreign investors has been shared far and wide, including at international trade meetings such as the 2009 Sierra Leone Trade and Investment Forum in London which attracted several large agro-industrial investors

Table 7.1 Sierra Leone agro-investment firms

Agricultural Investment	Chiefdom and District
Socfin Agricultural Company	Malen Chiefdom, Pujehun District
Addax Bioenergy	Makere Gbanti Chiefdom, Bombali District
Sierra Leone Agriculture Limited	Bureh Kasseh Makonteh Chiefdom, Port Loko District

(Palliere and Cochet 2018; Phoenix et al. 2019). The Oakland Institute (2012) estimates that 500,000 ha of concessions or contracted land was turned over for agro-industrial production in 2012. Some major agro-investment firms in Sierra Leone are listed below in Table 7.1.

Two districts, Port Loko and Pujehun, are particularly affected by the growth in long-term agricultural land lease agreements. Some 40% of the total land area of Port Loko, accounting for 231,326 ha in seven of the 11 chiefdoms, has been leased. For Pujehun, 61.15% of the district land area (246,923 ha) in eight of the 12 districts has been leased (Baxter and Schaefter 2013) (Fig. 7.1). The SOCFIN Agricultural Company (SAC)'s land deal was unique in a number of ways in comparison to other LSLAs arrangements across the country. As of December 2017, the agreement involved a cumulative lease area of 18,473 ha and was between two levels: (1) a "head lease" between landholding families and the former Ministry of Agriculture, Forestry, and Food Security (renamed the Ministry of Agriculture and Forestry) and (2) a sub-lease between the same Ministry and SAC (Phoenix et al. 2019).

The involvement of the Ministry of Agriculture and Forestry in the negotiation of such a large land acquisition did not go without criticism, especially in a district with the highest incidence of poverty and a chiefdom that is socially and economically reliant on its agricultural activities. The land deal was denounced as illegitimate by local community members who stated that the process lacked consultation and transparency. Community members alleged that they faced pressure and intimidation from the chiefdom authorities, including the Paramount Chief, among others. This coercion resulted in the creation of the Malen Affected Land Owners and Land Users Association (MALAO) (The Oakland Institute 2012). Community concerns surrounding the risk of increased impoverishment and food insecurity following the ceding of

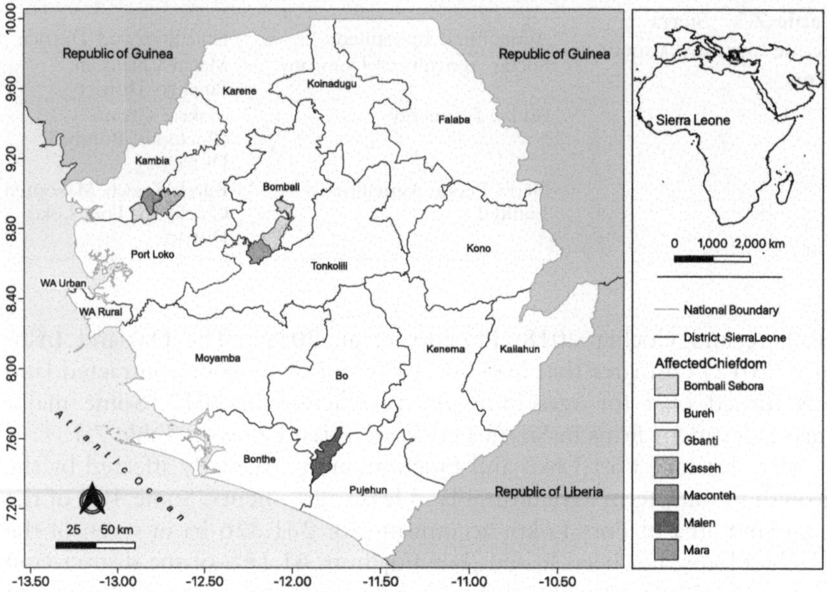

Fig. 7.1 Map of Sierra Leone

such a large track of land and for such a long period of time attracted the attention of national and international civil society organizations, including Green Scenery, the Oakland Institute, FIAN Belgium, and Welthungerhilfe (Phoenix et al. 2019). SAC managed to obtain a 50-year lease for an initial 6500 ha (which later increased to 18,743 ha in 2017) with the possibility of two 25-year extensions, an arrangement which supersedes the 25-year renewal option specified by the statute (Pheonix et al. 2019).

Findings and Discussions

As discussed earlier, LSLA proponents employ a job creation and economic development 'mantra' that permits them to access land in developing countries. National governments collude with such proponents in characterizing their lands as productive and abundant but empty and underutilized (Yengoh and Armah 2016). Statistics from the literature suggest that Addax Bioenergy possesses a concession between 40,000 and 57,000 ha of pristine agricultural land in the Bombali and Tonkolili Districts in the Northern Province of Sierra Leone, for the cultivation of sugar cane and bio-ethanol, respectively. Addax Bioenergy plans to both export biofuel and allocate it to the national grid as "green" electricity (Maconachie 2019; Mann and Bonanomi 2017; Millar 2015). Addax Bioenergy leased these land areas for an initial 50-year period with possibility of extension on two renewable 21-year periods (Maconachie 2019; Millar 2015).

The Environmental Health and Social Impact Assessment (EHSIA) reports conducted by the various large-scale agricultural investors in Sierra Leone, including Addax Bioenergy and SAC, are replete with futuristic assumptions about the benefits of LSLAs—usually based on the premise that land is currently underutilized as propagated by SLIEPA. Official employment statistics from LSLA investors are few and far between, and those that are available vary in credibility depending on the source of the data. For instance, the Memorandum of Understanding (MoU) between Addax Bioenergy and the affected landholding families states that some 3000 individuals will be employed by the company in the first phase of operations (2010–2013) and an additional 1000 individuals in the second (2013–2015) (Palliere and Cochet 2018). Addax Bioenergy's official website, however, only records approximately 2000 direct jobs. Meanwhile, the EHSIA promises an estimated 2200 permanent positions and 2500 locally recruited seasonal workers (Ryan 2018). SAC, on the other hand, promised 2414 jobs by 2020 in its MoU with landholding families, and claimed to have provided 3583 jobs in the Malen Chiefdom by 2017 (Phoenix et al. 2019). Apart from the promise of local job creation in the operational areas of these companies, the MoUs contain clauses that have later been viewed as anti-progressive, especially for the communities where these agricultural investments are established. For instance, Addax Bioenergy is exempted from any amendments to the law that are considered to adversely effect its operations (Millar 2015). The company will not comply with amendments—even when geared towards revenue mobilization—so long as the relevant changes are assumed to be contrary to the interests of its investors. Moreover, the two MoUs lock landholding communities in the lease agreement for a potential 50 + years.

Further, there is no particularization as to the types of jobs created by large-scale agricultural investments. The available literature suggests that most jobs are seasonal and low paid (Maconachie 2019; Hansen et al. 2016). SAC's MoU is vague about what constitutes a "direct job."

For instance, an estimated 32,842 people are considered to be directly and indirectly affected by SAC operations in the Malen Chiefdom; yet, only 1178 permanent jobs have been created and very few local people hold management or supervisory positions (Phoenix et al. 2019). Recent research by Maconachie (2019) documents the disappointment of those living in the Addax Bioenergy project area who are not satisfied with remuneration received for their labour. If local people are dispossessed of their livelihoods through LSLAs, adequate compensation or remuneration through labour should be provided. Sierra Leone's 2019 Financial Budget increased the minimum monthly wage from 500,000 Leones (US$50) to 600,000 Leones (US$60). However, the average salary of SAC's casual seasonal workers is between 150,000 and 250,000 Leones (Phoenix et al. 2019), making a mockery of wage regulations and the ability of the Sierra Leonean government to uphold the law.

According to Addax Bioenergy estimates, the creation of 2000 jobs will inject US$3.5 million into the local economy each year. This figure is by no means insignificant, but questions remain: what type of jobs are being offered, for what salary, and for how long? This last question is particularly important since farming operations stop during the rainy season. How will families met their livelihood needs during this period if they can no longer cultivate land for subsistence purposes? It is common for workers to be laid off, particularly in non-productive periods, which is perhaps unsurprising given that SLIEPA explicitly promotes Sierra Leone's flexible labour laws. The practice of laying off workers during non-productive times undoubtedly creates suffering for unemployed casual labourers who have been deprived of the land that they previously relied on for decades. These issues are relevant beyond the Sierra Leonean context. The inability of African governments to generate adequate employment opportunities and fufill livelihood needs is particularly dire in a continent where 7–10 million young people enter the labour force each year; this situation coerces a disproportionate amount of rural youth to migrate to urban areas (Turok 2012; Thornton and Rogerson 2013, 1).

Addax Bioenergy and SAC, like many other LSLA investors doing deals in developing countries in sub-Sahara Africa, Asia and beyond, insisted that their projects would benefit locals through direct employment, new infrastructure, and the provision of social services. These promises resonated with local people in affected project areas, as men and women of all ages dreamed of transformative opportunities for their communities (Maconachie 2019). However, the investigations of academics, global anti-land grabbing campaigners such as the Oakland Institute, and national civil society organizations such as Green Scenery reveal the negative impacts of LSLAs on local communities and ecosystems alike. A huge gap exists between the promises of multinational agro-industrial companies, contained in their ESHIAs, corporate social responsibility literature and elsewhere, and actual outcomes on the ground.

An EHIA study conducted by Addax Bioenergy in 2009 proposed a Smallholder and Out Grower (SHOG) scheme in the Makeni project area aimed at developing farmer-managed food, sugarcane, sorghum, and cassava production (Coastal & Environmental Services, 2009). Addax Bioenergy also promised a Farmer Development Programme aimed at training some 2000 individuals in modern farming techniques. The company allocated 2000 ha of land for the cultivation of local food, including rice and cassava (Maconachie 2019). Like Addax Bioenergy, SAC proposed a SHOG scheme between 2014 and 2025 with a budget of US$7,824,000 (Phoenix et al. 2019). The SHOG would theoretically enable landholding families affected by oil palm plantations to produce and sell palm fruits to SAC. Although the SHOG looked good on paper, SAC did not meet its commitments. Under its cooperate social responsibility programme, US$2,608,000 was expected to have been invested by 2017. However, the 2015 Social Due Diligence Assessment Study concluded that there was no SHOG scheme in SAC's operational areas. SAC also proposed a US$16,433,375 budget line for the benefit of 32,000 people from 52 villages in its concessional areas between 2011 and 2017. A study by Phoenix et al. (2019) shows that only 16% (US$2,583,784) of the planned budget has been spent. Debates about where and how individuals and communities affected by agro-industrial projects can gain access to farmland for food crop production persist.

Despite statutory requirements for all large-scale agricultural investors to undertake an ESHIA and execute an environmental management plan, these studies fail to provide accurate cost–benefit analyses and do not adequately account for the losses experienced by community when landholding families sign away their land to foreign firms for at least five decades. The agrobiodiversity values of rural farmlands areas are of significant importance to the local communities. Individuals and families benefit from genetically rich plants, fish proteins, bush meat, and water resources. LSLA proponents and the Sierra Leonean government, however, do not fully appreciate or understand the value of agrobiodiversity and biodiverse resources to rural communities who depend on farmlands, bush meat, domestic livestock, and a wealth of genetically rich plants.

The tenure and lease payment arrangement under which land deals have been signed in Sierra Leone is a cause of concern. To reiterate, land rents are divided as such: 50% to the landholding family, 20% to the District Council, 20% to the Chiefdom Council, and 10% to the central government. Families whose farmlands are leased for large-scale agro-industrial projects should arguably receive a disproportionate percentage of the rent payments, given the widespread impoverishment of rural communities, and especially considering that land is held in trust by the Paramount Chief who already has a 20% interest in such deals. Theoretically, Chiefs can manipulate land deals to maximize their own share of the rent. For instance, MALAO considers the Paramount Chief of the Malen Chiefdom as the "King Pin" in the deal between SAC and the Government of Sierra Leone, with land owners left in the dust (Baxter and Schaefter 2013; Phoenix et al. 2019; Ryan 2018).

Conspicuously absent in the LSLA memoranda discussed above is the possibility to re-negotiate land rents over the duration of the lease period. Given that land as a factor of production appreciates with time, it is absolutely necessary for prolonged land lease agreements to contain a re-negotiation clause at specific intervals. Such a clause will properly account for the increase in land value over time. The issue of payment for permanent crops is another issue seemingly absent in the memoranda and the relevant legislation. While evaluations are undertaken regarding the commercial value of permanent crops, these evaluations do not consider the commercial value of permanent crops over time, that is, the entire lifespan of cultivation. In rural Sierra Leone, farm families cultivate crops over a number of years, but only receive restitution for one-time harvests. This oversight is perhaps one reason why farm-dependent families remain impoverished.

Conclusion

LSLAs across Sierra Leone are facilitated by the central government through the SLIEPA. Agro-industrial investors interact with customary land laws which state that land cannot be sold to non-indigenes but instead must be leased for an initial 50-year period, at a payment of US$12 per ha/year, with the possibility of two lease extensions at 21-years each. This attractive arrangement has resulted in over 500,000 ha of land leased, in many cases for nearly 100 years. Rural communities now rely on lease rents rather than their farmlands to provide the basic necessities for their families.

While LSLA investors promised jobs to the local communities and the chance to improve their livelihoods, evidence suggests that few of these promises have been upheld. Farm families who previously depended on their land for subsistence have become seasonal workers and are paid wages below the country's minimum requirement. In other words, rural people have very little to show for the relinquishment of their land to LSLA investors. Lease payment arrangements do not adequately compensate for rural families' loss of land. Meanwhile, groups not directly affected by LSLA land deals, such as the Chiefdom Council and the District Council, receive a disproportionate share of land rents. Both agribusiness and government alike have fallen well-short of their purported pro-poor development objectives.

The outcomes of large-scale investments in Sierra Leone's agricultural sector provide a window into the broader landscape of land grabbing across Africa. For the most part, the continued duality and informality of African land tenure systems, between customary and state regimes, benefits governments and foreign investors to the detriment of rural and indigenous peoples.

References

Ayelazuno, Jasper Abembia. 2019. Land governance for extractivism and capitalist farming in Africa: An overview. *Land Use Policy* 81: 843–851.

Baxter, Joan, and Schaefter, Elke. 2013. Who is benefitting? The social and economic impact of three large-scale land investments in Sierra Leone: A cost-benefit analysis. *Report for the Action for Large-Scale Land Acquisition Transparency*. https://curtisresearch.org/wp-content/uploads/who-is-benefitting-Sierra-Leone-report1.pdf. Accessed 12 May 2020.

Borras, Saturnino (Jr.), and Jennifer Franco. (2011). Political dynamics of land-grabbing in Southeast Asia. *Amsterdam: Transnational Institute*.

Coastal & Environmental Services. 2009. (Sugar cane to ethanol project, Sierra Leone, Project Description). Grahamstown.

Cotula, Lorenzo. 2013. The international political economy of the global land rush: A critical appraisal of trends, scale, geography and drivers. In *The new enclosures: Critical perspectives on corporate land deals*, edited by Ben White, Saturnino Borras Jr., Ruth Hall, Ian Scoones, and Wendy Woldford, 43–74. Routledge.

Danish Trade Council for International Development and Cooperation. 2017. *Labour market profile Sierra Leone*. Danish Trade Council for International Development and Cooperation.

Deininger, Klaus, and Derek Byerlee. 2011. *Rising global interest in farmland: can it yield sustainable and equitable benefits?* The World Bank.

Fairhead, James, Melissa Leach, and Ian Scoones. 2012. Green grabbing: A new appropriation of nature? *Journal of Peasant Studies* 39 (2): 237–261.

Gbanie, Solomon Peter, Amy L. Griffin, and Alec Thornton. 2018. Impacts on the urban environment: Land cover change trajectories and landscape fragmentation in post-war Western Area, Sierra Leone. *Remote Sensing* 10 (1): 129.

Hansen, Marc, Mohamed Conteh, Martina Shakya, and Wilhelm Löwenstein. 2016. *Determining minimum compensation for lost farmland: A theory-based impact evaluation of a land grab in Sierra Leone*. Working paper 211, Ruhr University Bochum, Institute of Development Research and Development Policy.

Kay, Silvia, and Jennifer Franco. 2012. *The global water grab: A primer*. Transnational Institute for Hands off the Land Alliance.

Li, Tania Murray. 2011. Centering labor in the land grab debate. *The Journal of Peasant Studies* 38 (2): 281–298.

Maconachie, Roy. 2019. Green grabs and rural development: How sustainable is biofuel production in post-war Sierra Leone? *Land Use Policy* 81: 871–877.

Maconachie, Roy, and Tony Binns. 2007. Farming miners' or 'mining farmers'? Diamond mining and rural development in post-conflict Sierra Leone. *Journal of Rural Studies* 23 (3): 367–380.

Mann, Stefan, and Elisabeth Bürgi Bonanomi. 2017. Grabbing or investment? On judging large-scale land acquisitions. *Agriculture and Human Values* 34 (1): 41–51.

Millar, Gearoid. 2015. We have no voice for that": Land rights, power, and gender in rural Sierra Leone. *Journal of Human Rights* 14 (4): 445–462.

Ministry of Agriculture, Forestry and Food Security. 2009. *Investment policies and incentives for private sector promotion in agriculture in Sierra Leone in 2009*.

Njoh, Ambe J., and Fenda Akiwumi. 2012. Colonial legacies, land policies and the millennium development goal: Lessons from Cameroon and Sierra Leone. *Habitat International* 36 (2): 210–218.

Palliere, Agustin, and Hubert Cochet. 2018. Large private agricultural projects and job creation: From discourse to reality. Case study in Sella Limba, Sierra Leone. *Land Use Policy* 76: 422–431.

Phoenix, Michael, Florence Kroff, and Manuel Eggen. 2019. *Land Grabbing for palm oil in Sierra Leone: Analysis of the SOCFIN case from a human right perspective*. FIAN Belgium.

Renner-Thomas, Ade. 2010. *Land tenure in Sierra Leone: The law, dualism and the making of a land policy*. Author House.

Ryan, Caitlin. 2018. Large-scale land deals in Sierra Leone at the intersection of gender and lineage. *Third World Quarterly* 39 (1): 189–206.

Schoenberger, L., D. Hall, and P. Vandergeest. 2017. What happened when the land grab came to Southeast Asia? *The Journal of Peasant Studies* 44 (4): 697–725.

SLIEPA. 2019. *Sierra Leone: An investor's guide a private sector perspective on the investment landscape*. SLIEPA. http://sliepa.org/wp-content/uploads/3380O_Sierra-Leone-Investment-Guide_d8_print.pdf. Accessed 25 November 2019.

The Government of Sierra Leone. 1927. The provinces land act: Chapter 122.

The Government of Sierra Leone. 2007. The Sierra Leone investment and export Promotion agency act.

The Oakland Institute. 2012. *Understanding land investment Deals in Africa Sierra Leone*.

Thornton, Alec, and Christian Rogerson. 2013. African cities and the millennium development goals: A case for applied geography. *Applied Geography* 36: 1–2.

Turok, Ivan. 2012. *Unleashing the economic potential for African cities*. Report prepared for the UN Habitat Workshop, Cape Town, South Africa 23–24 February..

UNDP. 2018a. *Sierra Leone multidimensional poverty index 2019:* https://www.statistics.sl/images/Sierra_Leone_MPI_2019.pdf. Accessed 11 May 2020.

UNDP. 2018b. *Human development indices and indicators: 2018 statistical update*. United Nations Development Programme New York.

Unruh, Jon D., and Harry Turray. 2006. *Land tenure, food security and investment in postwar Sierra Leone*. Working Paper 22, FAO.

Weeks, S. B., & Bah, S. 2017. *Sierra Leone 2015 Population and Housing Census; Thematic report on population structure and population distribution*.

Yengoh, Genesis Tambang, and Frederick Ato Armah. 2016. Land access constraints for communities affected by large-scale land acquisition in Southern Sierra Leone. *GeoJournal* 81: 103–122. https://doi.org/10.1007/s10708-014-9606-2.

CHAPTER 8

The Politics of "Land Grabs" and Development Contradictions in Zimbabwe: The Case of the Chisumbanje Ethanol Project

Prosper B. Matondi and Blair Rutherford

Introduction

The dramatic and politicized land reform in Zimbabwe, wherein the state forcibly redistributed the vast majority of white-owned farms to black smallholder farmers in 2000, is a momentous event in this southern African country and a unique case in the global "land grab" debate (Moyo 2001; Scoones et al. 2010; Matondi 2012). This turbulent context continues to inform understandings of and response to "land grabs" in the country. The Zimbabwean government's Fast Track Land Reform Programme (FTLRP) is rooted in a long history of struggles for land that

P. B. Matondi (✉)
Ruzivo Trust, Harare, Zimbabwe

B. Rutherford
Carleton University, Ottawa, ON, Canada

L. Cochrane and N. Andrews (eds.), *The Transnational Land Rush in Africa*, International Political Economy Series,
https://doi.org/10.1007/978-3-030-60789-0_8

stretches back the 1800s. The period of legally enforced displacement by the Rhodesian colonial government between 1900 and 1950 is of particular import. Zimbabwe gained independence in 1980 and embarked on a modest land resettlement effort focused on re-distributing land to black resettlement farmers (Moyo 1995; Moore 2005; Alexander 2007). By 1997, an estimated 3.6 million hectares (ha) of land out of the 15 million hectares previously owned by white farmers was redistributed.

The FTLRP severely exacerbated longstanding economic problems in Zimbabwe. The contribution of the agricultural sector to the economy declined across the board. Overall maize production declined from 2.6 million metric tonnes in 1996 to 2.1 million metric tonnes in 2000 and reached as low as 495,000 metric tonnes in 2008 (Matondi 2012). Sugar production fell from a peak of 583,000 metric tonnes in 2000 to as low as 259,000 metric tonnes in 2010. Livestock, cotton, and other commodities are characterized by a similar story of decline. The diversity that previously existed in the agricultural sector dramatically shrunk.

The net effect of the economic decline following the implementation of the FTLRP is mired in contradictions. Many people lost formal employment on large-scale farms (Waeterloos and Rutherford 2004), yet perhaps an equal number "re-populated" the agricultural sector. At the start of 2000, the agriculture sector held about 1 million farmers, of which 4,500 were white large-scale farmers, 8,000 small-scale commercial farmers, and an estimated 76,000 farmers in old resettlement areas. The sector radically changed thereafter, with an additional 200,000 new farmers directly displacing 4,500 large-scale commercial farmers. Despite the increase in the number of smallholders, food security crops (particularly maize, wheat, and other small grains) declined in production and poverty levels rose. The government sought to tackle these economic and social problems with new forms of investment in agriculture, particularly public–private partnerships. The ethanol production sector was one key area where domestic investors showed interest, and Green Fuel, a private company, formed to operationalize the Chisumbanje ethanol production project.

Apart from government investment in agriculture, the Chisumbanje ethanol project in the Eastern Highlands of Zimbabwe is the largest investment in agriculture by the private sector (to the tune of $US300 million), largely driven by a Zimbabwean businessman, Billy Rautenbach. Whereas there was capital and donor flight from any state land and commercial farms under FTLRP, the Green Fuel and associated financial companies (e.g. Macdom Investments and Ratings Investments) took the risk of investing in agriculture in communal areas (postcolonial name for the colonial native reserves) upon "invitation" from the state and in agreement with representatives of local communities. There was, however, intense resistance to the large-scale land takeover by the company, as rights to ownership were unclear between the community and the government. The government administration in charge of managing the land was the Agricultural and Rural Development Authority (ARDA), a parastatal body that is involved in large-scale commercial production. The parastatal is modelled as a producer and offtaker of agricultural commodities, namely through outgrower land contracting arrangements. It retained ownership rights in the communal areas and "leased" land to communities because it had no "present interest" to produce in the 1960s, when it was first established. The communities, however, felt they were the rightful owners of the land, as the "first to occupy," over the government parastatal. This contention has been the main sight of struggle in the last 8–10 years (Fig. 8.1).

Existing studies view the Chisumbanje project as characteristic of a "land grab" (see Scoones et al. 2010, 138; Hall 2011; Zamchiya 2011; Mutopo and Chiweshe 2012). Some studies have focus on the political connections of Rautenbach, devoid of analysis of what the investment and its impacts might mean in the broader political economy of Zimbabwe (Mujere and Dombo 2011).[1] We argue that such studies fail to situate the Chisumbanje ethanol project in its proper context historically, materially, and politically. The "land grab" discourse was rapidly appropriated in the Zimbabwean context following the flux of foreign investors seeking to buy or lease land in the Global South for speculation, food production, tourism enclaves, mining claims, etc. (Matondi et al. 2011; Hall 2011; Cotula 2013). Many scholars fell into a similar trap of taking line, hook, and sinker of the popular media's view, without analytical rigour (Kaag and Zoomers 2014). Existing studies and reports do not accurately assess whether the companies involved in the Chisumbanje project are truly "international." In this chapter, we present detailed research findings on

[1] Perhaps it is only Zamchiya (2011, 2013), who has done serious grounded field work in the area, though more could be done by looking at the site struggles from a national lens, where he speaks to a variety of actors who are engaged politically in this project. Otherwise the rest of the writers its hearsay, political undertones derived from the media than serious scientific research work.

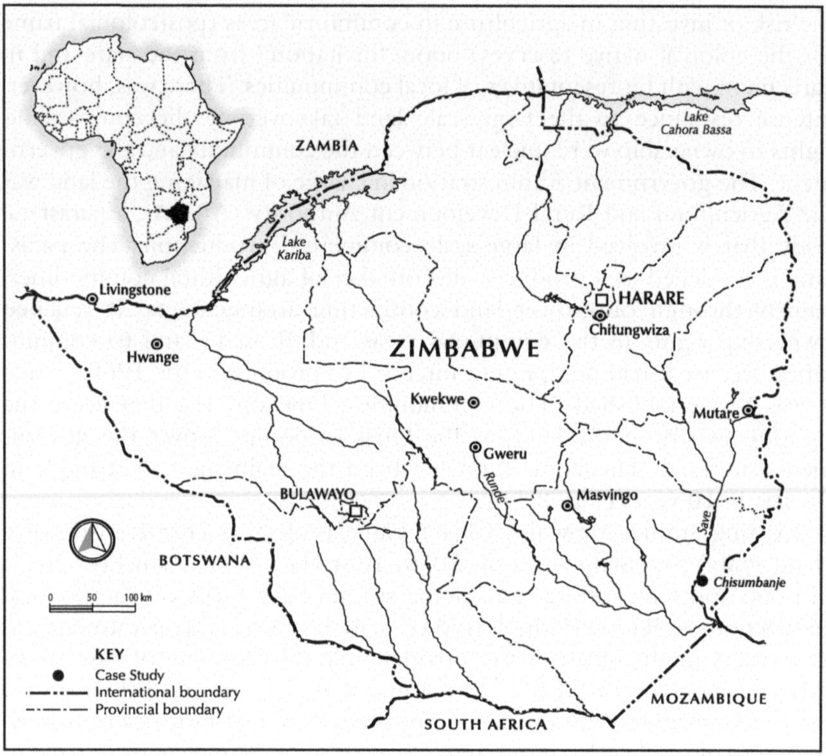

Fig. 8.1 Map of Study site in Chipinge District, Manicaland, Zimbabwe (*Source* Ruzivo Trust cartography (2015)

land "ownership" and use, and determine that the lease arrangements underpinning the project are largely state-owned.

Ruzivo Trust Land Investment Research conducted field research between 2013 and 2015 in Chisumbanje in collaboration with the Programme for Land and Agrarian Studies (PLAAS) at the University of Western Cape in South Africa. This three-year research programme put the theoretical definitions of a "land grab" to test within Zimbabwe's context. Several months of fieldwork in the three years of study in the Chipinge district of south-eastern Zimbabwe elicited a more nuanced understanding of this "land grab." Fieldwork entailed a variety of tools that included: a quantitative survey of 120 smallholder farmers in Chisumbanje and 60 in Chinyamukwakwa; a business enterprise survey (10 respondents); 5 focus group discussions; 4 key informant interviews; and informal meetings with key actors in the district and bio-ethanol project production site. The team also conducted an extensive literature of materials from Green Fuel website, various media resources, and working papers.

This chapter provides a snapshot of a larger research project which focuses on the impact of domestic and international large-scale investments in agriculture on livelihoods. We begin this chapter by situating the Chisumbanje project within the wider political economy of state investments in land in a specific region of Zimbabwe. Next, we examine the overlapping institutions and players involved in land governance that shaped both the investment and the diverse responses to the project. Finally, We analyse some of the socioeconomic consequences of the Chisumbanje project thus far.

Context and Scope

In 2008, the Chisumbanje bio-ethanol project leased land from ARDA for sugarcane planting, the main feedstock for ethanol production. Over 9,000 ha was leased from ARDA through a public–private partnership. The government classified the deal as a national project and thus the state possessed sole production rights to sugarcane for ethanol, in addition to the mandatory blending of imported petrol with ethanol. However, from the very beginning stages of the ethanol project, the communities raised the issue of land ownership and their historical disagreements and negotiations with the ARDA. The bio-ethanol project encroached on customary land where people settled some 50 years ago. Moreover, the transactions involving the land purchase and/or lease agreements were highly opaque and few details have been made public. The Chisumbanje ethanol project captured the imaginations of the Zimbabwean people and drew the citizenry into dialogue on land governance, particularly the meaning of land ownership in the context of the FTLRP. Underpinning this intense dialogue was the broader development goals of the country, where people's livelihoods were jeopardized by a "state-owned" project. Communities believe that they have ultimate ownership to the land and resources of Chipinge, and that any state-driven project must balance economic growth objectives and human well-being.

The land for the Chisumbanje project is formally "owned" by the government which provides usufruct rights to the land users. Both the pre-existing local communities and the partners in the new investment possess the right to cultivate land based on the lease arrangement. However, the usufruct rights in the communal area, defined by the Presidential Trusteeship clause of the Communal Lands Act (1982), provide local communities with "qualified rights" to the land. Community members used and improved the land over a long period of time and developed social and cultural ties to specific places, a situation which creates major obstacles to investment in the current context.

The legal uncertainty between usufruct rights and the state's sovereignty over land is compounded in Chisumbanje by the fact that people live on the land "owned" by the ARDA. The traditional leaders are wary of the conditions of the land lease given the government's apparent lack of interest in the development of their communities. The ethanol project altered understandings of the land ownership where communities assumed their rights were protected and legally guaranteed. The ARDA, armed with an investor and the authority and economic ambitions of the central government, prioritized private financial interests in the production of sugarcane for ethanol production over local rights. Any investment, be it government or private sector, must proceed carefully in Zimbabwe given the socio-cultural meaning of "land rights" and the practices of communities for generations. Large-scale land investments primarily affected smallholder farmers with pre-existing forms of farming. The existing user rights, include a variety of crop production and livestock grazing lands. The forests, constituted an important ecosystem for the gathering of wood, fruits, medicinal plants, and related natural resources products. These resources often constituted a critical source of economic livelihood, especially for women, who are often disproportionately affected by land takeovers given the dominance of patriarchy in Zimbabwe's social cultures and power relations between men and women.

The investment in the Chisumbanje ethanol project continues and has remained largely immune from the wider challenges facing the country, namely rising poverty and unemployment levels. This context, however, compounds the concerns and sensitivities of communities when land is targeted for investment given the potential of displacement without clear compensation policies. They risk losing both their livelihoods and historical identity.

The Chisumbanje ethanol project was formulated at a time when the country was in a deep economic and energy crisis (Matondi et al. 2011). When the project gained traction in Chipinge around 2008, the potential "multiplier effects" in the areas directly impacted by the project became apparent. Further, the demand for ethanol to make hand sanitizers in the context of the COVID19 pandemic provides the company additional business opportunities. However, the expected spin-off benefits for local communities in terms of reach, quality, and equality remains a key area for future investigation.

The Chisumbanje project is designed to make healthy profit for private investors while also meeting state objectives to reduce fuel import bills and create local and national employment. These objectives differed fundamentally from the Rhodesian colonial government. For example, the Chisumbanje Experimental Station, an irrigation project that began in 1965, aimed to provide Zimbabweans with a minimum level of agricultural development in the hopes of quelling growing protests against colonial land thefts (injustices that ultimately fuelled the liberation struggle against the white minority regime). Colonial officials often negotiated with a traditional chief for land, but most often usurped land from communities without negotiation (Kelly 1973).

At independence in 1980, ARDA took over much of the land acquired by the colonial regime. In the early 2000s, as FTLRP was being enforced, ARDA invited Macdom and Ratings under the Zimbabwe Bio-Energy Company to invest in sugarcane production for ethanol (Matondi et al. 2011). The company moved into Chisumbanje in 2008 and commenced production of sugarcane, relying on the ARDA's estates and an outgrower scheme, as well as an ethanol processing plant. This project began at a time when an inclusive government formed between the Zimbabwe African National Union Party–Patriotic Front (ZANU–PF) and the two Movement for Democratic Change (MDC) parties, forced by international mediation after the contested and violent 2008 election. A brick wall emerged as the new transition government refused to force blending of fuel purportedly to promote one company.

While the national politics over blending was being played out, Green Fuel continued to invest in a US$300 million plant, the largest investment in Zimbabwe's agriculture sector since 2000. The rights of local communities were supplanted by a perceived need for economic growth as per the government's stated national priorities. Establishing who owned what land was a dramatic political exercise at both the local and national levels, leading to media and scholarly interest in the project.

The land for the Chisumbanje project, belonging to the ARDA through a lease agreement with the Chipinge Rural District Council (RDC), was accessed by Green Fuel through two separate twenty-year Build, Operate, and Transfer agreements, which later morphed into a joint venture between the two private agricultural companies: Macdom Investments (operating at Chisumbanje) and Rating Investments (operating at Middle Sabi). The ARDA invested US$36.7 million of state funds into land and immovable assets. Macdom Investments holds a 90% stake in Green Fuel while the Zimbabwean government holds a 10% stake. The total investment into Green Fuel is US$350 million.

The Chisumbanje Ethanol Project consists of 6500 ha of sugarcane plantations in Chisumbanje (with a potential of 45,000 ha) managed by Macdom Investments and 3,500 in Middle Sabi (with a potential of 10,000 ha) managed by Ratings Investments. The Ethanol processing plant is located in Chisumbanje. In 2015, the mill employed about 300 people on a permanent basis, while approximately 2000 were part-time workers invited on a seasonal basis. Overall, there is a total of 55,000 ha allocated for potential sugar cane plantations, with 10% (5,500 ha) reserved for community development projects in either sugarcane production or horticulture depending on local preferences. However, much of the plantation land is already under communal usage, creating completing claims to land ownership and governance. The general manager of the project is reportedly claimed that the land in question was identified in the 1960s for commercial purposes: "They (villagers) have been using council land to do their own cropping. They don't have land anywhere here and that's why we will give them 10% (4000 ha) irrigated land so that they will be able to sustain themselves."[2] This seems to imply that the total land area (65,000 ha) was always designated for a grand project like Green Fuel's Ethanol proposal.

In addition, as part of the project's design, over 2,000 ha of flood irrigation was developed for 4,000 smallholders. Some 176 small-scale farmers benefitted in Chisumbanje and 388 in Chinyamukwakwa. In

[2] Both the private (*Newsday*) and public (*The Herald*) media had the same caption and captured the same issues in their reports: https://www.newsday.co.zw/2011/07/04/2011-07-04-villagers-dispute-ethanol-project-land/; http://www.herald.co.zw/villagers-cry-foul-over-green-fuel/.

2014, a further 50 ha of land was developed for the Chinyamukwakwa community. The irrigation schemes are managed by the Irrigation Block Committee formed by the farmers themselves, with the assistance of a manager and irrigation supervisor from Green Fuels, the ARDA, and Agritex officers (a state agency for the provision of agricultural extension services). Pumping units and waterways for 18 schemes were refurbished at the Middle Sabi site, covering 1,863 ha and divided into small plots for 2,681 small-scale farmers in July 2014. Development projects aside, this complex, large-scale investment converted a large stretch of land to sugar production in the "national interest," with no emphasis of food crops for local communities. The project generated significant conflict as areas designated for cultivation were already populated with people dependent on agriculture for their livelihoods (i.e. crop and livestock production).

The major limitations of the Chisumbaje ethanol project are the efficiency of the conversion process (or lack thereof) and the availability of suitable land and water resources for biofuel production (White et al. 2012). The Save River in Zimbabwe shows decreasing levels of water availability, which has been happening for many decades. The Save River is experiencing multiple stressors not only from Green Fuel, but from local people who rely on its water for domestic chores, bathing, fishing, irrigation, and other ecosystem services such as reeds used in the basket-making industry. The possibility of water-related conflicts is thus substantial.

In addition to growing competition for land and water resources, other potential challenges that will need to be addressed as more land is cleared and used for sugarcane production include aquifer depletion, soil erosion, and the loss of biologically diverse ecosystems relied upon by local communities. In the case of Chisumbanje, field surveys show that local communities produce a range of commodities on land in a complementary fashion, an equilibrium threatened by monoculture production.

Land ownership disputes between the ARDA and local communities are at the centre of the conflict in Chisumbanje, with the latter claiming that their lands were unjustly taken. Green Fuel is enmeshed in this controversy since they are the primary users of the land leased from the ARDA (which originally leased the land from the Chipinge RDC). The existing tenure system in the area is "communal," which means there are a range of differing authorities. Communities claim that they have cultivated the land for a long period of time and thus assert ownership over the disputed. They also claim to have co-existed with the ARDA long before Green Fuel entered Chisumbanje.

Governance Entanglements

There are numerous governance gaps and complications arising in Chisumbanje. The ethanol project is an illustrative case of the range of official and unofficial stakeholders involved in land governance in Zimbabwe, as discussed below.

Land investment policy guidelines in Zimbabwe were developed by multilateral agencies like the World Bank and the African Union through discussions at the global level. The Land Policy Initiative, a joint programme between the African Union, the African Development Bank, and the United Nations Economic Commission for Africa, involves "testing" and implementing the instruments devised to promote processes of development. These policy instruments "from above" have not been taken on board at the national and regional levels; in many cases, there are no sector-specific guidelines for governments and investors alike.

Biofuels investments require expansive pieces of land for good economic returns. As seen in the case of Chisumbanje, the economic model requires at least 45,000 ha of land for sugarcane production, whereas an additional 10,000 ha is required in Middle Sabi. Without a land policy to guide the investors, Zimbabwe relied on the FTLRP as a programme to direct management decisions. The company had little to no other options than to use the ARDA estates, despite local communities' pre-existing use of the designated land. No homes were built on the land since the ARDA informed traditional leaders that it could repossess the land at any time in the future, however, community members still use the land and its resources for subsistence. This is politically volatile situation perhaps could have been avoided if there had been a clear land policy at the time.

Given the policy gaps and the weakness of the inclusive government, the investors relied on support from local communities to get the project started. At the same time, they also experienced resistance from local stakeholders; some Non-Governmental Organizations (NGOs) such as the Platform for Youth Development complained about issues of displacement, inadequate employment, and environmental pollution. The ARDA signed an leasing agreement with Green Fuel with the expectation that the government agency would clarify land ownership issues. However, this has not fully happened, leaving the Green Fuel to defend the project amidst the failings of the state.

Communities allege that the company has not provided clarity on questions of beneficiation. For example, it was questioned how the community benefits if the company continues to operate only on ARDA (5,112 hectares), because for the project to reach optimal levels it requires no less than 45,000 ha. The ARDA land can sustain 10% of the blending process, which means that no matter the niceties conveyed in the negotiations, the community land is under threat. Communities are asking Green Fuel where they will get this land because if the company expands it will have to absorb 6 wards of south Chipinge that are heavily populated.

Green Fuels informed community members that it would receive 45,000 ha for its project so that Zimbabwe could rely exclusively on a domestic fuel source (as opposed to importing fuels). There are understandable economic and security rationales for this project, however, the people of Zimbabwe's Manicaland Province are adversely affected without recourse. The company has offered alternative land to communities, specifically 0.5 ha per household under irrigation schemes along the Save River. The details of this arrangement, and its projected economic benefits, have not been fully explained. Communities may find that they lose more in the process, which is why local people are pushing for their land rights to be defined and recorded amidst company–community negotiations. There are multiple battle fronts, and although there is a significant amount of political will propping the project up, local discontent is abound.

There is also overlap within the government, as there are several ministries with an interest in biofuels as a strategic resource. The ARDA, through the Ministry of Agriculture Mechanisation and Irrigation Development (MoAMID), was central in securing the initial leasing offer to Green Fuel. Yet, all land in Zimbabwe is owned by the state and administered by the Ministry of Lands and Rural Resettlement (MLRR) and various other ministries depending on the enterprise. Communal land has been under president trusteeship since 1982 and is administered by RDCs under the Ministry of Local Government and National Housing. Traditional leaders also play an administrative role, though they must liaise through RDCs.

The ARDA has not clearly demarcated land ownership rights in the area of Chisumbanje where the project is being implemented, in part due to the multiple government stakeholders with a vested interest. Statutorily, MoAMID owns the land. The third player in this complicated "puzzle" is the Ministry of Energy and Power Development, which regulates all energy in Zimbabwe through the Zimbabwe Energy Regulatory Authority (ZERA).

Governance in Zimbabwe, particularly when it comes to land, is intimately tied to politics and power (Alexander 2007; Rutherford 2017). At the local level, only actors with access to certain skills, networks, and resources are able to influence the project. The Chipinge RDC seemed to suffer from a lack of local participation and, thus, legitimacy in the eyes of the community. Moreover, the RDC is supposed to represent the varying local perspectives but it has no clear role in the project.

The company found itself in a quandary, sometimes with political support and at other times without. When the inclusive government came to power in 2009, it enacted a style of governance more clearly based on market principles compared to earlier governments. As such, it was at odds with the still powerful technical bureaucratic state that operated in the shadows of the ZANU–PF's more politicized administration (Sachikonye 2011). The most dramatic position on the Chisumbanje project was taken by the former Minister of Energy and Power Development in 2012 who rejected the legislation of forced blending.

The returning Member of Parliament for Chipinge South perceived the broader dynamics at play in Zimbabwe's political economy. In an interview with Matondi on July 16, 2015, the MP accurately predicted instabilities with the start-up of Green Fuel's project due to the engenderment of competition. Competitors in the fuel sector raised ostensible concerns about the harmful effects of blending, to protect the high prices they enjoyed. The Member of Parliament noted that:

> There was resistance to the company. This was because there are many players in the fuel industry, and some fear is competition. There are people with tankers who go as far as Beira and Durban to collect fuel. If there is a 20% reduction in fuel imports, it means that these people have lost. Blending has been going on in triangle and there is nothing new. People are afraid of competition and transporters and fuel dealers fear loss of business.

For their part, traditional leaders expressed in group discussions and in individual meetings strong and emotionally laden affinities to land

(Fontein 2015). Fear of losing land as an important cultural resource motivated action on the part of traditional leaders. Yet, many of their constituents were also critical of them. Some 1,008 farmers lost their land to the company, ranging anywhere from 2 ha to 40 ha. Out of the 1,008 farmers from Chisumbanje who lost land, only 172 were compensated with 0.5 ha of irrigation schemes per family.[3] A key informant interviewee noted that:

> The coming of Green Fuel saw one thousand and eight (1008) farmers losing their land that ranged from 2ha-40ha to the company and out of the 1008 from Chisumbanje; only 172 farmers were compensated with 0.5ha irrigation schemes per family. The company had slashed down crops that belonged to the farmers during land clearance and takeover and only compensated the farmers with US$3.00/ha. Now the community is failing to send their children to school because they do not have the land to till and have no jobs. The few who have been employed are not being paid up; employees at Green fuel have gone for more than three months without pay despite the company now selling the ethanol produced."[4]

When the Green Fuel project began, it was apparent that the affected communities had tenuous relations with all their leaders. Many complained that their leaders, be they members of the RDC, Members of Parliament, or traditional chief, were not defending the people "enough." There were accusations that the company "bought" leaders and that frustrations about the lack of inadequate information on the project and its roll-out plans.

Fontein found that the weakest link in the project were technical bureaucrats. Bureaucrats drew blanks in their interviews, and ordinary community members could often articulate the substantive issues better than people who worked in government. That said, civil servants are bound by the Official Secrets Act and can only release information in the public interest that does not incriminate them or bring their office into public disrepute. In addition, there are procedures civil servants must follow to allow interviews and provide statements. Although Matondi received official approval for his research, civil servants did not willingly provide interviews. This resistance is somewhat problematic since the

[3] Key informant interview, 11 May 2014, Chisumbanje.

[4] Key informant interview, 11 May 2014, Chisumbanje.

research was about a programme of national importance, whose structures, character, and vision are important to citizens. It is likely that civil servants are fearful of becoming entangled in the politics of the project; an understandable concern given the increased politicization of the government (McGregor 2002).

War veterans from the guerrilla armies that fought for independence against the Rhodesian regime are also been important players in governance disputes related to the Chisumbanje project. The power and influence of war veterans in rural areas was strengthened in the late 1990s due to the introduction of the FTLRP (Kriger 2006; Matondi 2012). The company supplied veterans with more land and support than others in the surrounding communities, despite their fewer numbers. According to current land policy in Zimbabwe, all allocations must meet a 20% quota to war veterans in terms of the number of plots or the size of land, whichever applies. The company was also worried by the potential for conflict and any form of mobilization that would disrupt the project. Communities then accused the war veterans of "selling out" and acting as spokespersons for the company given the benefits provided to them.

High unemployment, the out-migration of young people, and weak local economies are compounding factors that heighten community resistance to the project. Land that once formed the traditional and sociocultural foundation of communities is usurped by commercial interests, however, opinions on this issue diverge widely depending the proximity of communities to the project sites. Not all livelihoods were affected equally and some could access to new opportunities created by the presence of Green Fuel. Others possessed more political power to make appeals directly to the government beyond their engagement with the company. Individuals and social groups (e.g. men, women, youth) possess differentiated capacities to influence policy outcomes. The hierarchical governance framework of Zimbabwe also means that some traditional leaders may not have unfettered access to central government. That said, these same chiefs leveraged the central government's presence in the Chisumbanje project as an opportunity to address the marginalization and development of their communities.

The people of Chisumbanje are creating new social structures to defend or gain a voice at the negotiation table. They have mobilized wider networks to engage national leaders and raise their questions, political opinions, and dissatisfaction with Green Fuel's project. At this point, most of community members do not want to see Green Fuel leave or for the project to be halted. While seemingly contradictory, marginalized communities have little choice but to leverage the investment in a way that minimizes their exploitation and maximizes potential benefits.

Some Socioeconomic Impacts of the Project

In this section, we briefly discuss the varied socioeconomic impacts of the Chisumbanje ethanol project in the region by examining who benefited, who did not, and some of the grievances that emerged in the process between the period of 2012–2014. While many grievances were of a local nature, for example, exclusion from employment and disagreements about whether to "partner" with the company, there was an equally contentious national debate over blended fuel.

Interviews by the Ruzivo Trust with a team of businesspeople reveal the Chisumbanje project's varied impact on Zimbabwe's volatile economic situation. The first beneficiaries of the Green Fuel project were the grocery store owners who had new and more customers with disposable incomes. The hiring of permanent and casual workers in the plant, in the fields, and also in the construction of the canals had immediate impacts in the region. Most of the spin-off shops were established from 2008 onwards in Chisumbanje, showing a causal link between the construction of the plant and new economic opportunities. This growth in local business also coincided with the slow recovery of the economy during the inclusive government from 2009 to 2013. During this time, a wider range of consumer goods became available in the area of the project, as national companies supplied their products to local retail shops. Affected communities no longer needed to travel over 200 kilometres to Mutare for grocery shopping, thereby reducing transport costs for many local consumers.

In general, economic diversification is key to the survival of many rural poor in sub-Saharan Africa (Bryceson 1999). Individuals, families, and communities use a combination of land resources for subsistence and casual wage labour to maintain or improve their livelihoods. For instance, a Headman for Chisumbanje presiding over 16 villages with 1,008 families indicated that livelihood options were lost when the land ranging from 2 to 40 ha was allocated to the company. He indicated that only 172 families were compensated with 0.5 ha of irrigated land. People used to grow maize for food and cotton as a cash crop; as shared by the Headman, "we were able to build our houses using proceeds from cotton." In productive seasons, community members would sell excess grain to the Grain Marketing Board. Since the project began, however, most families in these villages could not grow food or cotton to sell due to a lack of land. Keeping cattle was also a challenge due to lack of grazing space. As a result, some households could not afford to pay school fees, and thus, school dropout rates increased. As a consequence, more people in these villages became involved in cross-border trade, while others relocated to South Africa for employment opportunities, leading to what the Headman characterized as "high levels of family breakdown."

This description of desperation sharply contrasts with the economic development narrative touted by the national government. Certain areas, such as ChecheChe Growth Point, have experienced positive impacts. Prior to the plant, there were only two financial institutions in the community; in just a short timeframe following the construction of the project, new banks opened branches. The number of shops, including hardware stores, also increased.

The plant is the biggest of its kind in Africa and directly employs 4,500 people, in addition to creating thousands of jobs through downstream and upstream services. The Ruzivo Trust research team conducted a survey on the ethanol value chain in 2014 which showed that there were about 45,00 employees working in Green Fuel's agricultural departments in both Chisumbanje and Middle Sabi and 300 people working on the mill who all work two eight hour shifts per day. The minimum wage per month for those working in the fields was US$80.00, while for those working in the mill earned US$1800 per worth (there are different national wage rates negotiated for the two sectors).

Problems arose in 2011 when the company closed due to the low uptake of ethanol in Zimbabwe. The expected blending did not occur during the time of the inclusive government. Zimbabwe introduced mandatory fuel blending in 2011 in a bid to reduce its huge fuel import bill, which hovers slightly above $1 billion annually. Yet, the performance of the economy and negative media articles about blending meant the uptake was very low. Hope was restored when the Ministry of Energy and Power Development enforced the 10% mandatory blending quota in 2013. State officials argued that ethanol fuel blending saved the country an estimated $26.5 million in 2017, representing 2.65% per cent of the import bill (ZERA 201). The poor performance of the ethanol sector in Zimbabwe mainly impacted local people who lost their jobs, with only a few professional and menial staff remaining to maintain the plant.

At this point in time, the key demand raised by affected communities is that of employment. Locals are seeking to secure permanent contracts so long as they meet the supplier's qualifications on a competitive basis. Certainly, shop-floor jobs such as cleaning, weeding, irrigating, and transportation could be reserved for locals. Without a transformation of the skills base of the local people, however, conflicts surrounding employment will likely continue between Green Fuel and the communities. Such matters are also easily politicized.

The Chisumbanje ethanol project affected women and men differently. Gender is an important mediating factor in terms of the impacts of large-scale investments in agriculture. The project initially curtailed the migration of men to South Africa in search of employment, which had a resultant positive effect on families. Those already in South Africa started to return to Zimbabwe, however, the exact numbers are difficult to obtain. For the first time, women started to feel the impact of "visible" cash benefits as men spent money in the local area; they could easily trace expenditure patterns and control a stake of the income. The project thus increased women's bargaining power in the household and led to greater investments in child education and health, as reported by key informants from some schools and health facilities.

While the bargaining power of women with regard to household finances increased, gendered norms surrounding household roles also changed. The reduction in land area meant the reduction in the resources controlled by women. Women became increasingly dependent on men who mostly controlled the 0.5 ha of irrigated land and the incomes proceeding from the sales of corps and other goods. Women and children are traditionally engaged in the labour-intensive manual activities of agriculture (hoeing, weeding, and harvesting), in addition to domestic labour, and so the return of men from South Africa did not change these responsibilities; instead, men now supervised their wives and children in these chores.

Many women were not pleased with the impacts of the project. They acknowledged that the company did invest some money into the community (e.g. bridge construction), but pointed out that this was not an intentional or benevolent impact. They indicated that the bridge was built mainly to permit the company to access water from the other side of the river and the community benefit was only by happenstance. The greatest issue raised by women is articulated by one interviewee:

> It was promised that projects will be establish for us, we applied for projects and to this day nothing has been done towards this. These projects include the construction of a chicken run with them giving us the chickens which in turn we would sell to the company for its workers. They promised us a market place, for other villages they have done so but for our village they have not. They said they would offer us employment to cook sadza (thick porridge) for the workers and [the company] would employ people to feed the chickens but all this was not done. They did however construct 3 boreholes in this village, 1 which is no longer being used as the water is contaminated, and the other one their pipes are not enough and has been shut down and the last one is the one working.

A dominant thesis around gender in Africa is that on any land deal, poor rural women lose out because they do not have reliable access to land, secure land tenure, or customary land rights. Matondi, (2012) found that where the state has done a "land deal" in the form of the Fast Track Land Reform Programme (FTLRP), women have largely lost out, not just land, but a second best when it comes to the resources to use the land. Nonetheless, investments in mega-projects on customary lands shift household dynamics in terms of their roles, income-generation activities, and property rights. However, a surprising finding was that women in Chisumbanje were not lobbying for access to irrigation plots or lost land as to be "their" personal property, but rather for their spouses who had been pushed out or incorporated in small-sized land of 0.5 hectares and very far from their places of residency. Only a small proportion of community members, 172 out of 1060 members, received 0.5 ha of irrigated plots; yet for even those who received such plots they were located more than 30 km away from their homes. The dams at the areas allocated for irrigation did not have access to water. Often those who did not receive plots of land often let their animals roam free, as they felt cheated out of getting land. When women and men see developments in other villages they then feel left out and vent anger towards the company. Yet, their anger reflects the desire for local beneficiation, which needs collective efforts of the communities, the company, and government and other leaders. It can be concluded that Green Fuel land did not contribute to shifts on gender property rights, but has affected the rights of family property, which brings together families to lobby against the company. This material point has been missed in most of the gender type analysis in most of the studies to date of this project.

The traditional leaders acknowledged that the company is involved in corporate social responsibility initiatives. The company renovated a classroom block that was destroyed by a hailstorm at Chisumbanje Primary School, made renovations at St Peter's Hospital, and is currently building a community library at Takwirira. There are complaints, however, that the company is side-lining locals in potential employment opportunities through such project. Further, although several local people are being employed in Green Fuel's agricultural sector as weeders, irrigators, and cooks, many of these workers are not receiving their salaries on time as many interviewees expressed; some had gone for three months without pay.

In sum, there is an uneven distribution of benefits and grievances at the local and national levels in Zimbabwe as a result of the Chisumbanje ethanol project. The unilateral seizure of communal land highlights the issues of tenure and legal ownership which surround large-scale land deals in the agricultural sector. Though communal land is held under customary tenure through chiefs who act as legal entities, the land is de facto state-owned. Customary land tenure and usufruct rights are acknowledged through the Communal Lands Act (1982) and the Rural District Council Act (1988), but not necessarily protected by national law, as the provisions remain under the trusteeship of the President as per the Constitution. Land ownership is not the panacea to development challenges given that resources are needed to increase the value of land. Although Green Fuel has implemented some corporate social responsibility, its core business does not significantly benefit the wider community and local economies. The picture of the Chisumbanje project's socioeconomic impacts is not as clear-cut as purported once one starts talking with the diverse stakeholders impacted.

Conclusion

There are conflicting messages about what projects, such as the infamous Chisumbanje ethanol project in Zimbabwe, mean for national economic development and the empowerment of local people. Like in Cameroon and Sierra Leone (see chapters by Hamann and Sneyd and by Gbanie and Thornton, this volume), among other countries, the Zimbabwean government advertises its public land for agriculture-related investments. The lessons of the Chisumbanje ethanol project provide insight into the strategies needed to mitigate the negative outcomes of large-scale agricultural investments, while enhancing the positive aspects.

The Chisumbanje ethanol project does not fit the "land grab" discourse for a variety of reasons. Though issues of displacement are raised abound, the contestation over land tenure should not be directed at Green Fuel but rather focused on the ARDA, the state agency who owns the land. Green Fuel is only leasing the land from ARDA for sugarcane production and has no say in land governance. As such, land-related matters should be addressed by the government and not the company.

At the same, the ARDA is a shareholder in the project with the same rights (and financial interests) as Green Fuel. The ARDA claims that much land of the land used for the project had been "empty" for generations and acknowledges only temporary uses by communities. In reality, communities were well-established on this supposed state-owned land, which is why delicate negotiations were required to actualize the project. Although the investors in Green Fuel are Zimbabweans employing domestic finance, the affected Zimbabwean communities also possess a strong stake in the land for their range of livelihood needs.

The Chisumbanje ethanol project stimulated spin-off activities, and a range of products are now available to consumers in local markets. This situation is slightly different from other cases like Ethiopia where international investors usurped land to produce commodities for export (Beyene 2011). The Zimbabwean public and various economic sectors have been reluctant to accept blended fuel due to the messages of different politicians and other critics. After the inclusive government lost power to a single party in 2013, the new administration addressed the lack of policy coordination and quickly clarified the position on fuel blending by enacting legislation allowing for progressive blending from E5%, to E10%, and finally E20%. Fuel service providers were given time to construct the relevant infrastructure and consumers still possess options about what type of fuel they purchase.

The land disputes are rooted in failed or non-existence consultation processes, which either exclude an entire community or neglect to consult certain affected groups. The ARDA and other stakeholders need to work collaboratively and provide communities with knowledge of the company's expansion plans, providing opportunities for input and reform. Given the acrimony around land, the Chisumbanje project does not comply with some of the responsible guidelines for agricultural investments developed and promoted by institutional investors. We agree with Hammar's (2007, 387) assessment:

> Whenever one writes about questions of land in Zimbabwe, there is already a great weight of history – and of history making – to consider. When one is writing on such matters in post-2000 era marked by severe political and economic crisis with land one of the central pivots, even if one is reflecting upon an event or a set of relations in Zimbabwe prior to 2000, there is nonetheless also the minefield of the present to negotiate.

Zimbabwe's land issues were "internationalised" well before the FTRLP (i.e. the colonial era). However, agrarian arrangements have largely been "de-internationalised" through the FTLRP since then. Sugarcane production for ethanol is a land intensive and economically transformative enterprise. Ethanol production in Zimbabwe involves not only Green Fuel and its sister companies, but also complex interactions among and between the state, quasi-government institutions, traditional leaders, local business people, interest groups from the community (e.g. war veterans and NGOs). These relationships are concrete but contingent and characterized by uneven power relations. Rural, agrarian-based communities come up against the influence of private–public partnerships, which combine the authority of the state with the capital of a large agro-industrial corporation determined to make profits.

Although we do not consider the Chisumbanje project as an example of a "land grab," it does showcase the positive and negative consequences of large-scale agricultural investments. There is a compelling case for community development approaches that are grounded in participatory methods and prioritize local livelihoods. The disempowerment and marginalization of local people is a serious cause for concern, despite the few who are successful in gaining menial jobs. In the long-term, there is a need to ensure that more benefits accrue to affected communities and not just the company, in an incremental effort to "level the playing field."

Communities identified the land issue as the necessary starting place for other issues to be addressed. This tactic resonates with international trends, where foreign and domestic investors alike have been seemingly unable to fully comprehend the socioeconomic, cultural, and environmental consequences of their investments and resultant resistance. The land problems of the Chisumbanje ethanol project are not new but rather represent unfinished business; iterations from the colonial and post-independence period, including the FTLRP (Hammer et al. 2003).

Identifying stakeholders who are considered legitimate is at times a difficult exercise, especially when political interference clouds the consultation process. This problem is compounded by the range of authorities in rural Zimbabwe, and obscure and/or competing institutional, administrative, and political structures, where national priorities at times run counter to local needs.

The public, activists, academia, policy makers, technical bureaucrats, and practitioners are all confronted with the complexities of land governance and mobilize particular discourses in response. Some characterize the Green Fuel project as an "international land grab"; however, we suggest that the term is inappropriate in the context of Zimbabwe. Nonetheless, the "hype" around the land grab in Zimbabwe demonstrates how localized agricultural investments quickly become internationalized, revealing the need for a greater understanding of the local, national, and international political and economic dynamics at work.

Acknowledgements The project undertaken by Ruzivo Trust, Harare, Zimbabwe on land investments in collaboration with The Programme for Land and Agrarian Studies (PLAAS) of the University of Western Cape is acknowledged. Staff members from Ruzivo Trust then, that is Clemence Mhliziyo, Rudo Chingono in 2014 in Chipinge, and a follow up by Justice Muchati and Micheal Ndimba is sincerely acknowledged. The community results feed back also benefitted from Wilbert Tendai Marimira, Theophilous Mudzindiko, and Ngaatendwe Murimba.

Bibliography

Alexander, James. 2007. *The unsettled land: State-making and the politics of land in Zimbabwe, 1893–2003*. Athens, OH: Ohio University Press.

Beyene, Atakilte. 2011. Smallholder led transformation towards bio-fuel production in Ethiopia. In *Biofuels, land grabbing and food security in Africa*, ed. P. Matondi, K. Havnevik, and Atakilte Beyene, 90–105. London and New York: Zed Books.

Bryceson, Deborah Fahy. 1999. African rural labour, income diversification & livelihood approaches: A long-term development perspective. *Review of African Political Economy* 26 (80): 171–189.

Cotula, Lorenzo. 2013. *The great African land grab? Agricultural investments and the global food system*. London: Zed Books.

Fontein, Joost. 2015. *Remaking Mutirikwi: Landscape, water and belonging in Southern Zimbabwe*. Rochester, NY: James Currey.

Hall, Ruth. 2011. Land grabbing in Southern Africa: The many faces of the investor rush. *Review of African Political Economy* 38 (128): 193–214. https://doi.org/10.1080/03056244.2011.582753.

Hammar, Amanda Julie. 2007. The day of burning: Land, authority and belonging in Zimbabwe's agrarian margins in the 1990s. PhD dissertation, Roskilde University Department of International Development Studies.

Hammar, Amanda Julie, Brian Raftopoulos, and Stig Eduard Breitenstein Jensen. 2003. *Zimbabwe's unfinished business: Land, state and nation*. Harare: Weaver Press.

Kaag, Mayke, and Annelies Zoomers. 2014. *The global land grab: Beyond the hype*. London: Zed Books.

Kelly, Sydney Paul Alexander. 1973. Chisumbanje and Mkwasine: A study of African and European settler estate agriculture in the South-Eastern Lowveld of Rhodesia. PhD dissertation, University of Natal.

Kriger, Norma. 2006. From patriotic memories to 'patriotic history' in Zimbabwe, 1990–2005. *Third World Quarterly* 27 (6): 1151–1169. https://doi.org/10.1080/01436590600842472.

Matondi, Prosper B. 2012. *Zimbabwe's fast track land reform programme*. London: Zed Books.

Matondi, Prosper, Kjell Havnevik, and Atakilte Beyene. 2011. *Biofuels, land grabbing and food security in Africa*. London and New York: Zed Books.

McGregor, JoAnn. 2002. The politics of disruption: War veterans and the local state in Zimbabwe. *African Affairs* 101 (402): 9–37. https://doi.org/10.1093/afraf/101.402.9.

Moore, Donald. 2005. *Suffering for territory: Race, place, and power in Zimbabwe*. Durham, NC: Duke University Press.

Moyo, Sam. 1995. *The land question in Zimbabwe*. Harare: SAPES Books.

Moyo, Sam. 2001. The Land occupations movement and democratisation: The contradictions of the neoliberal agenda in Zimbabwe. *Millennium* 30 (2): 311–330.

Mujere, Joseph, and Sylvester Dombo. 2011. Large scale investment projects and land grabs in Zimbabwe: The case of Nuanetsi ranch bio- diesel project. Paper presented at the International Conference on Global Land Grabbing 6–8 April 2011, Organised by the Land Deals Politics Initiative (LDPI) in collaboration with the Journal of Peasant Studies and hosted by the Future Agricultures Consortium at the Institute of Development Studies, University of Sussex.

Mutopo, Patience, and Manase Chiweshe. 2012. Large scale land deals, global capital and the politics of livelihoods: Experiences of women small-holder farmers in Chisumbanje, Zimbabwe. International Conference on Global Land Grabbing II, Ithaca, NY (17–19 October).

Rutherford, Blair. 2017. *Farm labor struggles in Zimbabwe: The ground of politics*. Bloomington, IN: Indiana University Press.

Sachikonye, Lloyd Mambo. 2011. *Zimbabwe's lost decade: Politics, development and society*. Harare: Weaver Press.

Scoones, Ian, Nelson Marongwe, Blasio Mavedzenge, Felix Murimbarimba, Jacob Mahenehene, and Chrispen Sukume. 2010. *Zimbabwe's land reform: Myths and realities*. London: James Currey.

Waeterloos, Evert, and Blair Rutherford. 2004. Land reform in Zimbabwe: Challenges and opportunities for poverty reduction among commercial farm workers. *World Development* 32 (3): 537–553. https://doi.org/10.1016/j.worlddev.2003.06.017.

White, Ben, Saturnino M. Borras Jr., Ruth Hall, Ian Scoones, and Wendy Wolford. 2012. The new enclosures: critical perspectives on corporate land deals. *The Journal of Peasant Studies* 39 (3–4): 619–647. https://doi.org/10.1080/03066150.2012.691879.

Zamchiya, Phillan. 2013. The role of politics and state practices in shaping rural differentiation: A study of resettled small-scale farmers in South-Eastern Zimbabwe. *Journal of Southern African Studies* 39 (4): 937–953. https://doi.org/10.1080/03057070.2013.858547.

Zamchiya, Phillan. 2011. A synopsis of land and agrarian change in Chipinge district, Zimbabwe. *Journal of Peasant Studies* 38 (5): 1093–1122. https://doi.org/10.1080/03066150.2011.633703.

PART III

Formalization, Domestic Agency and Legacies of Legal Pluralism

The Power of Policy and the Entrenchment of Inequalities in Ethiopia: Reframing Agency in the Global Land Rush

Melisew Dejene and Logan Cochrane

Introduction

Existing estimates suggest that an area between 49 and 227 million hectares has been acquired by foreign investors on a global scale since 2007 (Cotula 2012; Hall et al. 2015; Land Matrix 2019; Oxfam 2011). The amount of land on the lower end of that spectrum equates to five times the land mass of Portugal. Africa is a central target for large land acquisitions and a significant site of contestations (ElHadary and Obeng-Odoom 2012). Accurate data on the global land rush is an ongoing challenge (Ali, Deininger and Harris 2017). While incomplete

M. Dejene
Hawassa University, Awasa, Ethiopia

L. Cochrane (✉)
Global and International Studies, Ottawa, ON, Canada

College of Public Policy, HBKU, Qatar

L. Cochrane and N. Andrews (eds.), *The Transnational Land Rush in Africa*, International Political Economy Series,
https://doi.org/10.1007/978-3-030-60789-0_9

(see Cochrane and Legault 2020), the Land Matrix clarifies the obscurity of foreign direct investment (FDI) involving large-scale land acquisitions. In Ethiopia, the extent of foreign land leases varies depending on the source consulted. Abbink (2011) reports that 1.2 million hectares were leased between 2007 and 2010; Cotula et al. (2009) suggest the figure is more like 602,760 hectares; while the Oakland Institute (2011) claims that 3.6 million hectares has been acquired. As of January 2019, the Land Matrix database collected reports on just over 1.6 million hectares of contracted, foreign large-scale land leases in Ethiopia. Some of these large-scale land acquisitions have been hotly contested and have centred on accusations surrounding the forced relocation of people and the leasing of national park lands (Cochrane and Skjerdal 2015).

This chapter critically analyses available data on land deals for the decade following the global commodity price spike of 2007/2008. While some refer to the massive transfer of land in the Global South to foreign investors as 'land grabbing' and as a contemporary iteration of neocolonialism, we find that these narratives often neglect the agency of national governments and sub-national administrations not only in approving these investments, but actively facilitating them. This study focuses on foreign investments, although the majority of investors in Ethiopia are domestic (for a broader analysis of commercial agriculture in Ethiopia, see Ali et al. 2017), since foreign investors acquired much larger contracts and therefore have a significant impact on the lives, livelihoods and the environment. National investors, while more numerous, acquire smaller plots of land, and in the aggregate lease less land than foreign investors. Our reliance on the Land Matrix database means that the data concerns large land acquisitions above 200 hectares and, as a result, primarily those that are foreign-owned. Our analysis is thus narrow in that it examines a specific set of investments in the agricultural sector by a specific set of actors. Our critical lens highlights the diversity of factors that enable and restrict foreign direct investment and thereby offers important lessons for policy practitioners. We begin our assessment with a brief overview of the Ethiopian context, followed by a description of the methods employed. We provide a history of relevant legal and policy changes in Ethiopia over time before discussing our findings. This chapter offers a macro-level landscape analysis that uncovers the intersections of inequality. Importantly, it demonstrates the power of the state in regulating investment and thus reframes conceptions of agency in the land rush debate, which to-date has largely focused on investors and their countries of origin. The state can perpetuate marginalization and inequality by enacting policies often in the name of the 'public good' or national interest without concern for the most vulnerable. Our chapters raises critical questions about who is benefiting by land investments and at whose expense.

The Ethiopian Context

For nearly a century, governments of Ethiopia (Imperial, Military, 'Democratic' alike) have viewed 'modernized' commercial agriculture as a strategy for improving national food security and economic development (Ali et al. 2017; Cochrane 2017). Government support for industrial agriculture began with the Imperial administration and continued during the military government, without many benefits accruing for the public (Belay 2003). During the current government (1991–present), there has been a rapid expansion of service provision and coverage for smallholder farmers, accompanied by increases in production and export levels (Cochrane and Bekele 2018a, b). As Abbink (2011) outlines, the continued emphasis on agriculture as the national economic engine is exemplified by a range of policies such as the Agricultural Development-Led Industrialization initiative (1996), which focus on commercialization and large-scale operations. Although the leasing of agricultural land to foreign investors is not a new phenomenon in Ethiopia, the scale of acquisitions has increased significantly under the ruling Ethiopian Peoples' Revolutionary Democratic Front (EPRDF) party. Abbink (2011) identifies the Rural Development Policy and Strategies of 2003 and the Plan for Accelerated and Sustainable Development to End Poverty (2005/2006—2009/2010) as marking the first formalizations of large-scale land acquisitions by government policy, a historical trend echoed in this research.

While the global 2007/2008 commodity price spike is often associated with growing investor interest in farmland around the world, practices of land grabbing began well before in Ethiopia. For example, Ethiopia saw significant foreign investment in the fresh cut flower industry in the early 2000s; the National Bank of Ethiopia added flowers as a key export commodity in its 2003/2004 annual report (there are 11 key commodities, six of which are agricultural; see Cochrane and Bekele 2018b). Weissleder (2009) argues that foreign investment in the agricultural sector rapidly increased in 2006, before the commodity price spike, which we also find. Foreign investment in agriculture and land pre-dating the commodity price spike primarily involved acquisitions for the fresh cut flower industry, with investors originating from Israel, the European Union (EU), India and the United States, and with exports flowing to

Europe. While fresh cut flowers were central to the Ethiopian economy prior to 2006, foreign investment subsequently diversified into biofuels, oilseeds, cereals, and vegetables from that point onward.

Abbink (2011) notes that the first investors in agricultural land were domestic investors, followed by foreign investors. According to Weissleder (2009), the reasons for the growth in foreign interest included currency depreciation and a supportive investment environment. The investors who entered the Ethiopian economy following 2007/2008 price spike were from the same countries as previous investors (Weissleder 2009). There are some exceptions, but investors from the EU, India, Israel, Saudi Arabia and the United States dominated the agricultural sector in Ethiopia well before and after the commodity price spike. One could also point to 2003—in addition to 2006—as a turning point for foreign investment (FDI rose from under US$20 million to over US$220 million), in alignment with the policy changes noted by Abbink (2011)). The Government of Ethiopia played a key role not only in approving land leases, but actively promoting and facilitating them. High-level government personnel, including the Prime Minister, spoke about the investment opportunities in Ethiopian agriculture around the world. The government also offered attractive packages to investors which included low annual land lease rates, income tax exemptions for a period of years, access to financing, guarantees for the full repatriation of capital and profits, and duty-free imports (Weissleder 2009).

Research on large-scale land acquisitions and 'land grabbing' in Ethiopia emerged several years after the commodity price spike of 2008. Among the early notable publications were Desalegn Rahmato's 'Land to Investors' (2011) report and Jon Abbink's 'Land to the Foreigners' (2011) article. Rahmato questioned if the government's stated development objectives could be met through industrial agriculture; his concerns materialized: rather than earning revenue, improving foreign exchange, and increasing exports, the result was a massive amount of lost revenue and a debt burden that poses systemic risk to the financial system. Rahmato, after publicizing his concerns in 2011, was deemed 'anti-development' and disregarded by the government. The state-owned television channel even ran content against the scholar. In the years that followed, non-governmental organizations reported on human rights abuses in relation to large-scale land leases, with the Oakland Institute playing a leading role (e.g. Hurd 2013; Oakland Institute 2011, 2013). In tandem, academic research began to provide insight into the complex set of outcomes and diverse actors involved in large-scale land acquisitions. For example, Maru and Rutten (2015) identified negative outcomes of commercial leases due to increased land competition, while Bamlaku et al. (2015) and Daniel et al. (2017) showed that job creation was minimal. Studies on the environmental impacts of industrial agriculture also revealed adverse outcomes (Teklemariam et al. 2016; Maru et al. 2016). There were arguments that some types of agricultural investments such as contract farming may have been better suited to improving food security (e.g. Negash and Swinnen 2013; Riera and Swinnen 2016).

Methodology and Methods

The data on foreign investments used in this study were obtained from the Land Matrix (2019), the largest publicly available collection of land deals globally. No additions were made to this data set in early 2019 (due to the migration to a new platform), and thus we frame the data set as covering the period of 2000–2018. The data is imperfect. Not all deals are made public, and those made public do not always specify the details of agreements, which change with time regardless. Many deals are missing (Cochrane and Legault 2020). The Land Matrix, and the data it supplies, should therefore be taken as being indicative of trends rather than as definitive and complete figures. As is the case in many countries, foreign investment is only one part of a more complex and longer story of land dispossession. In some parts of Ethiopia, domestic or diaspora investors dominate in terms of landholdings and the number of investors (Daniel et al. 2017). However, these deals largely go accounted for in the data set because (1) they are not considered foreign investments, and (2) in many cases, the land size falls beneath the Land Matrix threshold of 200 hectares. We focus primarily on foreign investments for these reasons, but further study is needed on other forms of investment in land, particularly domestic and diaspora investors. We collected the Land Matrix data on 18 January 2019. The database is regularly updated and the data we present may have changed by the time of publication. Given this fluidity, the findings of this paper are reflective of the date on which the data was obtained.

We cleaned the data for potential duplicates before analysing the data from the Land Matrix (see also Cochrane and Amery 2017). The identification of duplicates was done by searching the investor's name and comparing the size and location of investments. If an investment possessed the same location, size, intention, investor, investor country, crop types, and negotiation year as another, then it was reported to the Land Matrix and removed from the database. After data cleaning, we found 107 completed land contracts, including those that have been cancelled, with an aggregate land size of over 3.47 million hectares of intended land deals, of which more than 1.6 million hectares (1,600,289 ha) was actually contracted. The intended contract size is nearly double what was actually contracted, indicating potential problems with reported statistics (which may be been reporting on intended contracts rather than actualized ones). To validate and complement this data set, we draw upon available evidence and existing literature, including both peer reviewed academic material as well as reports from non-governmental organizations and governmental agencies.

Legal and Policy Changes

Land in Ethiopia holds important value in the economic, political, and social spheres. In the 1960 s and 1970 s, a student movement advocated that land be given back to the tillers in a context where many parts of the country were dominated by large landholders who operated in a feudal form (Bahru 2014; Gebreselassie 2006; Pankhurst 1966). One of the first major changes made by the military government (1974–1991) was land reform. All tenure agreements were nullified and land was nationalized and redistributed to farmers throughout the country. This reform enabled the majority of the country's citizens to access land not previously available to them. However, land reform also challenged alternative systems of land use and organization, such as collective or communal approaches to tenure that involve seasonal uses of land for groups such as pastoralists.

The present government institutionalized land as state property in the constitution, a move which has drawn a multitude of criticism (see Gebreselassie 2006; UNECA 2002; Nega and Degfe 2000; Abbink 2011). One of those criticisms centres on the large-scale leasing of land to foreign investors which has only been possible through the usurpation of rights of Ethiopian people (Abbink 2011; Rahmato 2011; Lavers 2012). So-called 'emerging' regions such as Benishangul Gumuz and Gambella have been particularly impacted by the sale of their land to foreign investors and have been neglected by government. People from marginalized regions are being 'resettled' to open up land for investors, which has been a source of contestation (Cochrane and Skjerdal 2015).

While all land has been held in trust by the government since 1975, there have been other legal and policy changes which have enabled greater opportunities for investors. When the current EPRDF government came to power in 1991, and Ethiopia's Constitution subsequently approved, in 1995, some previously disallowed forms of land use became legal, including short-term land rentals. Later, in 2005, the government issued a legal reform regarding the expropriation of land for public purposes which included compensation provisions for those who lost their land (FDRE 2005). The controversial proclamation gave the government the power to expropriate land with 30 to 90 days-notice to the landholder (30 days for holdings without invested properties and 90 otherwise). Landholders had no right to contest expropriation, only the level of compensation. The proclamation defined compensation as 'payment to be made in cash or in kind or in both to a person for his property situated on his expropriated landholding' (FDRE 2005, 3125). Rates of compensation are low, as land holders are not compensated for the value of the land (viewed as owned by the government) but only for what is on the land. This is what led Makki and Geisler (2011, 2) to view 'land grabbing' by foreign investors as 'socio-spatial enclosures in a global context characterized by sovereign states and the ever-continuous process of capitalist commodification and valorization'.

In 2008, the federal government issued a directive proclaiming that all leases over 1000 hectares were to be handled by the federal government. The federal government used purported administrative inefficiencies and corruption at lower levels of administration to justify this change. The regional states, although vested with the power of self-determination as per Ethiopia's Constitution, were marginalized by this policy change, which prevented them from effectively working in the interests of their populations. The reduced power of the regional states to manage and control investments, and the increased power of the federal government, reflected an ideological shift of the ruling political party. The 'developmental state' modality strengthened the influence of the central government in land governance, management, and administration (Cochrane and Mandefro 2019; Dejene and Cochrane 2019). Such practices led some researchers like Lavers (2012, 105) to conclude that the government's approach to large-scale land transfers to foreign investors conflicted with its own political strategy of ethnic self-determination. When this policy change took place in 2008, a procedure was put in place requiring investors to obtain a federally issued investment license before seeking land from a regional investment authority; the state was effectively setting itself up as a gatekeeper for all foreign leases (Abbink 2011). The introduction of this procedure was also a question of financial control as investments rose significantly beginning in 2006.

It became clear once the federal government seized control of large-scale land acquisitions that there was significant foreign investment interest in Ethiopia. The Government of Ethiopia began actively promoting the country as an ideal place for agricultural investment globally. Investors were presented with an attractive package of incentives, which included tax exemptions on imports (especially on capital goods), direct export of crop production without value addition (i.e. from the farm to the airport), and exemptions from custom payments. The government claimed that land transfers were made in consultation with affected local people, though it prioritized 'unused' land for foreign investment (Oakland Institute 2011). One investigation of ten investments involving large-scale land transfers found that nine of the ten resulted in a loss of access to farmland; five of the ten resulted in a loss of access to communal pasture; and three of the ten resulted in a loss of access to forest (Schoneveld 2017, 123). Other studies (e.g. Oakland Institute 2011; Rahmato 2011; Terefe 2016; Weissleder 2009) challenge the approach of the Government of Ethiopia to land and agricultural investment, citing its failure to meet stated objectives and the negative impacts on rural residents.

In 2012, the Ethiopian Investment Agency (EIA) published a study that called for investment in palm oil production, referencing the positive experiences of leading producers like Malaysia. The EIA identified potential places for this specific type of investment, including 300,000 hectares in the Southern Nations Nationalities and Peoples (SNNP) region, 100,000 hectares in Gambella and 5000 hectares in Oromia, with lease prices ranging from ETB 111 (approximately US$4) to ETB 3077 (approximately US$107) per hectare. The EIA also announced incentives for investors, including complete customs exemption on import duties for capital goods and construction materials, as well as tax exemptions for two to eight years (see the Council of Ministers Regulation No. 270/2012; FDRE 2012a). This federal push for investment in palm oil specifically targeted domestic investors, signalling a shift in the government's approach.

In that same year (2012), the government's enthusiasm began to wane as problems become more apparent and its objectives (stated and unstated) were not being met. One investment proclamation (Proclamation No. 769/2012), which complemented the Council of Ministers' Regulation No. 270/2012 (FDRE 2012b), introduced new restrictions on foreign investment. Foreign investors could no longer be legally involved in the export of raw agricultural products such as coffee, chat, oil seeds, pulses, precious minerals, natural forestry products, among others. In the following year (2013), the Director of the Ministry of Agriculture, Bizualem Bekele, explained that, 'no company has fulfilled the government's expectations' (African Intelligence 2013). An internal investigation found that many investors had not begun operations; as a result, the government gave investors a 6-month period to demonstrate activity or their contract would be cancelled and the allocated land seized (African Intelligence 2013). A second major legal change took place in 2013, namely the option for very large leases ended. Foreign investors would be given a maximum of 5000 hectares and no additional land until proven successful. Priority would also be given to domestic investors (the land limit for domestic investors was 3000 hectares; Africa Intelligence 2013). In their study of large commercial farm operations, Ali et al. (2017) identified that only 55% of land was being used. The underutilization of leased land was one of the contributing factors that spurred these legal revisions regarding large-scale land leases in 2013.

By the end of 2018, the Government of Ethiopia revoked a number of contracts. Mostly notably, one of the most controversial and largest investments (Karuturi) was annulled in 2015. At least six large-scale contracts were cancelled, totalling a contracted land area of 133,200 hectares (with an intended land size of 550,000 hectares). There are reports of other investment license cancellations, such as those granted to MIDROC Group (as reported on the domestic, state-owned news station on 27 March 2018), but these do not yet appear as cancelled or failed in the Land Matrix database. We anticipate that many more cancellations have occurred than what appears in the Land Matrix. Cancellations are hard to track since there is much less reporting on cancellations.

The Landscape of Investments and Ongoing Issues

India is Ethiopia's single largest source of foreign direct investment for large-scale land acquisitions. Indian investors have acquired the largest amount of land in Ethiopia: nearly half a million hectares in 20 acquisitions (representing 22% of large-scale foreign land acquisitions). Domestic investors lease the second largest amount of land in Ethiopia, though this figure is likely under-reported in terms of deals listed in the Land Matrix (Cochrane and Legault 2020). Here, domestic investors includes all private investors as well as government-owned entities. For example, half of the total amount of land leased to domestic investors (203,000 ha) was granted to the Ethiopian Sugar Corporation. After investors from India, investors from the EU and the Gulf Cooperation Council (GCC) countries stand out as the next biggest foreign acquirers of land (see Fig. 9.1). Of the EU nations, the United Kingdom (UK) and Italy completed the largest land deals in hectares. Israel finalized seven acquisitions, making it an important source of investment, but these deals were relatively small (total land acquired: 39,800 hectares). Overall, it is investors from India and Saudi Arabia that are the largest land holders. While there are multiple investors from India, nearly all of the investments

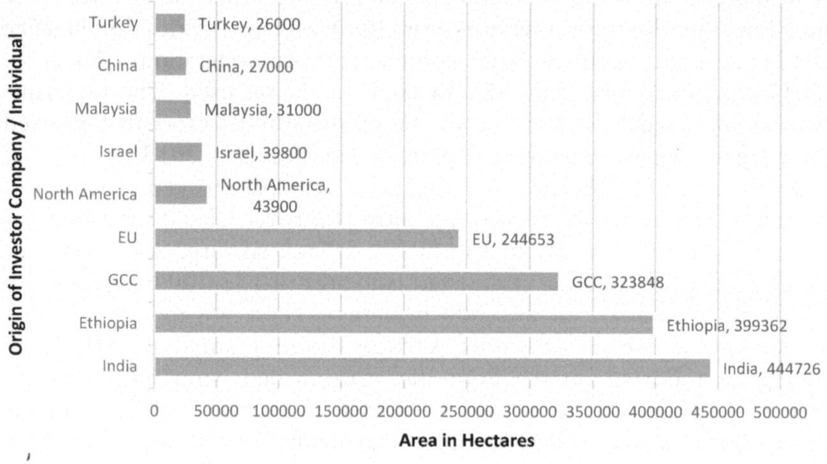

Fig. 9.1 Sources of Foreign Investment of Land Leases (Contracted in ha), 2000–2018 (*Notes* Figures are based on contract size [not intended deal size] and include contracts that were finalized but cancelled afterward. The data does not include negotiations that failed and contracts that were not finalized. If there were multiple investors [e.g. Denmark, Ethiopia], we listed the investor country using the first listing. The status of Brexit was uncertain at the time of data analysis; the UK was considered as part of the EU calculations. Not shown, due to small size: Pakistan [1000 ha], Iran [2000 ha], Singapore [5000 ha] and Djibouti [10,000 ha])

from Saudi Arabia (318,204 of 323,848 ha) *and* the GCC (98% of GCC investments) were made by a single investor, al-Amoudi, an Ethiopian-born businessman with Saudi citizenship, who is the country's single largest investor. He is one of the few investors with multiple holdings (10 in total). No other investor has finalized contracts for more than three large-scale land acquisitions. al-Amoudi and his companies (MIDROC and Saudi Star) is an exceptional case. Depending on the narrative being constructed, al-Amoudi is portrayed either as an Ethiopian success story, an Arab neocolonialist, or a privileged elite with unfair access to land and economic opportunities (Clapham 2018; Cochrane and Amery 2017; Vidal 2010; Zenebe 2009).

A qualitative assessment of the Land Matrix sheds light on some of the challenges of data reliability. For example, there are varying reports of the Karuturi land deal and its size (100,000 ha, 200,000 ha, 220,000 ha and 300,000 ha), yet the contracted amount listed in the Land Matrix is 1200 ha. The issue is not one of incorrect data per se, but that contracts were designed such that additional land might be granted to the investor over time. In this case, the intended land acquisition was 300,000 hectares, with 100,000 hectares pledged at the outset and the option of an additional 200,000 hectares in the future. In the end, only 1200 hectares were developed, but there are also reports of 12,000 hectares as being in production (EJA 2019; Oakland Institute 2011). Ultimately, the deal was cancelled by the government in 2015, but the story continued. In April 2019 Karuturi was (re)granted land in Gambella after lengthy legal proceedings, this time a size of 15,000 hectares. These changes in 2019 were not recorded in the data set examined (2018 year-end). The case of Karuturi highlights the complexities involved in tracking land acquisitions over time.

The 2007/08 food commodity price spike is situated in the literature and throughout this collection as a critical moment in the growth of foreign interest in large-scale land acquisitions. However, the trend began earlier in Ethiopia, where the government actively created and facilitated an investor-friendly environment in the years prior to 2007 (see Fig. 9.2). Alemu (2018) notes that these efforts began as early as 2002, with the Investment Proclamation No. 280/2002 which offered generous incentive packages to investors. The regulatory changes of 2003 (No. 84/2003, Articles 4 and 5) further enhanced incentives by offering tax exemptions and stipulating that 75% of produce could be exported (Alemu 2018). Additional incentives were offered to investors willing to

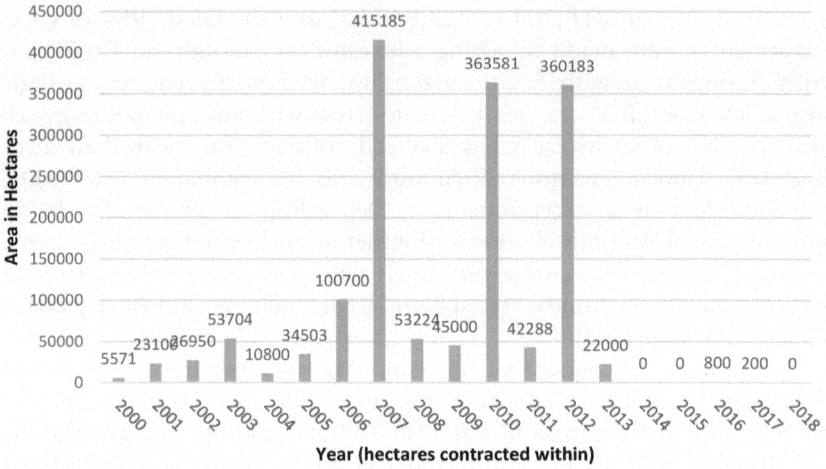

Fig. 9.2 Timeline of Investment, by Contract Size in ha (*Notes* Data are based upon the date that the contract agreement was concluded. Ten contracts did not contain this data and so we sought additional sources to verify the year of contractual agreements. In some cases, the earliest reference was used as we were unable to identify the specific contract year. Data was not available for five contracts, totalling a land area of 42,500 ha.)

work in less developed parts of the country—a contributing factor as to why some regions such as Gambella Regional State attracted many large-scale land investors. Efforts by the Ethiopian government to attract private investors into the agricultural sector continued with federal legislation in 2005 (RLAUP 456/2005) designed to facilitate development activities. This federal principle was adopted by regional states thereafter. Notably, when the regulatory environment changed in 2013 to favour domestic investors, large-scale land acquisitions by foreigners effectively ended according to the Land Matrix data. The decline in foreign investment is also possibly linked to the decline of food prices and the lessening of speculative land leasing. These trends highlight the critical importance of domestic law, regulation, and policy to the extent and longevity of large-scale land acquisitions.

While more research is required, the correlation between investment trends and regulatory changes suggests a 'race to the bottom' mentality among governments seeking to increase large-scale land acquisitions.

When Ethiopian authorities began to enact stricter regulatory requirements, investors looked elsewhere. For instance, American investors did not lease any land in Ethiopia in 2014, however, that same year American investors acquired over 600,000 hectares in the Democratic Republic of the Congo where regulation is extremely weak (Land Matrix 2019). Contributions to this volume (e.g. Chapter 4 on South Sudan) demonstrate that certain investors possess some minimum requirements in their pursuit of the cheap land and labour. In 2011, Cotula et al. highlighted the important role that national policy and regulation play in ensuring fair and mutually beneficial agreements between corporations, governments, and affected citizenry. Stricter regulatory processes, Cotula et al. (2011, S111) write, might result in missed opportunities, but countries may experience greater harm when competing in the 'race to the bottom' by offering the cheapest land, least regulation, lowest labour costs, and highest tax breaks. Abbink (2011) also suggests that the right regulatory environment could increase successful outcomes and reduce the negative impacts.

In the Ethiopian case, the data suggests that domestic law, policy, and regulation influenced the rate and trends of foreign direct investment. Ethiopia's investment promotion policies and the transfer of large tracts of land for low prices (see Abbink 2011; Rahmato 2011; Oakland Institute 2011) served as 'pull' factors for foreign investors. Foreign investment in the country hit a historic high just as world food crises skyrocketed in 2007 (see Fig. 9.2). The restriction to foreign investments following the changes enacted by the Council of Ministers' Regulation No. 270/2012 is also reflected in the Land Matrix data, with no large-scale land transfers on record from 2013-2015. Political processes influence foreign investment on multiple levels through both international (e.g. bilateral and multilateral trade agreements) and national (e.g. laws, policies and regulations) avenues. The existence of bilateral and multilateral trade agreements prior to the 2007/2008 commodity price spike was one of the reasons foreign investors were already present in Ethiopia. As outlined by Weissleder (2009), Ethiopia entered into trade agreements with the EU before 2007, namely the 2000 Africa, Caribbean and Pacific-EU Partnership Agreement which allowed investors near duty-free access to the EU market. This agreement was challenged by the World Trade Organization as non-reciprocal preferential treatment and subsequently replaced by the new Economic Partnership Agreement). The trade relationship between the United States and Ethiopia, on the other hand, is defined by the African Growth & Opportunity Act and the Trade & Investment Framework Agreement between the United States and the Common Market for Eastern and Southern Africa (Weissleder 2009). The pre-existence of these agreements might explain the presence of European and American investors in Ethiopia before the 2007/2008 price spike in agriculture. In theory, the Common Market for Eastern and Southern Africa enables trade within the region and facilitates investment. However, foreign investment by member states remains limited; only one country, Djibouti, completed a single large-scale land lease (10,000 ha) in Ethiopia. With regard to bilateral investment agreements, Ethiopia signed deals with China, Malaysia, the United States and a number of EU states (Weissleder 2009), which are key sources of investment in agriculture. Therefore, in addition to the role of domestic policy and regulation, international agreements play an important facilitating role for foreign direct investment.

An alternative, or additional, reason why investment may have dropped in 2013 was due to the emergence of public protest. Many accounts of civil society resistance focus on protests against the 2015 Addis Ababa Master Plan. Although the government-initiated plan was an important ignitor of protest, resistance predated this period. In early 2012, the Muslim community began regularly protesting against perceived government interference in religious affairs. Seventeen prominent religious leaders were arrested in 2013, which only served to multiply the intensity and size of the protest. While civil unrest does not appear to be the primary deterrent of foreign investment in land and agriculture, it may have contributed to investors lack of enthusiasm when assessing potential risks.

The reasons behind the concentration of foreign, large-scale land acquisitions in specific areas of Ethiopia are speculative. However, the ethno-federalist structure of Ethiopia's administrative borders sheds light on the central government's decisions in the leasing process. Table 9.1 aggregates the contracted land by regional state and then compares those figures with the size of the region and the percent of the region leased by foreign investors. The regional states of SNNP, Benishangul Gumuz, and Gambella are characterized by large aggregate areas and high percentages in terms of land leased to investors. These regional states are not considered traditional (Amhara and Tigray) or emerging (Oromia) powerholders in the nation. They are unique in that they are ethnically diverse regional states. Regional states with lower percentages of land leased to

Table 9.1 Location of Investments, by Regional State (Aggregate Contract Size), 2000–2018

Regional State	*Contracted Land (ha)*	*Size of Region (ha)*	*% of Region*
Afar	20,600	7,205,278	0.3
Amhara	54,622	15,470,896	0.4
Benishangul Gumuz	261,026	5,069,868	5.2
Gambella	156,012	2,978,282	5.2
Oromia	305,212	28,453,784	1.1
SNNP	630,448	10,547,600	6.0
Somali	2000	27,925,200	0.0
Tigray	10,300	5,363,800	0.2
Unknown	53,069	–	–

Notes No large-scale foreign investments were recorded in the federal City Administrations of Addis Ababa and Dire Dawa. Harari was excluded as no investments were recorded in the very small regional state

investors possess greater ethnic homogeny. The regional state most associated with political power (i.e. those associated with the ruling elite since 1991), Tigray, has seen few large-scale land acquisitions. The ethnicities with the largest populations, and therefore political power, the Amhara and the Oromo, also experienced relatively less large-scale land acquisitions. Afar and Somali regional states are considered 'emerging regions' and have been historically neglected by the state, (see Cochrane and Rao 2019), but also experienced low levels of land leases. In our view, this outcome relates more to the environmental context in these arid areas than to political power.

Large-scale land transfers and accompanying agricultural investments have not delivered on their promises and, in some cases, have clearly produced more negative impacts than positive ones. For example, a supervisory body of the federal legislatures (Revenue, Budget and Finance Standing Committee members) from the House of Peoples' Representatives visited investments in Gambella regional state in March 2019. The team of legislatures reported many problems in relation to land transferred for agricultural investment. According to their investigation, 36 of the agricultural projects that were granted large tracts were abandoned and the 'investors' left the land they invested in after taking loans amounting to ETB 654,320,044 (US$22.7 million). In many cases, investors abandoned their projects after clearing forests, leaving behind damaged lands and less biodiversity. The supervisory body also found that 44 projects went bankrupt, holding loans amounting to ETB 902,779,464 (US$31.4 million). The situation in Gambella left the Ethiopian Development Bank in crisis. According to the data from the National Bank, 117 projects that took loans amounting to ETB 2.5 billion (US$86.8 million) were unable to pay back their loans (as reported on national, state-owned television on 27 March 2019). The Governor of the National Bank, Dr. Yinager Desse, briefed the House of Peoples' Representatives that his organization was working to address the crisis, however, outstanding loans surpassing ETB 45 billion (US$1.6 billion) put the government agency at substantial risk. Of the outstanding loans, agricultural and manufacturing investment projects were among the biggest borrowers (as reported on national, state-owned television on 28 March 2019). This was the outcome Dessalegn Rahmato (2011) warned about. The change of government in 2018 and its invitation of Rahmato to serve as a speaker at an event on rural development organized the Prime Minister's Office suggests that officials began to take his words seriously (Ethiopia Observer 2019).

Conclusion

In the last decade (from the 2010 election to the present), the issue of large-scale land leases has drawn significant scholarly attention in Ethiopia. Our findings shed light on the origin of foreign investment in Ethiopia, predominately investors from India, Saudi Arabia, and the EU, alongside domestic investors. Although Ethiopia experienced peaks in levels of land leasing in 2007, 2010, and 2012, the rush effectively ended in 2013 following the introduction of regulatory reforms which placed new restrictions on foreign investment. The concentration of land leases in specific regions of Ethiopia highlights how power influences whose land is leased. Ethnically-diverse regions with less political power experience more land leases than the demographically and historically dominant ethnic groups. The intersections between political power and inequality in relation to land grabbing practices require more research, especially considering the negative impacts of large-scale land leases. Future studies are also needed to assess the role and impact of national and diaspora investors; at present, this data is not publicly available.

Dominant narratives on the global land rush focus on the commodity price spike of 2007/2008 as the main factor for increased interest of foreign investors in large-scale land acquisitions. However, the Ethiopian case presents a different story. Investment began well before the 2007/2008 commodity price spike, a time when bilateral agreements and policies were developed to foster a favourable investment environment. The pre-existing regulatory environment is one of the reasons why foreign investment in Ethiopia's land skyrocketed in 2007. The global land rush discourse diminishes the agency of host countries and local people far too often. Their erasure equates to assumptions of powerlessness or victimhood. The Ethiopian story presents a much different narrative. The Government of Ethiopia first attracted foreign investors and then enacted policies and regulations to set the terms of their engagement.

Bibliography

Abbink, Jon. 2011. 'Land to the foreigners': Economic, legal, and socio-cultural aspects of new land acquisition schemes in Ethiopia. *Journal of Contemporary African Studies* 29 (4): 513–535.

Africa Intelligence. 2013. Land policy revised. Available https://www.farmlandgrab.org/post/view/22621-ethiopia-land-policy-revised.

Alemu, K. T. 2018. Agricultural investment alternatives and the smallholder farming sector. In *Agricultural transformation in Ethiopia*, ed. A. Beyene, 45–62. Zed: London.

Ali, Daniel Ayalew, Klaus Deininger, and Anthony Harris. 2017. Using national statistics to increase transparency of large land acquisition: Evidence from Ethiopia. *World Development* 93: 62–74.

Bahru, Zewde. 2014. *The quest for socialist Utopia: The Ethiopian student movement c. 1960–1974*. Addis Ababa: Addis Ababa University Press.

Bamlaku, Alamirew, Harald Grethe, Khalid Hassan Ali Siddig, and Tesfamicheal Wossen. 2015. Do land transfers to international investors contribute to employment generation and local food security? Evidence from Oromia Region, Ethiopia. *International Journal of Social Economics* 42 (12): 1121–1138.

Belay, Kassa. 2003. Agricultural extension in Ethiopia: The case of participatory demonstration and training extension system. *Journal of Social Development in Africa* 18 (1): 49–84.

Clapham, Cristopher. 2018. The Ethiopian developmental state. *Third World Quarterly* 39 (6): 1151–1165.

Cochrane, Logan. 2017. Strengthening food security in rural Ethiopia. PhD diss., University of British Columbia, Kelowna.

Cochrane, Logan. 2018. Food security in Ethiopia: Review of research, 2005–2016. *Ethiopian Journal of Applied Sciences and Technology* 9: 1–11.

Cochrane, Logan, and Hussein Amery. 2017. Gulf cooperation council countries and the global land grab. *Arab World Geographer* 20 (1): 17–41.

Cochrane, Logan, and Yeshtila W. Bekele. 2018a. Average crop yield (2002–2017) in Ethiopia: Trends at national, regional and zonal levels. *Data in Brief* 16: 1025–1033.

Cochrane, Logan, and Yeshtila W. Bekele. 2018b. Contextualizing narratives of economic growth and navigating problematic data: Economic trends in Ethiopia (1999–2017). *Economies* 6 (4): 64.

Cochrane, Logan, and Hone Mandefro. 2019. Discussing the 2018/19 changes in Ethiopia: Hone Mandefro. *NokokoPod* 2019 (2): 1–15.

Cochrane, Logan, and Danielle D. Legault. 2020. The rush for land and agricultural investment in Ethiopia: What we know and what we are missing. *Land* 9 (5): 167 (1–13).

Cochrane, Logan, and Terje Skjerdal. 2015. Reading the narratives: Resettlement, investment and development in Ethiopia. *Forum for Development Studies* 42 (3): 467–487.

Cochrane, Logan, and Nitya Rao. 2019. Is the push for gender sensitive research advancing the SDG agenda of leaving no one behind? In *Forum for Development Studies* 46 (1): 45–65.

Cotula, Lorenzo. 2012. The international political economy of the global land rush: A critical appraisal of trends, scale, geography and drivers. *Journal of Peasant Studies* 39 (3–4): 649–680.

Cotula, Lorenzo, Sonja Vermeulen, Rebeca Leonard, and James Keeley. 2009. *Land grab or development opportunity? Agricultural investment and the international land deals in Africa*. Rome: Food and Agriculture Organization.

Cotula, Lorenzo, Sonja Vermeulen, Paul Mathieu, and Camilla Toulmin. 2011. Agricultural investment and international land deals: Evidence from a multi-country study in Africa. *Food Security* 3 (Suppl 1): S99–S113.

Dejene, Melisew, and Logan Cochrane. 2019. Ethiopia's developmental state: A building stability framework assessment. *Development Policy Review* 37 (S2): O161–O178.

EJA. 2019. Karuturi global plants sugar and other crops in Gambella. Available online https://ejatlas.org/conflict/karuturi-global-plants-sugar-and-other-crops-in-gambela-ethiopia.

ElHadary, Yasin Abdalla Eltayeb, and Franklin Obeng-Odoom. 2012. Conventions, changes, and contradictions in land governance in Africa: The story of land Grabbing in North Sudan and Ghana. *Africa Today* 59 (2): 58–78.

Ethiopia Observer. 2019. Appropriate policy that places small producers at the centre required: Dessalegn Rahmeto. *Ethiopia Observer*, March 27. Available https://www.ethiopiaobserver.com/2019/03/27/appropriate-policy-that-places-small-producers-at-the-centre-required-dessalegn-rahmeto/. Accessed March 28, 2019.

FDRE. 2003. *Council of ministers regulations on investment incentives and investment areas reserved for domestic investors*. Council of Ministers Regulations No. 84/2003. Addis Ababa: Government of Ethiopia.

FDRE. 2005. *Expropriation of landholdings for public purposes and payment of compensation proclamation*. Proclamation No. 455/2005. Addis Ababa: Government of Ethiopia.

FDRE. 2012a. *A proclamation on investment*. Proclamation No. 769/2012. Addis Ababa: Government of Ethiopia.

FDRE. 2012b. *Investment incentives and investment areas reserved for domestic investors*. Council of Ministers Regulations No. 270/2012. Addis Ababa: Government of Ethiopia.

FDRE. 2014. *A proclamation to amend the investment proclamation*. Proclamation No. 849/2014. Addis Ababa: Government of Ethiopia.

Gebreselassie, Samuel. 2006. Land, land policy and smallholder agriculture in Ethiopia: Options and scenarios. *Future agricultures*. Discussion Paper 008: 1–13.

Hall, Ruth, Ian Scoones, and Dzodzi Tsikata. 2015. *Africa's land rush: Rural livelihoods and Agrarian change*. James Currey.

Hurd, Will. 2013. *Understanding land investment deals in Africa: Ignoring abuse in Ethiopia*. Oakland: Oakland Institute.

Land Matrix. 2019. https://landmatrix.org/en/get-the-detail/by-target-country/ethiopia/.

Lavers, Tom. 2012. 'Land grab' as development strategy? The political economy of agricultural investment in Ethiopia. *Journal of Peasant Studies* 39 (1): 105–132.

Makki, Fouad, and Charles Geisler. 2011. Development by dispossession: Land grabbing as new enclosures in contemporary Ethiopia. Paper presented at the International Conference on Global Land Grabbing 6–8 April 2011, LDPI: University of Sussex, UK.

Negash, Martha, and Johan F.M. Swinnen. 2013. Biofuels and food security: Micro-evidence from Ethiopia. *Energy Policy* 61: 963–976.

Maru, Shete, and Marcel Rutten. 2015. Impacts of large-scale farming on local communities' food security and income levels—Empirical evidence from Oromia Region, Ethiopia. *Land Use Policy* 47: 282–292.

Shete, Maru, Marcel Rutten, George C. Schoneveld, and Eylachew Zewude. 2016. Land-use changes by large-scale plantations and their effects on soil organic carbon, micronutrients and bulk density: Empirical evidence from Ethiopia. *Agriculture and Human Values* 33 (3): 689–704.

Nega, Berhanu, and Befecadu Degfe. 2000. *Annual report on the Ethiopian economy*, Vol. 1, ed. Befecadu Degfe and Berhanu Nega. Ethiopian Economic Association: Addis Ababa.

Institute, Oakland. 2011. *Understanding land investment deals in Africa—country report: Ethiopia*. Oakland: Oakland Institute.
Institute, Oakland. 2013. *Omo: Local tribes under threat*. Oakland Institute: Oakland.
Oxfam. 2011. The growing scandal surrounding the new wave of investments in land. Oxfam Briefing Paper 151, Oxford, Oxfam.
Pankhurst, Richard. 1966. *State and land in Ethiopian history*. Addis Ababa: Institute of Ethiopian Studies.
Rahmato, Dessalegn. 2011. *Land to investors: Large-Scale land transfers in Ethiopia*. Addis Ababa: Forum for Social Studies.
Riera, Olivia, and Johan Swinnen. 2016. Household level spillover effects from biofuels: Evidence from castor in Ethiopia. *Food Policy* 59: 55–65.
Schoneveld, George C. 2017. Host country governance and the African land rush: 7 reasons why large-scale farmland investments fail to contribute to sustainable development. *Geoforum* 83: 119–132.
Teklemariam, Dereje, Hossein Azadi, Jan Nyssen, Mitiku Haile, and Frank Witlox. 2016. How sustainable is transnational farmland acquisition in Ethiopia? Lessons learned from the Benishangul-Gumuz Region. *Sustainability* 8 (3): 213.
Terefe, Altayesh T. 2016. The negative impact of foreign direct investment on people's right to food: Ethiopia's horticulture/floriculture industry. LLM Short Thesis, Central European University.
UNECA. 2002. *Ethiopia—Good policy, Decent outcomes. Economic report on Africa 2002: Tracking performance and progress*. Addis Ababa: ECA.
Vidal, John. 2010. How food and water are driving a 21st-century African land grab. *The Observer*, March 7, 2019. https://www.theguardian.com/environment/2010/mar/07/food-water-africa-land-grab.
Weissleder, Lucie. 2009. Foreign direct investment in the agricultural sector in Ethiopia. *EcoFair trade dialogue*, Discussion Paper No. 12.
Zenebe, Wudineh. 2009. Al-Amoudi's efforts to initiate Saudi Agro investments. *Addis Fortune*, November 24. http://farmlandgrab.org/post/view/9188.

CHAPTER 10

Overlaps, Overestimates and Oversights: Understanding Domestic and Foreign Factors in the Land Rush in the Democratic Republic of the Congo

Chris Huggins

Introduction

The Democratic Republic of Congo (DRC) is prominent in literature on the 'global land rush.' Between 2008 and 2011, several media articles claimed that foreign firms were acquiring huge land concessions in the DRC. Much attention was paid to land acquisition for commercial agricultural production. One source claimed that the 'land rush' in the DRC involved a total of 11 million hectares (ha), which represents 48% of the total agricultural land in the country; approximately 8 million ha was leased by South African companies (Global Land Project 2010; see also 'Buying farmland abroad' 2009). As explained by Asanzi (2014), the

The original version of this chapter was revised: The author name "Marie Gangé" has been changed to "Marie Gagné". The correction to this chapter is available at https://doi.org/10.1007/978-3-030-60789-0_12

C. Huggins (✉)
University of Ottawa, Ottawa, ON, Canada
e-mail: chuggins@uottawa.ca

L. Cochrane and N. Andrews (eds.), *The Transnational Land Rush in Africa*, International Political Economy Series,
https://doi.org/10.1007/978-3-030-60789-0_10

plans of Chinese investors were also featured heavily in media reports, in part due to the faulty assumptions and biases of Western analysts that characterize Chinese strategies in Africa as 'different' from or in competition with the West (Curtis 2013; Bräutigam and Zhang 2013).

In practice, the global land rush in the DRC was smaller in scale than originally reported, though still significant (as was the case in Cameroon, Senegal, and South Sudan, see Hamann and Sneyd, Gagné and Fent, and Wight, this volume). The role of South African companies in the DRC in particular was smaller than forecasted. One study of agro-industrial concessions, based on fieldwork in the DRC, estimated that only 260,000 hectares (ha) were in production in 2013 (Feintrenie 2014). In late 2019, by contrast, the total amount of land under foreign control for all land uses was reportedly around 7.5 million ha under 53 land deals (Land Matrix 2019).[1] Currently, the vast majority of deals reported in the Land Matrix involve forestry (i.e. logging) projects. Mining concessions also represent a fairly significant proportion of large-scale land acquisitions. As described below, land acquisitions by domestic companies and individuals are also highly significant.

There are several reasons for the differences in the statistics reported by various sources. *First*, some deals were abandoned before leases were signed, while others were signed but ended up being either smaller than planned or unsuccessful. For example, one reported 2.8 million ha negotiation resulted in only 100,000 ha being acquired (Cotula 2013). In other cases, Chinese investors secured support from central government in Kinshasa but were unable to secure access to land due to opposition from local leaders and so they moved into agri-processing roles instead (Asanzi 2014). Some sources include only concluded land deals, while others include deals currently under negotiation; some include only hectares under production, while others include all land acquired. *Second*, some sources on the land rush in the DRC include land acquisition for several different land uses (such as oil exploration, mining, and forestry), while others focus only on agricultural projects. *Third*, some figures include land acquisition by large-scale domestic companies while others include only transnational deals. *Fourth*, there are different criteria on scale—the Food and Agriculture Organization (FAO) of the United Nations (UN) considers any deal involving 1,000 ha or more to be a 'large-scale land

[1] This figure includes contracts for oil, gas, and mineral concessions. Excluding oil, gas and minerals, there are 7.08 million ha under foreign control.

acquisition' (Batterbury and Ndi 2014), while many other international organizations use a figure of 5,000 ha or more (Cochrane 2016). *Fifth*, the secrecy surrounding many land deals makes it difficult for researchers to verify reports.

These issues are also found in the broader literature on the 'land rush' around the world. As documented by Pedersen and Burr (2016), the 'first phase' of research into land grabbing tended to rely on unverified media reports and described land grabbing as largely the result of the initiatives of large multinational companies moving into countries with weak legal frameworks. A second phase paid closer attention to verifying reports and hence reconsidered the 'hype' around the rush (Kaag and Zoomers 2014) and the inflated figures previously published.

Despite the differences between initial and current estimates of foreign land acquisition, the trend is clear: foreign acquisition is significant. This reflects a broader global reality, 'not of a short-lived 'land panic,' but of a trend of growing competition for land that is likely to continue for the foreseeable future' (Anseeuw et al. 2011, 60). The other clear trend is the acquisition of large landholdings by domestic (Congolese) stakeholders, whether companies or individuals, which is a widespread and sometimes problematic issue. This is due to weaknesses in Congolese laws and institutions (explained below) as well as longstanding imbalances of economic and political power that enable unjust and corrupt practices. Communities are often evicted without compensation. Such 'domestic' land rushes have yet to be revealed by the 'second phase' of global land grab research, even though domestic land grabbing practices may result in more land changing hands than the 'global' dynamics (Cotula 2013). The domestic 'land rush' may need different remedies from those promoted by international agencies.

This chapter is based on an extensive review of published and unpublished (i.e. grey) literature on the DRC's land tenure system as well as the impacts of the land rush in the DRC. It builds on previous work by the author on land issues in the DRC (e.g. Huggins and Paluku 2019; Huggins 2015; Vlassenroot and Huggins 2014; Huggins 2010; Vlassenroot and Huggins 2005) which was based on a combination of fieldwork, particularly semi-structured interviews with key stakeholders, and literature reviews.

The rest of the paper proceeds with an explanation of the conceptual framework, which is followed by an outline of the key laws and policies on land and related natural resources. Four case studies are then presented, representing land acquisition by multinational companies in the oil palm, mining, forestry, and agricultural sectors. The discussion section emphasizes the importance of cooperation between different stakeholders; the need to cultivate a high level of political will to tackle land grabbing and support the land rights of local communities; the importance of funding decentralized institutions that can monitor and regulate land grabbing by foreign and domestic actors; and changing discourses around land and agriculture to move away from a simplistic 'modernization' argument that justifies the land rush. The conclusion briefly considers whether the international responses to the global land rush (such as non-binding guidelines and principles for 'responsible' agricultural investment) are likely, on their own, to result in effective regulation of the land rush in the DRC. The final argument is that, particularly given the extent of land grabbing by Congolese actors, only coordinated legal, political, and institutional action in the DRC (driven by pressure from local communities) can make a real difference.

Conceptual Framework

This paper uses a broad political economy framework, which takes account of material flows and discourses that shape debate and decision-making over land and resources. It is also informed by gender analysis frameworks, as the ways in which land is acquired, used, and given value are highly gendered (Collins 2014). Its approach to land rights is guided by ideas of legal pluralism (Griffiths 1986) which acknowledge that within a single state or geographical territory there may be numerous systems of land governance and different sources of authority which claim decision-making rights over land. For example, Overbeek and Tamás (2018, 3) characterize the land sector in the DRC as a space of hybridity in which, 'diverse and competing governance structures, sets of rules, logics of behaviour, and claims to power co-exist, overlap, interact, and intertwine in the access to and control over resources.'

While I consider international laws and norms around land tenure systems binding on states, such international laws and principles often fail to provide specific guidance of their relevance to particular local contexts; while necessary, these legal frameworks are insufficient to guide analyses of the 'land rush.'[2] Furthermore, and following other literature on

[2] The right to housing and the right to property is included in the 1948 Universal Declaration of Human Rights which provides that, 'no one shall be arbitrarily deprived

the 'land rush,' this chapter does not use the strict legal definition of land grabbing (i.e. the *illegal* acquisition of land through intimidation, corruption, fraud, or other criminal activities) but rather considers 'land grabbing' to be the large-scale acquisition of land through processes that exclude certain parties and/or which take place in contexts of economic, political, and social inequality. Land grabbing may therefore be technically legal but still highly problematic. While large-scale land acquisitions may have positive impacts, such as the creation of formal employment, both theoretical and empirical work suggests that it is more likely to have negative impacts on local populations (especially the most vulnerable) as well as the local environment. A comprehensive understanding of land rush dynamics is therefore multi-scalar, multi-resource (or 'multisectoral'), informed by intersectional gender frameworks, and based on an understanding of historical trajectories.

Country Context

Known as 'a rich country of poor people' (Trefon 2016, 2), the DRC is a large country with extensive natural resources, including one of the most biodiverse forested areas in the world, valuable minerals, ample water resources, and fertile land. However, 'poor natural resource management handicaps efforts to rebuild the state, and because the state is weak, it cannot assert authority of sovereignty over its natural capital' (Trefon 2016, 2). These resources have not been transformed into opportunities for the majority of the population of 80 million, who struggle to make a living. The country is ranked 176th of 189 countries in the Human Development Index[3] and 112th of 113 countries in the Global Food Security Index.[4] Its Gross Domestic Product (GDP) growth rate has been quite high, averaging around 6% per annum since 2003, though this rate was lower in 2016–2018 due to the crash in the prices of its major

of his property' (Article 17). Similar rights have been recognized in international treaties including the International Covenant on Economic, Social and Cultural Rights (ICESCR); the International Convention on the Elimination of All Forms of Racial Discrimination (ICERD); the Convention on the Rights of the Child (CRC) and the Convention on the Elimination of All Forms of Discrimination against Women (CEDAW), as well as many other international conventions, declarations, and other documents.

[3] http://www.hdr.undp.org/en/2018-update.

[4] https://foodsecurityindex.eiu.com/.

export commodities (especially minerals) (World Bank 2019). However, this relatively high economic growth rate has resulted only in 'a moderate reduction in poverty,' and the extreme poverty rate in the DRC was estimated at 73% in 2018 (World Bank 2019). The average Congolese citizen is able to consume only 1,500 calories a day (rather than the 2,500 recommended by the FAO) (Trefon 2016, 42).

The DRC is separated into 26 Provinces (see Fig. 10.1). Several provinces in the east of the country remain insecure following the official end of the Second Congo War in 2003. Conflict between numerous non-state armed groups is often related to disputes over land (Huggins 2010). An outbreak of Ebola in North Kivu Province in 2018 was declared over only in June 2020, which is a sign of weak state presence and capacity.

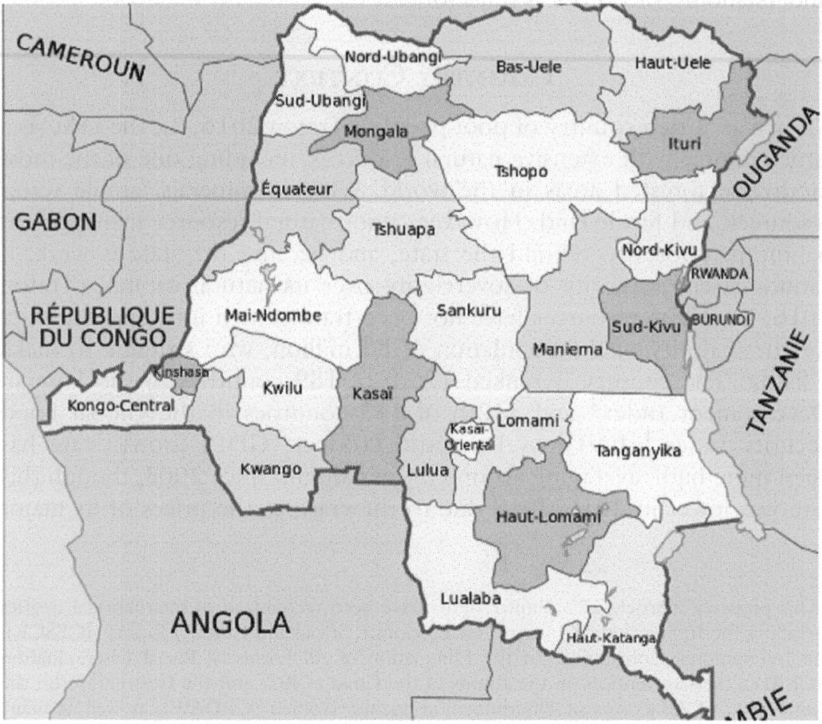

Fig. 10.1 Administrative Map of the Democratic Republic of the Congo (Creative Commons/Moyogo)]

The government also struggled to deploy testing for COVID-19 outside of the capital city, Kinshasa.

The DRC government does not use land use management plans, which results in poor coordination. There are frequent overlaps between land use rights granted by different ministries. Many zones assigned for government use include areas inhabited or used by communities and families for subsistence. Given the overlaps, ambiguities, and political disagreements between the jurisdictions and mandates of various government agencies, contemporary acquisition of large land concessions is often problematic. According to Peemans (2014, 28) central authorities grant land to foreign players though opaque processes, without consulting the local population. Land surveys are rarely carried out to ensure that the land is not already settled. Land is a popular investment for wealthy Congolese, who instead of working with farm managers to make it productive, may lease landholdings to local farmers, purchase land for speculative purposes, or use it as collateral for bank loans. Large landholdings may therefore remain idle.

Land disputes are therefore endemic and represent more than 80% of the overall number of cases in courts (Bayengeha 2014). Disputes, particularly those involving members of different ethnic groups, frequently become linked to broader political tensions and become militarized or violent (Vlassenroot and Huggins 2014; Huggins, 2010). Poor coordination between different state agencies in the land rights, forestry, mining and agriculture sectors, calls for 'integrated land use plans and zoning at the landscape level' (Samndong and Nhantumbo 2015, 35), ideally as part of a broader reshaping of governance.

Most Congolese smallholder farmers lack regular access to agricultural inputs and technologies, and poor transport infrastructure impedes the marketing of food. In some places, such as the densely populated Kivu Provinces, access to land is problematic and highly unequal. A generalized agrarian crisis is exacerbated by inadequate agri-processing infrastructure and the uneven implementation of various policies, which together undermine and deter domestic or foreign investment. While a host of policies have been developed for the agricultural sector, 'institutional reforms... have been thwarted by poor conceptualization, political squabbles for control of resources and the unwillingness of political elites in the capital to relinquish revenues to the provinces' (Asanzi 2014, 81). There is a longstanding political culture of leaders controlling multiple businesses, leading to self-serving policy-making, and other forms of corruption.

Nevertheless, some analysts are optimistic that governance is improving (Trefon 2016), especially since a partial handing-over of political power occurred following the long-delayed elections in late 2018.[5]

Chronological Overview of the Land Tenure Legal System in the DRC

During the colonial period, Belgian administrators imposed a dual land rights system on the DRC: a state-run title deeds system and customary laws. As in many other colonial states, land not clearly and visibly under the control of the Congolese population (i.e. land that has been cleared for cultivation or with existing infrastructure) was seen as 'vacant' land and thus put under state control.[6] Large areas were transferred to private companies and the colonial regime either encouraged or forced large movements of people to provide labour for plantations. The colonial period is described by Peemans (2014) as a period of the first three waves of land grabbing in the DRC.

The General Property Law of 1973

After Independence, the General Property Law of 1973 (amended 1980) attempted to increase central state control over land. While Article 389 of the law stated that a presidential ordinance on customary land would be issued, this ordinance never appeared, leaving customary rights in legal limbo. Customary rights remain largely 'invisible' to the state because they are undocumented and hence often ignored by government entities in land use planning or land rights registration. Although the 1973 law confers ultimate ownership of the land to the State, it is estimated that 70 per cent of the land is still held under custom in practice (Bayengeha 2014). Many indigenous communities, such as the Bacwa, Bambuti, and Batwa, possess only 'user rights' rather than rights of control or ownership (Musafiri 2009). This reflects a global pattern, where 'pastoralists, fisherfolk, hunter-gatherers, and forest-dependent people, whose land use

[5] The elections, widely held to have been rigged, resulted in a power-sharing agreement between the parties of opposition leader Felix Antoine Tshisekedi and former President Joseph Kabila.

[6] Under the State Land Decree of 1885 (Peemans 2014, 15).

and management practices are not recognized, are particularly vulnerable' to losing access to land in various ways (Anseeuw et al. 2011, 60).

Moreover, the costs of registering even a small plot of land are expensive for the average Congolese citizen. For example, surveying costs $US100 per day for farmland (Syn and Paluku 2015, 22). Once the land has been surveyed and the sale has been approved by a land administration office, a certificate is issued which guarantees a renewable and inalienable right of use for 25 years. Congolese citizens are able to convert this into a perpetual use certificate. Once issued, such a certificate can be challenged in court only for two years thereafter until it becomes legally unassailable.[7] In many cases, land administrators fail to verify that the land is unoccupied by other claimants before approving the sale, leading to the eviction of customary rightsholders without compensation.

In many cases, Congolese citizens may use both the custom and formal land administration systems to claim or contest land ownership, a situation known as 'forum shopping.' While some may benefit, this situation of legal pluralism is problematic for most (see also Hamann and Sneyd in this volume). Women are less able than men to succeed in either customary or state-run land governance institutions due to financial and socio-political barriers.

The 1973 law reduced local customary chiefs to the status of administrators, legally barred from benefiting directly from land sales. However, in practice many chiefs used their local knowledge and networks to take a 'commission' from facilitating land deals, privatizing community properties. The 1973 law therefore accelerated the dispossession of entire communities for the creation of new plantations and ranches by economic and political elites (Vlassenroot and Huggins 2005). This has been identified by Peemans (2014, 19) as the fourth 'wave' of land grabbing, which was followed in the 1980s and 1990s by structural adjustment policies and other approaches which sought to provide 'efficient' businesspeople with credit and commercial agri-inputs so that they could drive rural 'modernization' (which Peemans calls the fifth wave).

Importantly, Peemans (2014) highlights the continuities between the colonial and post-colonial periods, including in the treatment of the concept of the 'peasant.' He argues that marginalization of the peasant

[7] Unscrupulous buyers often acquire a land ownership certificate without informing local residents, wait for two years, and only then physically take occupation of the land, knowing that the certificate cannot be challenged.

way of life, both in material and discursive terms, started during the colonial period and continues until today. This marginalization, he contends, takes many forms, including prioritizing a 'modernization' approach (large-scale, mechanized, and high-input agriculture); reducing smallholders to 'beneficiaries' in need of external assistance; and generally demeaning discourse about their potential role(s) in national economic development. In this sense, any acquisition of land from smallholder farmers (or the acquisition of state land that could have been redistributed, instead, to landless or land-poor rural households) is not only an attack on the resource-base of the peasantry, but also on their very identity.

The DRC does not have a land policy to assist in the interpretation of the Land Law, neither does it have land use management plans, which results in poor coordination. There are frequent overlaps between land use rights granted by different ministries and many zones assigned for government use include areas inhabited or used by communities and families for subsistence, including areas of cultural and religious significance.

Given the overlaps, ambiguities, and political disagreements between the jurisdictions and mandates of various government agencies, contemporary acquisition of large land concessions is often problematic. According to Peemans (2014, 28) 'concessions are often granted by central authorities through quite opaque negotiations with foreign players without consulting the local population. Moreover, the land transfers are based upon a superficial evaluation of its value, without considering the specificities of local occupation.'

The 2006 Constitution

The 2006 Constitution potentially allows for greater community involvement in the management of natural resources by decentralizing many responsibilities to the provinces. It provides the state with 'sovereignty' over natural resources rather than 'ownership' (as was the case previously). Some NGOs and customary leaders interpret this as a legal opportunity for local communities to take greater control over their natural resources, including land. In addition, it provides that the individual or collective land rights of those claiming land, through the statutory law or through custom, will be guaranteed by the state (Article 34). However, the implications of these clauses have yet to be worked out through legal or policy-level processes. The Constitution also requires the Congolese state to ensure the elimination of all forms of discrimination against women and ensure the respect and promotion of their rights (Article 14).

Conseil Agricole Rural de Gestion (CARG)

Established from 2010 onwards, the CARG is a multi-stakeholder forum for rural land use management at various administrative levels. CARGs have been established in different Provinces with responsibility for advising the government on rural development issues (Tshiebwe 2015). They could therefore play a potentially important role in monitoring large-scale land acquisition at the local level. They could work in tandem with Provincial Parliaments and NGOs, some of which have commissioned studies into large-scale land acquisitions. To succeed, CARG will require political and financial support from the Congolese state as well as technical assistance from Congolese civil society.

The 2011 Agricultural Law

The Agricultural Law of 2011 was the culmination of sustained lobbying by a coalition of Congolese NGOs and provided a clear vision for the sector for the first time (Tshiebwe 2015). It contains several elements which have been viewed positively by Congolese and international specialists on rural development and smallholder agriculture. Unfortunately, the Agricultural Law has only partly been put into practice.

Article 16 of the law seems to be a response to the 'global land rush'; it was reportedly added to the law by the President's Office after the draft had already been approved by Parliament and the Senate. The article specifies that only 'natural persons of Congolese nationality' or 'legal persons governed by Congolese law' may acquire land; this means that foreign individuals or companies may only acquire land indirectly, through partnering with Congolese companies. In addition, social and environmental impact assessments must be conducted. This article was popular with many local NGOs, as they argued it would prevent land grabbing by multinational firms (Chaco 2012). However, NGOs were concerned with other clauses that restricted control over land to certain stakeholders, that is, those who can demonstrate economic capacity to develop the land, making it difficult for Congolese smallholder farmers to register their property. Furthermore, a clause restricting land ownership for purposes of speculation, which might be a useful tool against the 'land rush,' has also raised concerns among local NGOs who worry that some smallholders will be unable to make their land productive due to economic limitations and hence would be at risk of having it confiscated by the state (Chaco 2012).

Despite some positive aspects of the Agricultural Law, it contains provisions which are ambiguous or undefined as of yet. Article 18 acknowledges that land can be held under customary land rights systems, in accordance with the Constitution, but does not indicate how they may be registered or otherwise formalized by the state (Article 19). Moreover, the law does not provide any new mechanism for providing women with greater rights or assets in the agricultural sector (Tshiebwe 2015).

Forestry Legislation

Like the other sectors covered here, the forestry sector demonstrates both positive developments and questionable political will within the central government. There has been a moratorium on new logging concessions since 2002, but the government has not always abided by it. The 2002 Forestry law introduced the possibility of community-owned and managed forest areas, but this was not supported by regulations or mechanisms until more recently. Following intense lobbying, a Ministerial Order on the management of community forests was finally published in 2016. Communities can apply for customary ownership rights over forest areas of up to 50,000 ha (RRI 2017, 24).

Because women tend to be primarily responsible for household food preparation, water collection, and gathering non-timber forest products, the impacts of 'land grabbing' of forested areas are particularly gendered. Congolese NGOs such as Coalition of Women Leaders for the Environment and Sustainable Development (CFLEDD) lobbied provincial-level governments to protect women's rights. In May 2018, Equator Province issued an official decree protecting women's rights to land and forests, giving them a role in family-level decision-making over the use of income derived from forests and land resources (Province de L'Equateur 2018). CFLEDD is currently advocating for similar decrees to be promulgated in several other provinces.

Land Law and Policy Reform

Due to the widely accepted weaknesses of the 1973 Land Law, efforts have been underway for years to develop a new land policy and land law for the DRC. While efforts are driven by domestic pressure (particularly from local NGOs representing smallholder farmers and indigenous communities), they have largely been facilitated and financed by UN-Habitat. These initiatives have been slow-moving (Huggins and Paluku 2019) but provincial land policy consultation sessions are currently being held in all 26 Provinces. Thematic groups within the National Land Reform Commission (CONAREF) will then synthesize the findings and a national workshop will be organized to finalize a policy. A similar process will then be followed in order to draft a land law. According to CONAREF personnel, the new law will not have retroactive impacts and will therefore protect land rights that have already been acquired (CONAREF 2019). The land policy reform process is currently being funded through Reducing Emissions from Deforestation and Forest Degradation (REDD +) funding, which may lead to an emphasis on forest conservation and land registration options (Huggins and Paluku 2019). REDD + programmes are controversial in terms of their impacts on local people and their effectiveness in carbon sequestration (see Sect. 6.3 below).

Consultations around the draft land policy have involved discussions of various forms of 'land grabbing,' including land grabbing by foreign actors. For example, a draft land policy document includes a section on 'speculation on rural lands, which results in private land grabbing and large-scale tax evasion' (République Démocratique du Congo 2018).[8] In the Ituri Province consultation, participants asked whether a foreign national who acquired Congolese citizenship would then be able to acquire a permanent title to land (UCBC 2019). Others asked why large-scale concession-holders were not directly involved in the provincial consultations themselves. In regard to what they called the 'unethical and immoral' acquisition of land, participants suggested that local land commissions could ensure that a standard procedure was followed, and that guidelines for land valuation were also developed and respected. Participants also complained about the cultivation of export crops on

[8] Section 1.2.4 (c). Translation from the original French.

concessions, rather than crops that could contribute to local food security (UCBC 2019). During the North Kivu provincial consultation, it was recommended that maximum land holding sizes be introduced in both urban and rural areas (specifically, 50 ha in rural areas); that non-Congolese be permitted to hold only 'concessions ordinaires' (temporary, renewable leases of 25 years) rather than permanent land titles; that large concessions which are underutilized be re-possessed by the state; that the legal validity of titles to land concessions be investigated by the state; and that limits to the size of livestock ranches be introduced (CONAREF 2019). It remains to be seen whether the land policy and land law will incorporate such suggestions.

Case Studies

There are a very wide range of large-scale land acquisitions in the DRC, particularly those owned by domestic actors. The case studies below are illustrative rather than completely representative and focus specifically on international dimensions.

Feronia Palm Oil Plantation

One of the best documented transnational 'land rush' cases concerns Canadian company Feronia. In 2009, Feronia acquired a palm oil plantation over 100,000 ha in size that was previously controlled by the multinational company Unilever.[9] Feronia is part-owned and financed by various European 'development banks,' including CDC (UK), Proparco (France), FMO (Netherlands), BIO (Belgium), OPIC (US), AECID (Spain) (see RIAO-RDC 2019), and has hence received large concessionary loans and grants. For example, it reportedly received $US49 million in loans in 2015 alone (World Rainforest Movement 2018).

Feronia acquired the land through several separate 25-year lease agreements. The legality of the acquisition, however, has been questioned; the original granting of the concession to Unilever during the colonial period was based on falsified documentation (KFW-DEG 2019; Vidal 2015). There are also disputes around more recent leases acquired by Feronia

[9] Unilever gained control over 750,000-ha of land in 1911 and the Belgian colonial regime granted the company a monopoly over commercial palm oil production and trade in these areas, enforcing it with typically high levels of violence (RIAO –RDC et al. 2016).

of smaller, privately owned parcels around 200 ha each. The company is accused of failing to make public its various contracts and leases. In 2015, over 60 customary leaders wrote an open letter declaring the oil plantations to have been illegally acquired during the colonial period; this was followed in 2016 by a letter sent to the Prime Minister by more than 500 community leaders (RIAO–RDC et al. 2016). Congolese NGOs, in collaboration with international NGOs, are also been involved in documenting local concerns. An official complaint was filed with the Independent Complaints Mechanism of the German Development Bank DEG (KFW-DEG 2019).

The ongoing operations of the plantation have also caused conflict and provoked legal disputes between local people and the company. There are reports that the company's security staff and local police beat, tortured and murdered individuals accused of stealing oil palm nuts (World Rainforest Movement 2018). Local people complain that they are not allowed to harvest non-timber forest products in the forested areas around their villages controlled by the company, even though foraged foods such as snails and mushrooms represent important sources of nutrients for the local population. The various impacts of Feronia's operations are highly gendered, with women less able to gain employment at the plantations (World Rainforest Movement 2018) and often forced to deal with the food insecurity challenges at the household level.

There are around 3,500 workers on the plantations, some of whom complain about unpaid or underpaid wages (RIAO-RDC 2019). Local community leaders and residents have reportedly been pressured to sign agreements with Feronia.

There are further accusations that Feronia expanded its palm oil plantations into areas logged by commercial forestry companies (Global Witness 2018). This fits with a broader pattern in the logging sector: 'as the stock of high-value trees gets depleted, the incentive to transform the concession into a plantation – and by doing so cause deforestation – increases' (Global Witness 2018, 18). Although the coordination between Feronia and the logging company (Norsudtimber) is unproven, this would fit with the conception that large-scale land acquisitions for agriculture, logging, and other extractive sectors are increasingly connected (Le Billon and Sommerville 2016).

The public relations discourses of Feronia emphasize that the Unilever plantation had been in decline and that Feronia's investment saved thousands of jobs. The company's website argues that, 'the business was in danger of fading inexorably back into the jungles from whence it was conceived' (Feronia Inc. 2019). In the media, ideas of Feronia 'saving' a struggling local economy are embedded in colonial 'exotification' of the Congolese countryside, such as in the headline, 'One Hundred Years Later, Reviving a "Jewel" Deep in the Jungle' (Wilson 2017:1). Such a rendering de-values the livelihoods of the rural population and relegates the countryside to the status of wilderness, while exaggerating the commercial value of oil palm. The Feronia strategy for legitimizing its activities is reminiscent of the arguments made by Li (2014) about the combination of material and rhetorical elements that are assembled in order to make the 'land rush' possible. Li argues that the process of making land a commodity 'requires regimes of exclusion that distinguish legitimate from illegitimate uses and users, and the inscribing of boundaries through devices such as fences, title deeds, laws, zones, regulations, landmarks and story-lines' (Li 2014, 589). In addition to the clear work involved in building a storyline of 'saving' the plantation, jobs, and communities, Feronia assembled a collection of different organizations, notably the development banks mentioned above, in order to finance and legitimize its activities.

Land Acquisition in the Mining Sector

The DRC has a vast abundance of minerals, including the world's largest deposits of cobalt and industrial diamonds (Trefon 2016, 121). Industrial mining has been significant economic sector in the DRC since the colonial period. In the post-colonial period, under President Mobutu Sese Seko, state-owned mining companies controlled large concessions. As the financial and governance capacity of the state eroded in the 1980s and 1990s, state-owned companies lost capacity, and many of their mining concessions were accessed by artisanal miners with the consent of the state. Following the First and Second Congo Wars in the DRC (1996–1997 and 1998–2003), private mining companies were able to operate in the country again, with 'hundreds of exploration permits' being granted by then-President Laurent-Desire Kabila in the late 1990s (Trefon 2016, 127).[10] Following the Peace Accords of 2003, large multinational companies such as Banro became operational.

[10] Some mines were operated during the conflicts by armed groups or by small companies allied to armed groups.

A mining cadastre (registry) was established by the 2002 Mining Code that maps and registers areas reserved for artisanal and small-scale mining as well as large-scale mining concessions.[11] The mining law set out to attract foreign capital through favourable rates of taxation and low tariffs for mining-related imports. The granting of mining concessions to large companies intended to recentralize the collection of revenue in the mining sector and allow the central state to establish a greater presence in mining zones (Geenen and Honke 2014). In practice, local actors such as customary leaders managed to retain significant influence and control in mining areas due to their ability to mobilize or constrain popular resistance to projects (Geenen and Honke 2014). There are contradictions between the Land Law and the Mining Code, particularly in how these laws address customary rights. As described above, the Land Law (Government of Zaire 1973) as well as the Agricultural Law (Republic of Congo 2011) acknowledge customary rights to land but do not put in place procedures or mechanisms for those rights to be secured. The Mining Code, in contrast, does not make any mention of customary rights to land, referring only to 'the rightful holders of enjoyment of the surface rights' (Article 281), which generally acts against the interests of customary land owners. The government has followed the Mining Code in cases where mining rights and land claims overlap. This means that local communities may lose customary rights to land without compensation. The Mining Law of 2018, largely seen as a 'resource nationalist' law, made changes to the fiscal regulations around large-scale mining. However, it did little if anything to better regulate the ways in which multinational companies acquire mining concessions or to ensure that communities and artisanal and small-scale miners are not swept aside in the process.

Land Acquisition in Forested and Protected Areas

In early 2018, the Ministry of the Environment granted permission to two Chinese-owned companies to commence logging operations in equatorial forest areas, in apparent violation of the Congolese government's 2002 moratorium on new industrial logging titles. The move, criticized

[11] Law No. 007/2002 of 11 July 2002 establishing the Congolese Mining Code and its implementation measures, published in the mining regulations under decree No. 038/2003 of 26 March 2003.

by conservation organizations, follows political tension over international criticism of the government's failure to enforce logging regulations (Global Witness 2015).

In 2018, then-President Kabila reportedly granted several exploration permits to oil companies. The areas identified in the drilling licences overlap with parts of the Salonga and Virunga National Parks (Paravincini 2019), which are areas of outstanding biodiversity. Maps produced by International Union for Conservation of Nature (IUCN) show that various mining concessions (both exploration and exploitation) are located within the boundaries of the Okapi Wildlife Reserve (OWR). Minutes of meetings of the World Heritage Committee mention that a large-scale mining company, Kilogold, has been allocated a permit in the OWR (World Heritage Committee 2016).

As mentioned above, the DRC is one of the countries in which projects under the REDD + scheme are being piloted (Aquino and Guay 2013). While for some stakeholders and observers, REDD + activities are positive in terms of their contribution to conservation and local livelihoods, others are much more sceptical and are concerned that REDD + may take land out of the control of local communities, leading to restrictions on important livelihood strategies (see, for example, Chapter 6 of this volume on community forests in Liberia). Sceptical actors are concerned that any benefits accruing to local community members will be insufficient to recompense them for the loss of access to forested areas; a related concern is that financial and other benefits will be monopolized by elite actors. Indeed, due to various legal and political weaknesses, negotiations over implementation of REDD + and related forestry activities in DRC have been suspended several times in recent years (FPP, RRN and DGPA, 2017, 10).

Agribusiness Parks

The Government of Congo launched the National Agricultural Investment Plan (known by its French acronym, NPIA) in 2013. This model was based on discussions between the government, private investors, and certain multilateral donors (Africa Lead Team 2014). The main focus of the NPIA are 'agribusiness parks,' which are large areas zoned for agricultural production and processing and which are designated as special economic zones. The NPIA plans to provide companies with leases in 21 agribusiness parks, totaling up to 640,000 square kilometres (247,100 square miles), equal to more than one-quarter of the total land area of the country (Clark 2014). These parks were designed to attract international investment while avoiding enclave economies through pre-planned upstream and downstream linkages. The first park, an 80,000 ha site at Bukanga Lonzo near the capital of Kinshasa, was put in place in conjunction with the cooperation of South African investors (Huggins 2015; Ulimwengu 2014).

The agribusiness parks model can be seen, on the one hand, as a government attempt to control and manage 'foreign investment' in the agricultural sector; on the other hand, it reflects the outcome of a high-modernist, production-oriented agricultural policy as well as neoliberal narratives of 'public-private partnerships.'

According to Congolese civil society organizations, 'at the operational level, the ministries with responsibility for the Environment and Land Affairs had been excluded from involvement in Bukanga Lonzo' (FPP, RRN and DGPA 2017, 49). This statement suggests institutional competition and fragmentation within the government. The agribusiness park model seems to have been driven by the personal influence of John Ulimwengu, a Fellow at the International Food Policy Research Institute (IFPRI) and advisor to the Congolese government, as well as the ambitions of the then-Prime Minister Augustin Matata Ponyo (Ross 2018). It is also a product of the efforts of South African farmers and agribusinesses to expand operations across the continent (the South African firm Africom was in charge of most technical elements of the project in Bukanga-Lonzo). NGOs raised concerns that the development of huge tracts of land may alienate customary landowners and displace local communities (Misser 2014). Those researching such issues raised the alarm regarding 'trickery and intimidation as means of land grabbing' at Bukanga Lonzo, the first agribusiness park to ever be developed (FPP, RRN and DGPA 2017, 48). Reports suggest that Bukanga Lonzo is failing to meet its targets and is essentially in collapse (AGRA 2019; Ross 2018). It seems unlikely that the other planned agribusiness parks will be implemented.

Discussion

The various case studies demonstrate that legal frameworks in the DRC are either systematically biased against customary rightsholders (such as the 1973 Land Law) or lack the regulations necessary to secure customary and smallholder land rights (e.g. the 2011 Agricultural Law). Moreover, the Congolese state machinery is, despite pockets of effectiveness, generally poor at inter-agency coordination and susceptible to corruption. It is vital therefore that the momentum created by the current land law and land policy efforts is harnessed to develop not only a law and policy which can facilitate Congolese citizens to secure their land rights, but also a network of stakeholders who can push to see the law and policy implemented. Effective cooperation between state agencies, NGOs, community organizations, farmers' associations, and international donors is crucial. In particular, it is important that the viewpoints of women are included through the direct representation of women in various roles.

There is a political culture in the DRC where leaders, including at the presidential level, use public resources for personal gain. Unless such corruption is constrained, land grabbing practices are likely to continue. Simply put, how can a government regulate large-scale land acquisition if its political leaders represent the most prominent land grabbers? The issue of 'political will' is paramount. This chapter identified a number of legal instruments and policy approaches that may result in either positive or negative outcomes for the average rural Congolese citizen, depending on how they are interpreted and implemented. One example is the provision for control over 'idle land' in the 2011 Agricultural Law, which, depending on the political orientation of politico-administrative elites, could be used against the rural poor rather than preventing land speculation. Another example is Article 16 of the same Agricultural law which could either represent an effective way of limiting a foreign 'land rush' or merely a mechanism for the enrichment of a 'gatekeeping' class of Congolese elites.

To reiterate, political will is needed to make the decentralization of natural resources governance a reality. Some of the greatest opportunities lie at the provincial-level (through the actions of provincial parliaments) and more local levels (through the CARG, for example). However, there are constant tensions between various administrative levels, and decentralized institutions require adequate funding from the central state if they are to be effective.

This chapter drew attention to some of the discursive aspects of the 'land rush' in the DRC. Peemans (2014) identifies continuities between the colonial and post-colonial periods, including in the treatment of the concept of the 'peasant' (associated with ignorance and a lack of skills). The knowledge and ideas around farming are shaped by the interests of large-scale agribusiness companies and the macro-economic focus of the central state. The rich indigenous knowledge of the Congolese peasantry is overlooked and actively undermined by an agenda of 'modernization' and commercialization. Other ways in which debates are shaped in the DRC include the falsity that much of the country is an uninhabited 'bush' or 'jungle' (Wilson 2017) which requires outside investment to become 'valuable'. The existing land uses and claims to resources of local communities are either devalued or simply ignored in such narratives. International stakeholders, including donors, multinational companies, journalists, NGO personnel, and scholars are enmeshed in these discursive debates and often reduce Congolese people to a 'victimhood' state or as a passive 'beneficiary' of assistance. A key part of the struggle against dispossession of communities must be an effort to recognize the existing strengths and achievements of Congolese communities and to identify the potential that could be unleashed through material and political support for their livelihoods.

Conclusion

This chapter focused on the laws, policies, and institutions of the DRC rather than the global dimensions of the 'land rush.' Whether international initiatives such as voluntary principles and best practices will have a positive impact on the DRC in relation to issues of land grabbing remains to be seen.[12] Public campaigns like those by NGOs such as Oxfam attempt to pressure multinational corporations to improve their policies and practices. Many of the principles and approaches developed in these voluntary guidelines could theoretically regulate domestic aspects of the land rush, but there are pre-existing challenges. Since domestic land grabbers do not have to register their activities in the same ways that foreign investors do, problematic cases may be more difficult to identify, except for maybe at the local level. This illustrates the importance of supporting capacity-building for local organizations, whether NGOs, state agencies, provincial parliaments, or multi-stakeholder platforms.

[12] These include the Voluntary Guidelines on the Responsible Governance of Tenure of Land, Fisheries, and Forests in the Context of National Food Security developed by the Committee on World Food Security (May 2012); the AU/ADB/UN-ECA Guiding Principles on Large Scale Land Based Investments in Africa (2014); the USAID Operational Guidelines for Responsible Land-Based Investment (March 2015); the Internal guidelines of the G8 New Alliance on Food Security and Nutrition; and industry guidelines for specific commodities (soy, biofuels, palm oil, sugar, etc.).

Domestic actors may not be affected by 'reputational risk' in the same way as multinational corporations who may be wary of the impacts of bad publicity on their share prices. The 'name and shame' tactics often used against multinational land grabbers may therefore not be as effective in a domestic context. Legal restrictions on ownership of land by foreign individuals or corporations are of course not relevant to the role of domestic actors in land grabbing. Instead, for domestic actors, political decisions and technical assessments must be made over what constitutes a problematic 'land grab' as opposed to a positive investment. This exercise may revolve around interpretation of the clauses in the 2011 Agricultural Law regarding the 'economic capacity' to develop land.

Rather than focusing only on the 'corporate social responsibilities' of those acquiring land, political efforts should focus on protecting and securing the rights of those already living upon and using land in the Democratic Republic of Congo. This requires not only legal and policy action, but also a broader shift in thinking about the roles of smallholder farmers in the national and global food system, and the roles of forest-dwelling communities and other indigenous and marginalized groups within society. Such changes are unlikely to come only 'from above' through the decisions of the central Congolese state, but also 'from below' through sustained struggle and activism by vulnerable communities and their allies. Communities and local organizations, and all those who want to challenge injustices around land acquisition in the DRC, possess a power that must be recognized and valued by the central state.

References

Africa Lead Team. 2014. *Institutional architecture systems assessment for food security policy change: Democratic Republic of Congo*, 2014. Washington, DC: USAID.

AGRA. 2019. *Africa agriculture status report: The hidden Middle: A quiet revolution in the private sector driving agricultural transformation* (Issue 7). Nairobi, Kenya: Alliance for a Green Revolution in Africa (AGRA).

Anseeuw, Ward, Liz Alden Wily, Lorenzo Cotula, and Michael Taylor. 2011. *Land rights and the rush for land: Findings of the global commercial pressures on land research project*. Rome: International Land Coalition.

Asanzi, Philippe. 2014. Understanding the challenges of Chinese agricultural Investments in Africa: An institutional analysis. *Journal of Agricultural Science and Research* 2 (5): 76–87.

Aquino, André, and Bruno Guay. 2013. Implementing REDD + in the Democratic Republic of Congo: An analysis of the emerging national REDD + governance structure. *Forest Policy and Economics* 36: 71–79.

Batterbury, Simon, and Frankline Ndi. 2014. Land grabbing in Africa. In *The routledge handbook of African development*, ed. Tony Binns, Kenneth Lynch, and Etienne Nel, 573–582. London: Routledge.

Bayengeha, Floribert. 2014. Harnessing political will to induce land reform: The story of the Democratic Republic of Congo land reform. Paper prepared for presentation at the 2014 World Bank Conference On Land And Poverty, Washington DC, The World Bank, March 24–27.

Bräutigam, Deborah Haisen Zhang. 2013. Green dreams: Myth and reality in China's agricultural investment in Africa. *Third World Quarterly* 34 (9): 1676–1696.

Chaco, Emmanuel. 2012. DR CONGO: Farmers' organisations slam new agriculture law. *Inter Press News Agency*, February 28 (IPS).

Clark, Simon. 2014. Congo seeks investors for farmland bigger than France. *Wall Street Journal*, October 28.

Cochrane, Logan. 2016. Land Grabbing. In *Encyclopedia of food and agricultural ethics*, ed. P. Thompson and D. Kaplan. The Netherlands: Springer.

Collins, Andrea. 2014. Refocusing governance from the 'bottom-up': Understanding the gendered dynamics of land deals for biofuel development in Kenya and Tanzania. In *New approaches to the Governance of natural resources: Insights from Africa*, ed. J.A Grant, W.R.N. Compaoré and M.I. Mitchell. London: Palgrave Macmillan.

CONAREF. 2019. *Rapport des Consultations provinciales sur le document de la politique au Nord-Kivu*. Goma: CONAREF.

Cotula, Lorenzo. 2013. *The Great African land grab? Agricultural investments and the global food system*. London, New York: Zed Books.

Curtis, Devon. 2013. China and the insecurity of development in the Democratic Republic of the Congo (DRC). *International Peacekeeping* 20 (5): 551–569.

Feintrenie, Laurène. 2014. Agro-Industrial plantations in central Africa, risks and opportunities. *Biodiversity and Conservation* 23 (6): 1577–1589.

Feronia Inc. 2019. Our plantations. https://www.feronia.com/plantations.

FPP, RRN, DGPA. 2017. Land reform and protection of communities' rights. Kinshasa.

Geenen, Sara and Jana Honke. 2014. Land grabbing by mining companies: Local contentions and state reconfiguration in South Kivu (DRC). In *Losing Your land: Dispossession in the Great Lakes*, ed. An Ansoms and Thea Hilhorst. Martlesham: James Currey.

Global Land Project. 2010. Land Grab in Africa. GLP Report 1. GLP International Project Office, University of Copenhagen.

Global Witness. 2015. Exporting impunity. June 3. https://www.globalwitness.org/en/campaigns/democratic-republic-congo/exporting-impunity/.

Global Witness. 2018. *Total Systems Failure: Exposing the Global Secrecy Destroying Forests in the Democratic Republic of Congo.* London: Global Witness.

Griffiths, John. 1986. What is legal pluralism? *Journal of Legal Pluralism and Unofficial Law* 24: 1–55.

Huggins, Chris. 2015. Land-grabbing, agricultural investment and land reform in the DRC. In *L'Afrique des Grands Lacs: Annuaire 2014–2015*, ed. Filip Reyntjens, Stef Vandeginste, and Marjike Verpoorten, 149–174. Belgium: University Press Antwerp.

Huggins, Chris. 2010. Land, power, and identity: Roots of violent conflict in Eastern DRC. International Alert.

Huggins, Chris and Christol Paluku. 2019. The political economy of land law and policy reform in the Democratic Republic of Congo: An institutional bricolage approach. *Canadian Journal of Development Studies* 41: 260–278.

Kaag, Mayke, and Annelies Zoomers. 2014. *The global land grab: Beyond the hype*. London, New York: Zed Books.

KFW-DEG. 2019. PHC (FERONIA) / 18-002. https://www.deginvest.de/%C3%9Cber-uns/Verantwortung/Beschwerdemanagement/Feronia/index-2.html.

Koen, Vlassenroot, and Christopher Huggins. 2005. Land, migration and conflict in eastern Democratic Republic of Congo. In *From the ground up: Land rights, conflict and peace in Sub-Saharan Africa*, ed. Christopher Huggins and Jenny Clover. Pretoria: Institute of Security Studies.

Le Billon, Philippe, and Melanie Sommerville. 2016. Landing capital and assembling 'investable land' in the extractive and agricultural sectors. *Geoforum* 82: 212–224.

Li, Tania Murray. 2014. What is land? Assembling a resource for global investment. *Transactions of the Institute of British Geographers* 39 (4): 589–602. https://doi.org/10.1111/tran.12065.

Musafiri, Prosper Nobirabo. 2009. *The dispossession of indigenous land rights in the DRC: A history and future prospects*. London: Forest Peoples Programme.

Overbeek, Fons Van, and Peter Anew Tamás. 2018. Claim-making through subjectivation: A governmentality analysis of associational performance to Claim land in the hybridity of peri-urban Bukavu. *Geoforum*. https://doi.org/10.1016/j.geoforum.2018.04.007.

Paravincini, Giulia. 2019. Congo's former president awarded oil block in UNESCO heritage site. *Reuters*, February 27. https://www.reuters.com/article/us-congo-environment-idUSKCN1QG22A.

Pedersen, Rasmus Hundsbaek. 2016. Access to land reconsidered: The land grab, polycentric governance and Tanzania's new wave land reform. *Geoforum* 72: 104–113.

Pedersen, Rasmus Hundsbaek, and Lars Buur. 2016. Beyond land grabbing. Old morals and new perspectives on contemporary investments. *Geoforum* 72: 77–81.

Peemans, J.-P. 2014. Land grabbing and development history: The congolese experience. In *Losing your land: Dispossession in the Great Lakes*, ed. An Ansoms and Thea Hilhorst. Martlesham: James Currey.

Province de L'Equateur. 2018. Edict 002/2018 portant reconnaissance des droits de possession et de jouissance des femmes aux patrimoines forestiers et fonciers. *Journal Officiel de la Republique Democratique de Congo, July 2018*. Kinshasa: Cabinet de President de la Republique.

République Démocratique du Congo. 2018. *Programme d'Appui à la Reforme Foncière Axe/Jalon 2 : Formulation de la Politique Foncière Nationale : Document de Politique Foncière Nationale, draft 1*. Kinshasa: Ministère des Affaires Foncières/Commission Nationale de la Réforme Foncière (CONAREF).

République Démocratique du Congo. 2011. *Loi no. 11/022 du 24 décembre 2011 portant principes fondamentaux relatifs à l'agriculture*. Kinshasa: Government Printers.

Rights and Resources Initiative, 2017. *From Risk and Conflict to Peace and Prosperity: The urgency of securing community land rights in a turbulent world*. Washington, DC: Rights and Resources Initiative.

RIAO-RDC. 2019. Violent tensions at Feronia's oil palm plantations in the DR Congo. *Grain*, March 21. https://grain.org/e/6182.

RIAO–RDC, Africa Europe Faith and Justice Network, Entraide et Fraternité, GRAIN, SOS Faim, UMOYA, urgewald, War on Want and World Rainforest Movement. 2016. Land conflicts and shady finances plague DR Congo palm oil company backed by development funds. *Grain*, November 2.

Ross, A. 2018. "Africa's green revolution stumbles at Congo project to solve food shortages." *Reuters*. Accessed at https://www.reuters.com/article/us-congo-agriculture/africas-green-revolution-stumbles-at-congo-project-to-solve-food-shortagesidUSKCN1IN0IJ on November 26, 2020.

Samndong, Raymond Achu, and Isilda Nhantumbo. 2015. *Natural resources governance in the Democratic Republic of Congo: Breaking sector walls for sustainable land use investments*. IIED: London, UK.

Syn, Julitette, and Christol Paluku. 2015. *Improving women's access to land in eastern DRC: Challenges and emerging opportunities, learning from emerging practices*. Nairobi: UN-Habitat.

Trefon, T. 2016. *Congo's Environmental Paradox: Potential and predation in a land of plenty*. London, UK: Zed Books.

Tshiebwe, Grégoire Ngalamulume. 2015. Décentralisation agricole, développement rural et gouvernance locale en République Démocratique du Congo. *African Journal of Democracy and Governance* 2 (1): 113–130.

Ulimwengu, John. 2014. DRC agricultural Business parks initiative: An integrated strategy to unleash economic development and address food insecurity in DRC and beyond. PowerPoint Presentation, the Corporate Council on Africa, Washington DC, April 9.

Université Chrétienne Bilingue du Congo (UCBC). 2019. Rapport de L'atelier Provincial de Consultation sur le Politique Fonciere en RDC: Province de L'ituri. UCBC/ PROJET CAFI (Central African Forest Initiative).

Vidal, J. 2015. UK development finance arm accused of bankrolling 'agro-colonialism' in Congo. *The Guardian*. Published online 5 Jun 2015.

Vlassenroot, Koen, and Christopher Huggins. 2014. Le foncier et les dynamiques de conflit à l'est de la république démocratique du Congo: définir des options d'intervention. In *République démocratique du Congo: Décentralisation et espaces de pouvoir*, ed. Jean Omasombo and Paule Bouvier, 159–167. Tervuren, Belgium: Royal Museum for Central Africa.

Wilson, Thomas. 2017. One hundred years later, reviving a 'Jewel' deep in the jungle. *Bloomberg*, September 15. https://www.bloomberg.com/news/articles/2017-09-15/one-hundred-years-later-heart-of-congo-ships-oil-again.

World Bank. 2010. *Rising global interest in farmland: Can it yield sustainable and equitable benefits?*. Washington, DC: World Bank.

World Bank. 2019. Democratic Republic of Congo: Overview. https://www.worldbank.org/en/country/drc/overview.

World Heritage Committee. 2016. 40th session of the committee on the convention concerning the protection of the world cultural and natural heritage. Accessed on 8 May, 2018 https://www.informea.org/en/decision/okapi-wildlife-reserve-democratic-republic-congo-n-718-90.

World Rainforest Movement. 2018. The untold suffering of women living in and around Feronia's industrial oil palm plantations in the DRC. *Bulletin* Issue 239—September.

CHAPTER 11

Beyond the Land Rush? Reflections on Transnational Interactions and the Future IPE of Africa

Logan Cochrane, John Hopeson Anku, and Nathan Andrews

Introduction

This volume set out to explore the transnational land rush in Africa. The breadth of countries impacted by large-scale land acquisitions (see Fig. 11.1 below) covered in this collection highlights the multiple manifestations of this global phenomenon in specific settings. In the Introduction, we noted that climate change, human rights-based perspectives, and social differentiation did not receive significant attention in this

L. Cochrane (✉)
Global and International Studies, Ottawa, ON, Canada

College of Public Policy, HBKU, Qatar

J. H. Anku · N. Andrews
Global and International Studies, University of Northern British Columbia, Prince George, BC, Canada
e-mail: nathan.andrews@unbc.ca

L. Cochrane and N. Andrews (eds.), *The Transnational Land Rush in Africa*, International Political Economy Series,
https://doi.org/10.1007/978-3-030-60789-0_11

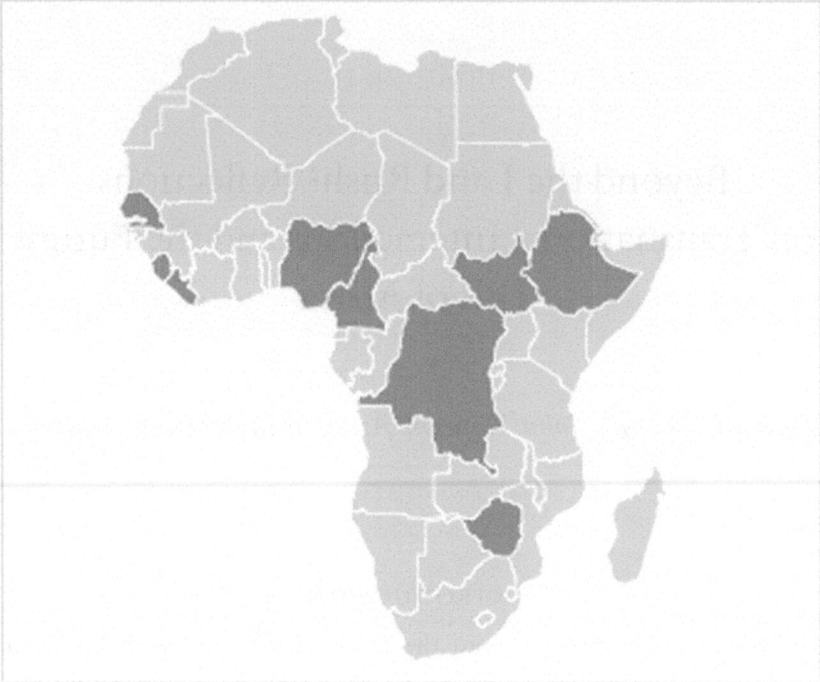

Fig. 11.1 Map of Countries Included in this Collection

volume, leaving room for future research. A recent review of the land rush in Ethiopia (Cochrane and Legault 2020) identifies a few additional areas for investigation. One limitation of the current literature on the land rush is its near-exclusive focus on foreign investors, when in some cases domestic and diaspora actors have been as, or even more, important. This volume addresses this gap by examining the role of national governments and domestic actors in large-scale land investments, alongside foreign investors. Some other intersecting factors, such as climate change, impacts to biodiversity and water, and traditional ecological knowledge and indigenous knowledge, continued to be understudied (see Cochrane and Legault 2020).

The mainstream International Political Economy (IPE) scholarship, in particular, has not devoted significant attention to ecological issues or, more specifically, the intricate relationship between the international political economy and the environment (Clapp and Helleiner 2012). The emphasis on the "IPE of money" (Cohen 2017) results in a systematic neglect of the intersectionality of these two topics. As noted in the introductory chapter, the prevailing Eurocentricism and positivism of IPE contributes to this dismissal of certain issues which bear directly on both the livelihoods of people and global political economy/ecology (Hobson 2013; Weber 2015). To be sure, our volume does not entirely address such gaps, but we point to these areas as avenues for future research either in the Palgrave IPE series or elsewhere in leading IPE journals such as *Review of International Political Economy*. Overall, we hope our volume contributes to discussions around the need for a critical and multidimensional exploration of the continuities and changes in the study of contemporary IPE (Mahrenbach and Shaw 2019).

The purpose of this concluding chapter is three-fold. First, we examine the context of large-scale land acquisitions in various African countries, including those not written about in this volume. This discussion is important for highlighting the contributions that this book has made as well as its limitations in terms of scope. Secondly, we compare and contrast the various case studies examined in this book by analyzing topics such as leasing and commodity trends, legal regimes, and land tenure systems, as well as the broad range of actors involved in the land rush. Thirdly, the final segment reflects on the question of "what is beyond the land rush" that is posed in the title of this chapter. We critically interrogate the crises and issues afflicting Africa and discuss whether moving "beyond" the transnational land rush is possible under current circumstances, especially considering the World Economic Forum's estimate that Africa has about 65% of the uncultivated arable land left in the world (see Monzon 2020). At the very least, this status quo points to a rather complex future IPE of land in Africa.

Inclusion Limitations and Regional Perspectives

Attempts to include all six key regions of the African continent (below) in a single book created limitations. The methodology employed in selecting countries resulted in uneven geographic coverage. We started with the countries most impacted by the land rush, in terms of hectares acquired using the largest database available, despite the limitations of the Land Matrix as discussed in several chapters of this volume. We invited authors to write chapters on the 10 countries most greatly impacted by the land rush (in terms of hectares acquired) and then expanded to the top 20 countries, though not all countries were included in the final publication. Examples of cases that met the criteria but for which we could not secure authors or finalized chapters include: Gabon, Madagascar, the Republic of Congo, Sudan, Mozambique, and Tanzania. As a result of our criteria and method for case selection, countries in the north and south of the continent as well as the small island states received limited attention. Although we do not attempt to offer comprehensive review of each region, we present highlights from the twenty countries most impacted by the land rush drawing on the Land Matrix database, with particular attention to those not covered in this collection. We hope to make more explicit the geographic gaps in this collection and direct future researchers to under-studied countries.

Central Africa. There are contributions on Cameroon (Chapter 2) and the Democratic Republic of the Congo (DRC) (Chapter 10) in this collection. What is missing are the chapters on the Republic of the Congo and Gabon, both of which experienced significant land acquisitions. For Congo, the Land Matrix lists over 2 million hectares of contracted land, an amount that is largely accounted for by two deals. The largest acquisition is 1.4 million hectares, acquired in 2011 by Olam International for the purpose of forestry and carbon sequestration. The second largest is 470,000 hectares, used for palm oil production. According to the Land Matrix, the implementation of this latter project appears to be moving slowly. Gabon is listed as having leased nearly 3 million hectares, and like the case of the Congo, there are massive contracts held by a few actors. In both countries, forestry accounts for the bulk of the investments. Recent research (Davis et al. 2020) points to significant tropical forest loss in the Congo basin. Among the nations most impacted by the land rush in Africa, Gabon appears to be the least researched (contributions include: Feintrenie 2014; Feintrenie et al. 2014). Searches on the Web of Science and Scopus produce no studies specific to Gabon. This gap ought to give academics pause for reflection with regard to the biases of researchers and hopefully encourage future studies.

East Africa. This volume included chapters on the most impacted nations in East Africa (Ethiopia in Chapter 9, South Sudan in Chapter 4). Other nations in the region with significant amounts of land acquired include Tanzania and Kenya. Of the 20 most impacted African nations, Kenya and Tanzania are relatively less impacted, yet they have been the subject of more research studies (particularly in comparison to countries like Gabon, Sudan and Zambia). This disproportionality raises questions about the geography of research, where accessibility, history, language, and relationships result in the neglect of some countries and thus a lack of grounded evidence to inform policy and decision-making (see Cochrane and Thornton 2018). In Kenya, the largest acquisitions are almost entirely for the purpose of biofuels and are largely stalled or failed. In Tanzania, the acquisitions are more diverse (forestry, food, mining, biofuels), domestic investors play a stronger role, and there is a lower failure rate. Based upon what is available via the Web of Science and Scopus, it does not appear that macro-level analyses have been conducted in either country, which represents a compelling and complementary area for future contributions.

North Africa. This volume did not include any country in North Africa. We attempted to include the most impacted nation in this region, Sudan, but were unable to for various reasons. There is a limited ability to conduct research in Sudan and almost no research has been conducted on the subject of land acquisitions (notable contributions include Elhadary and Abdelatti (2016) and Zambakari (2017)). The country's political changes in 2019 have made an opaque situation even more challenging to access and assess. From what the Land Matrix has been able to collect, it appears that investors from the Gulf Cooperation Countries (Qatar, Kuwait, Saudi Arabia, United Arab Emirates) possess several of the largest projects. It is unclear what the status of many of the investments are and much more research is needed to understand even the basics of the situation in Sudan. Morocco also appears among the top 20 impacted nations, although this is largely due to one large but failed investment (700,000 ha).

Small Island States. By virtue of their size, the small island states of Africa (e.g. Cape Verde, Comoros, Mauritius, Saõ Tomé and Principé and the Seychelles) did not feature as countries with large amounts of leased hectares, particularly when compared to geographically vast countries. However, another way of analyzing the impact of investments is by examining the percentage of the overall land leased. From this perspective, the small island states of Africa *are* significantly impacted by the land rush. For example, a single deal in Saõ Tomé and Principé accounted for approximately 5% of the country's land mass (a palm oil investment covering 4917 ha). For comparison, heavily impacted nations featured in this collection (e.g. DRC and Ethiopia) possess a lower percentage of their overall land leased (2.5% and 3.2% respectively). The focus placed on very large deals in terms of hectarage has resulted in less attention paid to small island states. This reflects yet another bias in the reporting and research of the land rush, and highlights another potential area for future investigations.

Southern Africa. One nation from Southern Africa was included in this book (Zimbabwe, Chapter 8). Mozambique is a significant omission in this work given the large amounts of land acquired in the country during the rush; although, in comparison to other nations (e.g. Gabon, Sudan and Zambia), Mozambique has been subject to more research (e.g. Arnall 2019; Bruna 2019; Porsani et al. 2019). The Land Matrix lists 11 contracts greater than 100,000 ha in Mozambique, five of which are in the start-up phase or have been abandoned. The intended uses of these acquisitions range widely and include mining, forestry, conservation, agriculture, and tourism. In Madagascar, over a million hectares of land have been acquired, however, two large deals primarily account for this figure: (1) 695,000 ha acquired by Varun Industries in 2008, primarily for mining uranium, and (2) 495,000 ha acquired by Hunter Resources in stages, beginning in 2005, primarily for biofuels, although the project was subsequently abandoned in 2011. Over a million hectares of land were acquired in Zambia, a country that is significantly under-researched. This lack of research attention may be due to the different profile of investors, the largest of which are mining (First Quantum with 255,101 ha in three acquisitions, Barrick Gold with 135,500 ha) and livestock (e.g. Zambeef gained 107,988 ha over five acquisitions).

West Africa. The greatest number of country case studies in this collection came from the West African region (Liberia in Chapter 6, Nigeria in Chapter 5, Senegal in Chapter 3, Sierra Leone in Chapter 7). Of the West African states not covered, Ghana is a notable gap as it is among the top 20 most impacted by the land rush. The country has seen significant interest in large-scale land acquisitions, with estimates suggesting over a million hectares involved in land deals. Out of this figure, the Land Matrix reports 400,000 ha contracted to a single entity, Inga Farms Ltd., for the production of crops such as coffee, oil palm, rubber, and sugarcane. Similarly, the Base for Industrial and Environmental Technology Ghana (BIET-Ghana) project acquired 50,000 ha, representing the second largest recorded deal (though the project has yet to commence). The Bui Power Authority also acquired some 44,400 ha for the purpose of constructing a hydroelectric dam (see Odoom 2017). Though the Land Matrix documents other large-scale land acquisitions in Ghana, there are not always specific figures attached to these transactions. A number of the recorded deals contain no data regarding the actual size of acquired land. Mali has also been significantly impacted by the land rush, with over half a million hectares acquired. Of that, 205,700 ha is a single deal with Agro Industrie Développement negotiated in 2011, the majority of which (200,000 ha) is allotted for conservation management through a public-private partnership. The next two largest land deals in Mali are public-private mining operations (37,200 and 30,200 ha, respectively). The next largest land deals are either not in operation or have failed (Southern Global with 30,000 ha; Agro Energy with 30,000 ha; Toya Holding with 30,000 ha, among others).

Understanding Sub-regional Comparisons of the Transnational Land Rush

Lease Trends

The scale of the corporate rush for land since the triple crisis of 2007/08 is unprecedented. However, this collection shows that land deals possess deeper historical roots, well before the triple crisis of 2007/8, with some leases having origins in the colonial era (e.g. see Chapter 2 on Cameroon). Examples from this volume demonstrate that an ahistorical focus on the contemporary period runs the risk of making invisible the evictions and expropriations of the past. Much of the scholarly attention focused on food commodities following the triple crisis, and the actions of particular investors and countries who exacerbated food insecurity in countries targeted for land acquisitions (see Cochrane and Amery 2017). While this narrative is not inaccurate, it presents only a part of the complex picture that has since emerged. Non-food commodities such as timber, carbon credits, minerals, tourism, and biofuels have also been key drivers of the land rush, as the regional summaries herein highlight (see also Chapter 2 on Cameroon, Chapter 3 on Senegal, and Chapter 8 on Zimbabwe). The diversity of the land rush challenges any continent-wide generalizations about its purposes and outcomes.

Large agricultural investments (i.e. food and fuel), despite being one of the key drivers of the land rush, experienced significant failure. For example, in Senegal, the 718,401 hectares of land projects announced in 2000 declined significantly by 2012, with many projects in the biofuel sector collapsing. Between the years of 2007 and 2010, only 15,000 ha out of the estimated 384,000 ha of lands allocated for biofuel projects were planted with jatropha. The situation was similar in Cameroon, where most intended projects (covering 2,771,406 ha) failed to materialize. In both cases, civil society played important roles in contesting the land grabs. While agricultural projects struggled to get off the ground due to local contestations, mining leases (in the DRC, Mozambique, Tanzania, and Zambia) and forestry plans (in Republic of Congo, Gabon and Liberia) continued to grow yet are under-researched in IPE; other disciplines, such as geography address these thematic areas more systematically. The complexity of the land rush across the continent is often simplified by sector or discipline, which in turn obscures and/or minimizes the diverse impacts on lives, livelihoods, environments, biodiversity, culture, and traditional knowledge. The challenge for the future of IPE is finding innovative ways to critically address these complexities and multiplicities, while also conveying them in engaging and accessible ways. In other words, the challenge is not only one of evidence generation, but of interdisciplinary, multi-sectoral engagement, and knowledge translation.

Commodity Trends

The need for developing countries to address poverty through export commodities is cited as one of the key enablers of the global land rush (Carmody 2011). Africa is no different: investors sought land across the continent and concentrated on a range of commodities. In the case of Cameroon, the large-scale concessions acquired were for the cultivation of food, biofuel crops, and timber. For the many countries in Central and West Africa, oil palm plantations dominate the cultivated crops sector. In Nigeria, there is an emphasis on agro-fuels, cassava plantations, and ethanol plants. The post-war countries of Sierra Leone and Liberia actively promoted rice and sugar cultivation, and palm oil plantations and logging, respectively, as part of their reconstruction process.

A review of the commodities targeted by land investors reveals the motivations behind the rush in Africa. For foreign and domestic investors alike, the search for alternative energy sources to meet the growing global demand for fuels was imperative. It was therefore not surprising to find that biofuels featured prominently across the country case studies discussed in this book. Discussions around the sustainability of current fuel sources and the quest to achieve a reduction in global greenhouse gas emissions brought biofuels to the fore as a viable alternative. The findings from the country case studies confirm earlier research on the role of biofuels in the global land rush (see Carmody 2011; Anseeuw and Taylor 2014; Boamah and Overa 2016; Lanz et al. 2018). Notably, this collection highlights that countries are not acted upon, but exert their own agency; national governments view biofuel crops as important elements in their economic development strategies, for instance, as avenues to boost their export earnings. Through the promotion of large-scale land acquisitions, African countries and governments are invariably seeking to "cash in" on associated economic and financial benefits. It is for this reason that a country such as Ethiopia would actively pursue a very intentional, deliberate policy of attracting investments into its biofuel sector. Likewise, for post-war countries such as Liberia and Sierra Leone, attracting desired foreign investment in the agricultural sector could kick-start economies that have been decimated by many years of civil conflict. While the parties involved in the transnational land rush (i.e. investors and host countries) hold varying motivations and incentives in pursuing large-scale land acquisitions, the promised economic benefits of this strategy in Africa remains a common denominator.

Legal Regimes and Land Tenure Systems

Countries in Africa possess varied legal regimes that regulate their land sectors, as the case studies presented in this book reveal. Though these regimes are often a source of contestation and ambiguity (see Home 2020), they circumscribe the framework within which large-scale land acquisitions take place. Examples described in this volume include Cameroon's 1974 decree (see Chapter 2), the 2009 and 2014 Land Act in South Sudan (Chapter 4), Nigeria's Land Use Act of 1978 (see Chapter 5), and Liberia's Community Rights Law of 2009 (see Chapter 6), among others. These different legal regimes result in land tenure systems that can be grouped into two categories, namely statist and dualist systems. Countries that subscribe to the statist system (e.g., Ethiopia, Nigeria, and to some extent Cameroon) experience a situation where decisions over land and access to land are primarily placed in the hands of the state and its allied agencies. Ethiopia's statist regime can be traced to its ancient history, when the emperor/empress exercised control over all land in the country, up until the current era where all land is considered state property, supposedly held on behalf of the people. The contemporary Ethiopian government put in a deliberate policy to attract foreign investors, providing them first with unfettered access and then ultimately restricting their operations through regulations prioritizing domestic and diaspora investors. In the case of Nigeria, the Land Use Act (1978) effectively terminated the rights of the people to their ancestral lands and placed power over land in the hands of the government. The Nigerian government, as a result, can easily allocate communal lands to private capital. In the case of Cameroon, there are three basic categories of land management in the country, established in 1974: the private, public, and national domains. The Cameroonian state plays a significant role in deciding land uses in these various domains, including for the "public good," and determines who has access to land and its resources.

In contrast, dualist systems share land management responsibilities between the state and the traditional/customary systems. In the case studies presented in this book, the DRC represents a prototype of a dualist system. The Belgians (former colonial power) imposed a dualist system that combined the state-run deeds system and customary laws. After independence and in the post-colonial period, the central state enhanced its role in negotiating land deals. The country's 2006 Constitution, however, restored the previous sense of dualism and outlined a role for communities on matters concerning land. Similarly, Sierra Leone inherited a dualistic land tenure system from the British colonial government. The communal and customary land ownership regime dictates that land is the property of indigenous extended families that can trace their lineage to founding ancestors and that is inherited from one generation to another. Liberia, however, presents a unique case in terms of how the state co-exists with customary institutions in the management of land and resources. The central government relinquished its power over logging concessions to community forest governance regimes through the Community Rights Law in 2009, which ceded ownership and management rights to communities with customary land. Though this approach has come with its challenges, it represents a refreshing departure from the colonially embedded practices of states in Africa.

The study of a country's land tenure system is important to understanding the institutional framework within which large-scale land acquisitions take place and can help predict the likelihood of project being accepted by a given community. For instance, the statist regimes in Nigeria and Ethiopia empower the government to define the scope and nature of land acquisitions. The Ethiopian government can, through policy, decide to attract or restrict foreign investments in the agricultural sector. The downside to this system, however, is the alienation of local people in processes of large-scale land acquisitions. Host communities tend to protest and rebel against investments due to a lack of consultation and collaboration. Sometimes the livelihood impacts of intended projects are ignored during negotiation processes. Those local people who have their livelihoods adversely affected expect to benefit from land transactions, yet they are often marginalized by the patriarchal and political structures related to land tenure in their respective countries (see Andrews 2018). The strength of the dualist system, in comparison to the statist system, lies in its ability to allow for communal input in the decision-making processes. This participatory approach minimizes the likelihood of protest and promotes community acceptance. That said, countries with dualist systems are also likely to experience situations of conflict, given the ambiguity produced by the two systems (i.e. state and customary) in terms of who has the authority to make final decisions over land access and use (Berry 2017, 2020; see also Andrews 2016). Therefore, investors can take advantage of this conflict and decide to not honour promised entitlements, such as financial compensation and land restitution for farmers. The dualist system does not delineate clear lines of responsibility and, in the end, individuals in host communities tend to "lose" in land deal negotiations.

"Glocal" Actors in the Transnational Land Rush

The scramble for Africa's land predates the 2007/2008 crisis and the more recent land rush it provoked. The chapters of this volume discuss how Africa's contemporary land tenure regimes are rooted in the colonial era and colonial histories. In post-colonial Africa, new powers seeking to "grab" the continent's land and resources emerged, such as the United States, China, India, and the Gulf Cooperation Council. There is also a confluence of "domestic actors" operating within specific countries and across the continent interested in acquiring land for all kinds of activities. For example, in the DRC, South African companies acquired large tracts of land. Similarly, the Nigerian state of Kwara seized land from local black farmers and contracted it to white farmers from Zimbabwe. Also significant is the role of national governments as land "acquirers." The Cameroonian government, through the Cameroon Development

Corporation, annexed large tracts of lands in the western provinces. Similarly, the Nigerian government acquired lands for its cassava and ethanol plantations.

In various communities, the role of traditional authority (i.e. chiefs) cannot be downplayed. For instance, the case of Liberia (Chapter 6) illustrates how the new governance structure put in place to regulate logging became a source of conflict between local political actors and the community members. The chiefs, having been empowered by the new system to act on behalf of their people, tend to abuse their position and therefore alienate community members from ongoing processes. The Liberian situation further supports findings from Ghana which show that chiefs have taken advantage of the dualist system to act arbitrarily in some cases, thereby provoking conflict in their communities (see Ahmed et al. 2017; Aha and Ayitey 2017; Kirst 2020). The role of the state and other "domestic actors" in the transnational land rush complicates mainstream narratives that suggest this phenomenon is driven almost exclusively by global forces. The contributions of this volume underscore what researchers have dubbed the "glocal" dynamics that relate to land issues in Africa (Collins et al. 2019).

The hegemonic influence of the state through its exercise of legal, sovereign power is not absolute. The chapter on Senegal reveals that non-state actors, in this case civil society organizations (CSOs), can exert considerable influence on state decision-making processes concerning land transactions. Here too, the "glocal" is important because there is a transnational network of CSOs (i.e.both domestic and international) who collaborated to successfully oppose land grabbing practices, like in the case of Grande Côte Operations and its adequate compensation for affected communities. Burnod et al. (2013) illustrate the influence of civil society over the state in land transactions through a study of the famous Daewoo affair in Madagascar. The government's decision to lease 1.3 million hectares of land to a South Korean company, Daewoo Logistics, to produce maize for export without the consent of the local communities produced a chain reaction that led to the fall of then-president Marc Ravalomanana. These two examples (Senegal and Madagascar) demonstrate that the power of the state over land transactions is not absolute but contingent. The case of Cameroon (Chapter 2) further highlights local resistance to land deals and communities' varying degrees of success in changing the nature of land transactions. For instance, the Herakles Farms incident was met with protests which led to reduction of the project size from 73,000 ha to 20,000 ha. This volume's focus on the power, agency, and influence of local communities and CSOs in processes of land acquisitions represents an important contribution to a discourse that often portrays Africans as victims.

Concluding Reflections: Beyond the Land Rush?

The global rush for land across the African continent was a "black swan"; the arrival of investors in finance, energy, and food was quickly followed by massive transfers of land from individuals and states to corporations, in the tens of millions of hectares. As we write, new crises are emerging on the continent, with uncertain impacts. In eastern Africa, where tens of millions of people already rely upon social safety nets and emergency aid (World Bank 2020), a locust plague has affected tens of millions of people (FAO 2020). Climate change is expected to push tens of millions into poverty (Hallegatte et al. 2016). The global pandemic of COVID19, and the drastic responses taken to contain it, are expected to push 71–100 million people into extreme poverty, 32–42 million of whom living in countries in sub-Saharan Africa (Mahler et al. 2020). This is in addition to the over 600 million people who were already living in extreme poverty, more than half of whom live in countries in sub-Saharan Africa (World Bank 2018). Global trade markets have been disrupted, with export-reliant nations feeling the brunt of the shock to the globalized system. Amidst these challenges, we are also witnessing the deepening of democracy across the continent, as seen in Burundi, Malawi, and elsewhere. The impacts of these changes are still unfolding, which bring us to the question posed at the beginning of this concluding chapter: what is "beyond the land rush"?

It is unclear what may emerge in the immediate and long-term following the multiple, intersecting crises described above. It was not until the dust began to settle several years after the initial rush for land in 2007/08 that the true scale and extent of this phenomenon came into clear view. The interruption to global supply chains and resultant shortages caused by the COVID19 pandemic has nations looking inward. The liberal idea of "competitive advantage" in a globalized market may lose whatever veneer remained; the vulnerabilities of inter-dependency in an unequal world more apparent. Countries are reevaluating what sectors are truly "essential," potentially decreasing investment opportunities for investors and export opportunities for African nations. Indeed, one of the immediate impacts of COVID19 was massive capital flight from Africa (OECD 2020). It seems possible that foreign investment will continue to drop significantly, yet one could have thought the same following the financial crisis of 2007/08. It is possible that these crises spur new races to the bottom, potentially in the manufacturing sector and on an intercontinental level. The high demand for health commodities and increased scarcity might drive growth in regionalized markets over globalized ones. Health systems are being stretched to their limits, and governments are coming close to their financial limits as they seek to expand social safety nets. African governments face the conundrum of declining foreign investment alongside weak domestic capital. The reluctance to rely upon globalized markets many mean greater regionalization, for, example, Kenyan capital in South Sudan and South African capital in Zimbabwe. What might this shift in political-economic relations mean for people, governments, and investors? Many lessons can be gleaned from the last decade. We know what laws, policies, and regulations do not work, regardless if the capital is domestic, diaspora, regional, or global.

This may be a critical moment, as some hope it is, for re-envisioning and re-imagining continental futures. A time for transformation. As Achille Mbembe (2020) describes, the global pandemic presents us with an opportunity not to fill-in the cracks of a broken wall, but to reinvent nearly everything. How can we expect a better outcome when casino capitalism simply shifts into new hands? When we reach into the snake hole, we ought not expect to pull out a dove. The future of IPE in Africa may reflect this metaphor. Indeed, well before this reckoning forced yet another "rethink," scholars were examining prefigurative questions, such as the future of sovereignty, the revaluation of agricultural and biodiversity wealth (Walshe 2019), and the transformation of urban areas into just and inclusive environments (Thornton 2018). While some of these questions take on new forms, others force us to return to questions from decades, even centuries past. Critical reflection about pasts and visions of possible futures are both necessary to our collective search for inspiration. We may return to questions of capitalism and global relations, as Samir Amin has done over the decades (1976, 1997, 2004), or we reassess the meaning wealth in its different forms, be it cultural (Cabral 1977) or linguistic (Thiongo 1986). "Looking back" does not mean romanticizing our pasts; however, we may need to look to previous generations to break free from the ideological blinders that limit our vision to our immediate, temporal peripheries. We may gallop ahead towards a new destination, only to arrive through the side door and encounter the capitalism casino still dealing the same blows. If we remove our blinders, however, we may dismantle already failing institutions and truly revolutionize the future (Fanon 1952, 1963). As we write, the dust of COVID19 has not even begun to settle. We are hopeful about IPE's ability to respond to the intersecting crises of globalization, capitalism, and racism, and look forward to the discipline's directions in the coming years and decade(s).

Bibliography

Aha, Bismark, and Jonathan Z. Ayitey. 2017. Biofuels and the hazards of land grabbing: Tenure (in)security and indigenous farmers' investment decisions in Ghana. *Land Use Policy* 60 (January): 48–59. https://doi.org/10.1016/j.landusepol.2016.10.012.

Ahmed, Abubakari, Benjamin Betey Campion, and Alexandros Gasparatos. 2017. Biofuel development in Ghana: Policies of expansion and drivers of failure in the Jatropha sector. *Renewable and Sustainable Energy Reviews* 70 (April): 133–149. https://doi.org/10.1016/j.rser.2016.11.216.

Amin, Samir. 1976. *Unequal development: An essay on the social formations of peripheral capitalism*, 70–71. New York: Monthly Review Press.

Amin, Samir. 1997. *Capitalism in the age of globalization: The management of contemporary society*. London: Zed Books.

Amin, Samir. 2004. *The liberal virus: Permanent war and the Americanization of the world*. New York: Monthly Review Press.

Andrews, Nathan. 2016. Challenges of corporate social responsibility (CSR) in domestic settings: An exploration of mining regulation vis-à-vis CSR in Ghana. *Resources Policy* 47: 9–17.

Andrews, Nathan. 2018. Land versus livelihoods: Community perspectives on dispossession and marginalization in Ghana's mining sector. *Resources Policy* 58: 240–249.

Anseeuw, Ward., and Taylor, Mike. 2014. Factors shaping the global land rush. In *Grabbing back: Essays against the global land grab*. ed. A.R. Ross. Oakland, CA: AK Press, 45.

Arnall, Alex. 2019. "Employment until the end of the world": Exploring the role of manipulation in a Mozambican land deal. *Land Use Policy* 81: 862–870.

Berry, Sara. 2017. Struggles over land and authority in Africa. *African Studies Review* 60 (3): 105–125.

Berry, Sara. 2020. On whose authority? Land reform, power and economic uncertainty in contemporary sub-Saharan Africa. In *Rethinking land reform in Africa: New ideas, opportunities and challenges*, ed. Cosmas Milton Obote Ochieng, 34–44. Abidjan: African Development Bank.

Boamah, Festus, and Ragnhild Overå. 2016. Rethinking livelihood impacts of biofuel land deals in Ghana: Rethinking livelihood impacts of biofuel land deals in Ghana. *Development and Change* 47 (1): 98–129. https://doi.org/10.1111/dech.12213.

Bruna, Natacha. 2019. Land of plenty, land of misery: Synergetic resource grabbing in Mozambique. *Land* 8 (8): 113.

Burnod, Perrine, Mathilde Gingembre, and Rivo Andrianirina Ratsialonana. 2013. Competition over authority and access: International land deals in Madagascar. *Development and Change* 44 (2): 357–379.

Cabral, Amilcar. 1977. (2016 translation). *Resistance and decolonization*. London: Rowman & Littlefield.

Carmody, Pádraig Risteard. 2011. *The new scramble for Africa*. Cambridge, UK; Malden Mass: Polity Press.

Clapp, Jennifer, and Helleiner Eric. 2012. International political economy and the environment: back to the basics? *International Affairs* 88 (3): 485–501.

Cochrane, Logan, and Hussein A. Amery. 2017. Gulf cooperation council countries and the global land grab. *Arab World Geographer* 20 (1): 17–41.

Cochrane, Logan, and Alec Thornton. 2018. The geography of development studies: Leaving no one behind. *Forum for Development Studies* 45: 167–175.

Cochrane, Logan, and Danielle D. Legault. 2020. The rush for land and agricultural investment in Ethiopia: What we know and what we are missing. *Land* 9 (5): 167 (1–13).

Cohen, Benjamin. 2017. The IPE of money revisited. *Review of International Political Economy* 24 (4): 657–680.

Collins, Andrea M., J. Andrew Grant, and Patricia Ackah-Baidoo. 2019. The glocal dynamics of land reform in natural resource sectors: Insights from Tanzania. *Land Use Policy* 81: 889–896.

Davis, Kyle Frankel., Koo, Heejin Irene., Dell'Angelo, Jampel., D'Odorico, Paolo., Estes, Lyndon., Kehoe, J. Laura., Kharratzadeh, Milad, Kuemmerle, Tobias., Machava, Domingos., Pais, Aurélio. de Jesus. Rodrigues and Ribeiro, Natasha. 2020. Tropical forest loss enhanced by large-ScALE land acquisitions. *Nature Geoscience*, 1–7.

Elhadary, Yasin, and Hillo Abdelatti. 2016. The implication of land grabbing on pastoral economy in Sudan. *World Environment* 6 (2): 25–33.

Fanon, F. 1952. *Black skin, white masks*. New York: Grove.

Fanon, F. 1963. *The wretched of the earth*. New York: Grove.

Food and Agricultural Organization (FAO). 2020. Desert locust response overview. http://www.fao.org/locusts/response-overview-dashboard/en/.

Feintrenie, Laurène. 2014. Agro-industrial plantations in central Africa, risks and opportunities. *Biodiversity and Conservation* 23 (6): 1577–1589.

Feintrenie, Laurène, Stéphane Akoa, Hélène Dessard, Iyabano Aboubakar Hayatou, Philippe Karpe, Patrice Levang, Eugene Ndong Ndoutoume, and Ludovic Miaro. 2014. Are agri-business companies responsible for land grabbing in central Africa? *World Bank Conference on Land and Poverty*, Washington DC, March 24–27.

Hallegatte, Stephane, Mook Bangalore, Laura Bonzanigo, Marianne Fay, Tamaro Kane, Ulf Narloch, Julie Rozenberg, David Treguer, and Adrien Vogt-Schilb. 2016. Shock waves: Managing the impacts of climate change on poverty. *Climate Change and Development Series*. Washington, DC: World Bank. https://doi.org/10.1596/978-1-4648-0673-5.

Hobson, John M. 2013. Part 1–Revealing the eurocentric foundations of IPE: A critical historiography of the discipline from the classical to the modern era. *Review of International Political Economy* 20 (5): 1024–1054.

Home, Robert. 2020. Law in African land reform: Contested areas. In *Rethinking land reform in Africa: New ideas, opportunities and challenges*, ed. Cosmas Milton Obote Ochieng, 132–141. Abidjan: African Development Bank.

Kirst, S. 2020. "Chiefs do not talk law, most of them talk power." Traditional authorities in conflicts over land grabbing in Ghana. *Canadian Journal of African Studies/Revue canadienne des études africaines*: 1–21.

Lanz, Kristina, Jean-David Gerber, and Tobias Haller. 2018. Land grabbing, the state and chiefs: The politics of extending commercial agriculture in Ghana: Land grabbing, the state and chiefs in Ghana. *Development and Change* 49 (6): 1526–1552. https://doi.org/10.1111/dech.12429.

Mahler, Daniel. Gerszon, Lanker, Christoph, Castaneda, R. Aguilar, and Wu, Haoyu. 2020. Updates estimates of the impact of COVID-19 on global poverty. Available online: https://blogs.worldbank.org/opendata/updated-estimates-impact-covid-19-global-poverty.

Mahrenbach, Laura C., and Timothy M. Shaw. 2019. Continuities and change in IPE at the start of the twenty-first century. *The Palgrave handbook of contemporary international political economy*, 1–23. London: Palgrave Macmillan.

Mbembe, Achille. 2020. The universal right to breathe. Available online: https://africasacountry.com/2020/06/the-universal-right-to-breathe.

Monzon, Luis. 2020. Tech is essential in developing a flourishing agriculture sector in Africa. Available online: https://www.itnewsafrica.com/2020/06/tech-is-essential-in-developing-a-flourishing-agriculture-sector-in-africa/.

Odoom, Isaac. 2017. Dam in, cocoa out; pipes in, oil out: China's engagement in Ghana's energy sector. *Journal of Asian and African Studies* 52 (5): 598–620.

OECD. 2020. COVI19 and Africa: Socio-economic implications and policy responses. Available online: http://www.oecd.org/coronavirus/policy-respon

ses/covid-19-and-africa-socio-economic-implications-and-policy-responses-96e1b282/.

Porsani, Juliana, Martina Angela Caretta, and Kari Lehtilä. 2019. Large-scale land acquisitions aggravate the feminization of poverty: Findings from a case study in Mozambique. *GeoJournal* 84 (1): 215–236.

Thiongo, Ngugi wa. 1986. *Decolonizing the mind*. London: James Currey.

Thornton, Alec. 2018. *Space and food in the city: Cultivating social Justice and urban governance through urban agriculture*. New York: Palgrave.

Walshe, Clare O'Grady. 2019. *Globalisation and seed sovereignty in Sub-Saharan Africa*. New York: Palgrave.

Weber, Heloise. 2015. Is IPE just 'boring', 1 or committed to problematic meta-theoretical assumptions? A critical engagement with the politics of method. *Contexto Internacional* 37 (3): 913–944.

World Bank. 2018. Decline of global extreme poverty continues but has slowed. Available online: https://www.worldbank.org/en/news/press-release/2018/09/19/decline-of-global-extreme-poverty-continues-but-has-slowed-world-bank.

World Bank. 2020. ASPIRE: The atlas of social protection. Available online: http://datatopics.worldbank.org/aspire/region/sub-saharan-africa.

Zambakari, Christopher. 2017. Land grab and institutional legacy of colonialism: The case of Sudan. *Consilience* 18: 193–204.

Correction to: The Transnational Land Rush in Africa

Logan Cochrane and Nathan Andrews

Correction to:
L. Cochrane and N. Andrews (eds.),
***The Transnational Land Rush in Africa*, International Political Economy Series, https://doi.org/10.1007/978-3-030-60789-0**

In the original version of the book, the following belated corrections have been incorporated: The author name "Marie Gangé" has been changed to "Marie Gagné" in Chapters 4 and 10. The book has been updated with the changes.

The updated version of these chapters can be found at
https://doi.org/10.1007/978-3-030-60789-0_4
https://doi.org/10.1007/978-3-030-60789-0_10

L. Cochrane and N. Andrews (eds.), *The Transnational Land Rush in Africa*, International Political Economy Series,
https://doi.org/10.1007/978-3-030-60789-0_12

Index

L. Cochrane and N. Andrews (eds.), *The Transnational Land Rush in Africa*, International Political Economy Series,
https://doi.org/10.1007/978-3-030-60789-0